The European Miracle

FOR JOHN HUGHES, REMEMBERING
OXFORD, PURDUE AND NORTHWESTERN

THE EUROPEAN MIRACLE

Environments, economies, and geopolitics in the history of Europe and Asia

SECOND EDITION

E. L. JONES

Professor of Economics, La Trobe University

CAMBRIDGE
UNIVERSITY PRESS

Published by the Press Syndicate of the University of Cambridge
The Pitt Building, Trumpington Street, Cambridge CB2 1RP
40 West 20th Street, New York, NY 10011-4211, USA
10 Stamford Road, Oakleigh, Victoria 3166, Australia

First published 1981
Reprinted 1981, 1982, 1983, 1985, 1986
Second edition 1987
Reprinted 1987, 1988(twice), 1990, 1991, 1992, 1993

Printed in the United States of America

Library of Congress Cataloging in Publication Data
Jones, E. L. (Eric Lionel)
The European miracle.
Bibliography: p.
Includes index.
1. Europe – Economic conditions. 2. Asia – Economic
conditions. I. Title.
HC240.J57   1987   330.94'02   87-8092

British Library Cataloguing in Publication Data
Jones, E. L.
The European miracle.
1. Europe – Economic conditions
2. Asia – Economic conditions
I. Title
330.94'02 HC240 80-41238

ISBN 0-521-33449-7 hardback
ISBN 0-521-33670-8 paperback

Contents

Preface and acknowledgements

Oscar Wilde expected to be met at the Pearly Gates by St Peter bearing an armful of sumptuously bound volumes and declaring, 'Mr Wilde, these are your unwritten works.' I have often felt that *The European Miracle* would turn out to be among St Peter's armful for me. As a narrative task the subject calls for unbounded reading; as an analytical challenge it inspires awe. Yet as a research topic there is a compensation that has been useful to me on my travels, that some pertinent material may be found anywhere, even in the mobile vans of rural library services. I am indeed indebted to assistants in many sorts of library in three continents, and especially, since all the material is never in any one place, to those who engaged in slow-motion wrestling with inter-library loan schemes for me.

Beyond portability, it seems to me important for the health of economic history that more of its practitioners should try to build houses with the bewildering variety of bricks baked in our individual researches, at the risk of dropping a few bricks on specialist toes. Recent works by a number of authors have indicated some renewed interest in universal and *very* long-term history (the term was first used by Hartwell (1969)). Not many of these writers have been professional economic historians, and I think that we too should try to reach the wider audience, if we believe that taken all together our work has something to say. Here is my own interpretation of *very* long-term development in Europe, paying special attention to the period from about A.D. 1400 to 1800 and to comparisons with Asia. The system which appeared then in Europe is obviously important for the history of that continent and as the progenitor of the United States, Canada, Australia, New Zealand, Latin America and South Africa as well as of much that has happened in the rest of the world.

I have not looked for a neat determinist or historicist model.

Criticisms of models of those kinds seem too strong (e.g. Bauer 1971). Neither have I necessarily pinned economic outcomes to pure choices of economic behaviour. The key influences in bringing the European economic system into being seem to have been political decisions made within a favourable natural environment, this environment imparting a direction but not precise marching orders. The choice of economic actions has to be examined within that evolving frame, at least for the periods under discussion. In brief, Europe appears to have had environmental advantages and while these did not guarantee particular responses, or any response, their absence in Asia may have made development harder there. I do not however favour the view that it would have been out of the question for parts of Asia to have industrialised spontaneously, even before Europe. It was just more difficult and a case may be made that it was becoming increasingly difficult in mainland Asia even in precolonial times. Asians lived under much worse and economically distorting oppressions. Europe alone managed the politically remarkable feat of curtailing arbitrary power, thus reducing risk and uncertainty, encouraging more productive investment, and promoting growth.

Were I to seek a general theory of history in the face of the arguments that this is the *ignis fatuus* of scholarship, I should stand further back and survey the world in the *very, very* long term, since the Palaeolithic. The prospect of an economic history of man as a successful species, articulated around the big population cycles identified by McEvedy and Jones (1978), the big overlapping migrations, and the fundamental advances in agriculture, is an exciting one. At that level there would be a class of phenomena from which generalisations might be drawn and against which the experience of independently creative cultures might be tested. But with Europe's achievement of sustained economic growth leading to the first industrialisation – by definition a unique case – there is no such class of phenomena and therefore no appropriate overarching theory. This necessitates a pragmatic retreat from the exposed outworks of theory pushed forward into history by Hicks (1969) and North and Thomas (1973; cf. Jones 1974b). For all the conceptual difficulties, anyone who has written on a topic like the present one is bound to hanker for someone who will take his work as *reculer pour mieux sauter*. For the present, in the absence of general theory, I have found the comparative method offers a measure of control over conjecture, and some hope of seeing the wood as well as the trees. Accordingly I have emphasised comparisons and contrasts between the experiences of Europe and Asia.

The current exercise seals my transformation from Hedgehog into Fox. The rites of that passage have embroiled my family and friends. None of them is to be held to account for the abandonment of scholarly caution that synthesising on this scale has required. I feel a special debt for their encouragement, nevertheless, to my former colleagues in the Department of Economics at Northwestern University, especially John Hughes and Joel Mokyr. Because I have since been working in Australia I am more than ordinarily grateful to those friends in Britain and the United States who have continued to write me letters, suggesting and even sending books, photocopies and clippings to help keep me in touch. Coming and going I have also been dependent on their hospitality, as on that of my parents. Thus my thanks go to Bob Dodgshon, Patrick Dillon, Malcolm Falkus, Max Hartwell, Michael Havinden, Geoffrey Hawthorn, Clifford Henty, Clifford Irish, Bill Kennedy, Noel King, Peter Large, Lew Lewis, Bob Machin, Derick Mirfin, John Naylor, Bill Russell, Colin Tubbs, Nick White, and Stuart Woolf in Britain; to Lou Cain, Stan Engerman, Matt Enos, and Bill Parker in the United States; as well as to Betty Vinaver and the late Eugène Vinaver in France. I have had memorable conversations with Betsy Hoffman at Northwestern, John Gould and Gary Hawke at Wellington, N.Z., Sir Frederick Russell, formerly Director of the Plymouth Marine Biological Research Station, James Lewis at the University of Bath, and Barry Turner at Exeter University. I have been glad, too, of the similar interests of John Anderson who has taught a course with me on economic change in the *very* long term.

Sabbatical leave entitlement under the terms of my Australian appointment, the first non-teaching leave I have had, enabled me to tackle this task. For my leave I was a Visiting Professor at the University of Exeter and I am grateful to Professor W. E. Minchinton and the members of the Department of Economic History for their courtesy. What Arnold Toynbee called the 'dumb show' of historical monuments, made real, in Somerset where I took a cottage, many of the events and processes discussed here. Physicists say that their best work is done in bed, bath, or 'bus, and while I might normally be tempted to retort with the Australian expression, 'half yer luck!', this year I was able to order my own thoughts while walking the Somerset orchards. The literate quality of English life proved stimulating, though in connection with literacy I must apologise for using the author–date system of referencing. It is ugly and interrupts the eye and reduces precision and flexibility in attributions, but does help to keep down publishing costs.

Another means of keeping down costs has been to have my wife and my children, Deborah and Christopher, fetch and carry library books and compile the bibliography. The works cited in the bibliography printed here are almost entirely restricted to those referred to in the text. My wife also went out to work to help pay for a visit we made to former colleagues in the United States during my leave. These are the least of the many debts she and the children are owed.

E. L. J.

Haselbury Plucknett, Somerset
January 1980

Introduction to the second edition

The subject of this book is a big one: Why did economic growth and development begin in Europe? They had after all been more likely to emerge in other parts of the world. The book, then, is concerned with how technical change, structural change, and income growth all got started, that is to say with a complex of issues at the heart of economic history. It is also concerned with historical geography insofar as place (in the sense of natural environment and the areal differentiation of political society) affected the shape of economic change. Comparisons with areas outside Europe are therefore made in an attempt to see what was special about the European case.

With a canvas as broad as this, touching on the experience of three-quarters of the world's population over several centuries and obliging us to rely on secondary sources, we should be prepared to consider all sorts of explanations. There is no completely satisfactory, uncontestable theory on this scale. The vehemence with which the exponents of one scheme or another assert that theirs is the answer shows that social scientific history remains immature, and that some of its practitioners are not yet mature enough to live with the uncertainty associated with hypotheses that are hard to bring to a conclusive test.

In the circumstances comparative history seems a less predetermined way than grand theory for weeding out explanations that may have local explanatory power but lack any general application. If we confine ourselves to studying the history of a single economy we may easily mistake its peculiarities for universal rules. The depth of research that the historian can attain by focusing on a single nation actually heightens this danger. Admittedly, as one reviewer of *The European Miracle* complained, a comparative approach does not guarantee that we will be able to tell exactly 'which pellet brought down the bird.' The only way to do that is by embracing a theory that has decided in advance which is the key variable. What comparison should do is eliminate a large part of the pattern of the shot (to adopt the same metaphor). There is, in any case, not the least reason to suppose that any single factor or relationship had an all-powerful effect on economic development. We will hang loose, as they say. This book is an exploration, not a gospel, and starts from the assumption that any broad historical evolution has a configuration of causes. In this Introduction I shall however mention a few minor changes of emphasis from the original picture I drew of that configuration.

WHAT, WHERE AND WHEN

Historical studies of growth typically seek to identify how a rise in average real income per head began – that is, the causes of an upturn in the trend of gross national product divided by population. This approach tends to home directly on presumed changes in income and cuts away the context of prior and facilitating change. In reality no sustained rise in per capita real income is likely to have begun in a stagnant and unaltered economy. It is fruitless to concentrate on growth shorn of its matrix of developmental and structural transformation, especially as there are virtually no figures on early movements of national income.

One of the reasons why there are few if any data aggregated at a level which modern economists take for granted is that the nation-state itself did not exist throughout most of history. Instead, it was a European political invention of the very period in which we are interested. Earlier economic changes must be referred to different and varying geographical units. Historical statistics are by no means lacking, especially those on taxes and prices, but we lack them at whole-economy levels. Few societies took even a population census before the present century. This means that miscellaneous, indirect indicators of economic change have to be discovered and compounded together.

Income growth for whole societies (or their 'average' members) may have begun quite early. Some major authorities claim that average incomes were rising in Europe as long ago as A.D. 1000, although the rise must have been glacially slow at first. Attaining economic growth is the means of solving the dire human problems caused by want, and it does matter desperately. 'A failure to maintain economic growth means continued poverty, disease, squalor, degradation and slavery to soul-destroying toil for countless millions of the world's population' (Beckerman 1974:3). If we deal with this subject, as we do here, via a discussion of shadowy, long-run, prestatistical, aggregate movements, we seem to be writing history far removed from the experience of individual people: dehumanized history, someone has called it. But consider, if we go to the other extreme and write biographies we can hope to deal with only a handful of people, and worse, we have no way of telling whether the chosen subjects were representative. Human strivings were no less agonizing because there were a lot of them. A statistician who was charged that his discipline was 'soulless' retorted that social statistics are frozen tears. Broad-gauge history makes good sense and is not as inhumane as it may look at first glance.

A concern with economic growth does not necessarily mean an indifference to questions of the distribution of income. (It may be fairer to see it as a matter of putting first things first.) One of the points stressed in the text is indeed that supplying more and better public goods had become almost a defining characteristic of European governments by the eighteenth century. The most significant were the actions classed here as disaster management. These included in particular the imposition of quarantines to halt the spread of epidemic diseases among human beings, of *cordons sanitaires* to shut out movements of infected cattle, the payment of compensation for the slaughter of infected herds owned by farmers, and the emergence of measures to redirect cereal surpluses to districts where high prices threatened to produce famine. In poor and vulnerable societies, the gains from administrative measures like these were large. The payment of compensation for beasts slaughtered because they had come into contact with sick animals suggests an altogether different picture of eighteenth-century administration and peasant life than is usually painted.

Europe came to outclass Asia and the rest of the world in its range of policies to avert or cope with disasters. Assertions to the contrary (Wong and Perdue 1983) do not stand up because they rely on the evidence of the remarkable famine precautions discovered for early Manchu China by Will (1980) while ignoring the context: famine was only one disaster; China was not Asia; and even the Chinese counter-famine measures shrivelled away just when Europe's competence became so apparent (Post 1977).

Public goods are defined as those from the use of which no one can be excluded. As a result of this nonexclusion principle, the unprecedented range and scale of provision by European governments improved welfare for the population at large. The implications of this for the well-being of Europe's poor are almost wilfully neglected in the historical literature. The significance should be assessed against the proper standards, which are those of most of Europe in the Middle Ages and those of most of the rest of the world until very recent times. It might be objected that the poor were taxed disproportionately to pay the costs of counter-disaster measures, but some public goods are so vital for life and health that even 'forced saving' to acquire them via taxation would have been a positive step.

Economic development may be viewed as involving change before gain. Development implies changes in the economic structure because of reduced employment in agriculture. This happened at first with the emergence of part-time manufacturing on farms and in farm cottages, which was a hidden form of structural change. The 'proto-industrial' sector created goods for sale, and reciprocally, among farmers specializing in growing food for the cottage workers, created the very market to absorb the goods.

Modern studies do show that development and growth run together, in the sense that structural change is positively associated with income growth. The association is not however very close, and there is more to development than just structural change. Other early aspects included investing in building roads, bridges and harbours and in river and canal navigation, to permit the wide distribution of bulk loads throughout Europe. Previously, bulk trade on any scale had tended to be confined to the Mediterranean basin, some of the Chinese waterways, the Sea of Japan, and (more in prospect than in reality) the 'Indonesian Mediterranean.' In all this we must see that Europeans were neither the only nor remotely the first active traders. Differences in trading activity around the world were in degree, not in kind, and many features of European development were those of a rather late-settled area catching up with the leading regions. What happened to distinguish Europe was the swollen emergence of bulk trade over quite long distances, multilaterally, in everyday commodities, and not simply in the luxuries that had always dominated long-distance trade.

We are not able easily to detect turning points in the early history of trade, for lack of statistical evidence, and as a result our explanations of the history of economic change are unlikely to be clear-cut. Economies are intricate things – there is now a literature which admits that their nature is better conveyed by biological rather than by the usual mechanical metaphors. Economies are related to the other features of social life in various and inconstant ways. The challenge is not that of fixing the focus on economic growth, which only becomes rapid or measurable in recent periods, but of judging which preceding developments were connected with the eventual rise of average income.

One phenomenon that was closely involved was the integration of markets, including the eventual merging of local, price-segregated markets. Commodity markets in Europe were integrated quite early, but while this was necessary it was clearly not sufficient for very significant growth to result. China long had integrated markets without any sustained rise in per capita incomes. The Islamic world would accept a single coinage. The banking system of Mughal India was capable of honouring drafts with which the very Marathas who were in revolt against the Mughal empire could for a time be bought off, like (to put it in European terms) a Dane-geld. By themselves, however, these sophisticated practices were not enough to bring about much growth.

Nevertheless the most fundamental change may still have lain in the emergence of markets, but not in commodity markets so much as in markets for land and labour. What Europe achieved in addition to bulk commodity markets was the formation of quite efficient factor markets able to transact in land and labour. This required a more profound dissolution of cultural and political rigidities, and thus deeper and more dangerous shifts in society, than the mere acceptance of extensive trading in goods.

Non-market exchanges of labour typically persist later than those of goods. It has been suggested that this is because the costs are higher as a result of difficulties in measuring a tenant's or worker's marginal product or in monitoring his effort (Posner 1981:181n.12). However, it would seem to have as much to do with considerations of appropriating the product – that is, with power relationships.

The history of economic performance is indissolubly bound up with the choices of geographical arena and precise period to be studied. The triad of questions, what, where, and when? is usually answered – the Gordian Knot is cut – by the almost un-thinking assumption that what really mattered in economic his-tory was the 'industrial revolution' originating in and diffusing outwards from late eighteenth-century Britain, together with the spread of imperialism, considered to have been solely a Western phenomenon and strictly negative to boot. 'In the beginning there was England. And contentment vanished from the world' (Berliner 1966:159). As a result of this orientation we have a trun-cated view of the stream of change, and the evolution of the pre-industrial and precolonial worlds has become hard to recognize and assess dispassionately.

The geographical issue splits in two. First there is the question of the proper scale of the units of study. Second, once that has been decided, there is the question of selecting the appropriate historical examples to be studied. The main contending units are regions, nation-states, and the empires which were sometimes virtually coextensive with culture areas or civilizations. Nation-states are the most popular but least suitable of these categories. They are artefacts of European historical process, hammered to-gether from job lots of feudal fragments. They had not come fully into being at periods when it is reasonable to seek the early experience of development. In short, they are anachronisms. They are also anatopisms. Having largely been forced on the rest of the world since 1945, they do not capture or contain the whole relevant historical experience outside Europe.

Economic activity is more plausibly regional, and it is interest-ing to note the rediscovery of the region by economic historians during the last few years, trumpeted as if an original finding. Yet regions present almost insuperable problems of definition (someone once dismissed them as metaphysical units used by geographers). They need to be redefined continually according to the fortunes of the economic activities they contain and for which they are often rather clumsy proxies. This makes them uncertain vessels in which to pour history, which is necessarily about change through periods over which the regional assemblages may not be stable. A further difficulty is that regions are not independent of larger or overlapping polities. Although farming, in particular, is quite usefully discussed in terms of ecological regions, it should not be forgotten that these remain subject to political influences such as taxation by incongruent units.

The conclusion is likely to be that we need multivariate geographical units, which are hard to identify or to find specific evidence about in practice. This somewhat tangled problem strikes me as comparable to the colligation problem – the problem of when to start – in historical analysis. No doubt the common-sense solution in both cases is to choose the date and unit most convenient to the analysis one has in mind, though since the chronological and geographical setting may set arbitrary bounds to the answers one can expect, it is important not to allow one-self to become a prisoner of the initial choice. Historical studies often do suffer in this respect because historians define themselves as students of periods and places rather than of problems. They rationalize this, understandably enough, in terms of the load of specific facts to be learned, but it too often constricts their thought about issues.

For our purposes the third major category mentioned, the empire, is the most suitable unit. We do have to remain aware of the possibility of contradictory economic fluctuations in the various subunits, and also add a consideration of the substitute for empire which emerged in Europe's case. The substitute was the states-system, whose common processes affected its constituent nation-states and regions alike.

The choice of unit for study in the history of growth has conventionally been the nation-state, and the first part of the world chosen has typically been Britain. Although lately there has been a breakaway which has carried with it a change in the unit of central focus, the largest body of thought does remain what I call the 'Little Englander' school. This school implies that England, or Britain, was or became so unlike everwhere else that she, and she alone, could spawn industrial revolution. This insularity has, or should have, suffered a hard knock from recent research on France, which turns out to have matched many of Britain's eighteenth-century achievements. Envisaging British economic history in a European context, instead of insisting that Popery and wooden shoes both began at Calais, almost seems a result of British scholars coming to terms with the Common Market. If so, there is still a surprisingly determined nationalistic opposition. The Little Englanders prejudge the issue of the timing of economic change by flatly assuming that all relevant change took the form of a late and decisive industrialization. The misfortune of this point of view is that if Britain truly were unique, her history could shed no light on the experience of other countries, even those near neighbours that industrialized so suspiciously quickly afterwards. It is much more instructive to look on Britain as affected by forces that were acting on the whole European continent, out of which she narrowly emerged as the first industrial power on the basis of technical change in the manufacture of cotton and iron.

At the opposite extreme are the 'One-Worlders.' They seem to be an extension, almost a reductio ad absurdem, of the world-system school of Immanuel Wallerstein and his followers. The original world-system view was Eurocentric. The system was envisaged as driven by an exploiting economic core of countries in northwestern Europe. This giant economic geography represented a liberating shift from internalist British or European work, although the central hypothesis of exploitative relations between the core, semi-periphery and periphery has not stood up to critical tests by independent scholars (e.g., O'Brien 1982). The train of thought is quite run off the rails by One-Worlders, who argue that all late premodern economies were permeated by the ripple effect of trade with Europe, and that this, rather than internal considerations, determined that the fate of the non-European world would seem to be dismal.

Mao Tse-tung pointed out that heat may be applied to a stone or an egg, but the fact that a chicken comes from one and nothing from the other is actually due to their internal structures. So it was with the non-European economies when European trade and violence touched them. They responded according to their own organization and circumstances, not merely according to the fierceness with which Europe laid hands on them.

The period before 1800, with which this book deals, was in any case free of massive European influences on most of the Middle East and Asia, especially China. An historian of Indonesia has spoken of the eighteenth century as Asia's own century (Van Leur 1955:271). A Turkish historian has observed that the Ottoman empire was an autonomous structure affected by international military rivalries rather than the plaything of commerce and relationships to the market (Sunar 1980:574–75n.2). The common assumption that the fate of Third World economies was always made more dismal by Western imperialists is in any case unwarranted. Lloyd Reynolds (1983; 1985) has amassed considerable evidence that many of these economies were already growing in the imperialist world of the late nineteenth century.

There seems little reason to suppose that geographically far-flung, but usually tenuous, trade contracts running back ultimately to Europe were what made the whole premodern world revolve. Certainly some of the distant repercussions have long been known, for instance the chain reaction of disturbances set up far to the west by fur traders on the east coast of North America, but an attenuated contact is not the same as a world market. One-Worlders tend to avoid the effort at quantification that might decide the point. Their argument in itself is not new. The geopolitician Halford Mackinder was accused of ignoring the experience of the 'people without history' who occupied the lands (almost) discovered by Columbus. Yet like Mackinder we do not need to study the entire world to grasp the beginnings of European development or even to provide adequate contrasts with European experience. As Mackinder's biographer savagely but tellingly retorted in his defence, insisting that people did dwell and make history outside the Eurasian land mass is like saying that a cupboard is not empty because it is full of air (Parker 1982:234–5). Such considerations led me to set Europe's economic emergence against a backcloth of the other major economies of the (European) early modern or late preindustrial period, defined as very large populations organized in single polities. Mackinder was dealing with the distributions of power, not culture; and we are dealing with major economic changes, not marginal cultures or obscure channels of trade. Small societies are anthropologically interesting and provide special opportunities to investigate economic behaviour under virtually controlled conditions, but they are by definition not the heavyweights of world history. It was the Europeans who rose to power and it was they, above all, who traded in bulk – mostly, it must be added, with one another.

The proper units for our purposes are therefore the European states-system and the great contemporary empires. The states-system was a set of interacting parts. The structure of individual nation-states, not to mention regions, of course influenced economic performance, but this was secondary to the systemwide influences of a common civilization, reactive politics, and supranational markets. Europe was bonded economically as much as politically. A better understanding may be gained of the total economy of the states-system by comparing and contrasting it with the other large economies of the time, organised as they were in political empires, situated in Asia or at any rate in Asia and the Middle East. Their different, and in Europe's early modern period ultimately downward, trajectories are not explained primarily by Western imperialism. A different imperialism is to be indicted. This was the command economics imposed by dynasties from the steppes of central Asia: Ottoman, Mughal and Manchu, all of them latter-day models of the Mongol onslaught. It was this, not the hydraulic agriculture of a timeless Asian Mode of Production, nor Western trade or conquest, that determined the fate of the East. Steppe imperialism was what made the difference, by clamping in its selfish grasp the customary agricultures and nascent trade sectors of the 'early modern' Islamic Middle East, India and China.

Why should we investigate these matters during Europe's 'long early modern period' from about 1400 to 1800? The deeper springs of Europe's growth certainly arose earlier, and earlier periods also need a glance if we are to notice the potential that had already been revealed by Eastern societies. The book does mention these former times, but concentrates on the period when Europe's acceleration became patent and overtook all others. That period permits a close look at the divergence.

Debate about the divergence is a silent, unexpressed, incoherent struggle. Various authorities make stern or impassioned comments about the timing of Europe's advance, with or without contrasting it to Asian experience, but they mostly ignore one another. They debate by default.

Transcurrent points, the dates when Europe forged ahead of China in the realms of science, were long ago calculated by Needham (1967). In more directly economic spheres, views about the passing points range over many centuries according to the authority. Part of the discrepancy stems from the choice of 'controls' (i.e., the precise other areas with which Europe is compared). The general issue is seldom addressed head on, but Issawi (1980) has devoted an article to 'what points in time and in what fields the West overtook and surpassed . . . the Middle East.' His answer is that in most respects, except the military, Europe was ahead by the fifteenth century at the latest.

Four leading authorities – Cipolla, Kuznets, Landes and Maddison – have separately stated the opinion or actually estimated that in strict growth terms Europe was edging up as far back as A.D. 1000 (collected in Maddison 1982:255n.3). This does not necessarily imply any particular trend elsewhere, but it does have implications very different from the Little Englander view of a 'great discontinuity' at the industrial revolution. One widely used industrial revolution textbook even claims that until the middle of the eighteenth century the British economy was 'relatively stagnant' (Deane 1979:18). Bairoch and his collaborators also indicate that the income gap opened only after 1750 (Bairoch and Levy-Leboyer 1981).

There are thus early and late schools of thought, geographical inconsistencies, and differences over the proper focus of economic enquiry. Syllabuses tend to be dominated by the 'late' school. Two otherwise different but widely held interpretations converge on a late discontinuity. The former is the Little Englander view, which sees Britain industrializing unaided in an income-stagnant world – in a phrase, 'taking off.' The latter is the imperialism view, which sees British or European industrialization achieved at the expense of non-Western societies, blighting growth prospects there, especially in India. The history of native Asian imperialisms is neglected in favour of implying that without Western imperialism the East might have achieved industrialization by itself.

The 'early' school may treat Europe's rise as an unfolding of possibilities latent wholly and solely within Europe, or it may set it against a backcloth of other societies. At least these scholars do recognize the early stirrings in Europe. 'An understanding of the subsequent widening gap in relative economic performance must be sought in the period when the gap originated, which was prior to 1500 A.D.,' declares one reviewer of *The European Miracle* (Crotty 1983:194). Others tend to narrow the critical period by depicting Europe as having been backward compared with T'ang or Sung China or the Abbasid caliphate of Baghdad, indeed from the Fall of Rome until the Middle Ages. They thus trace Europe's relative success to the High Middle Ages, long before there were dominant trading interactions with other cultures. In this vein North and Thomas (1973:157) proclaim that 'the industrial revolution was not the source of modern economic growth. It [i.e. the growth] was the outcome of raising the private rate of return on developing new techniques and applying them to the productive process.'

The most cogent summary by an economist may be that of Kuznets (1964:21). His opinion is that the European countries in their preindustrial phase, which he defines as before the share of the work force in agriculture fell below 60 percent, enjoyed per capita incomes several times higher than most less-developed countries in the 1960s. They were more developed than most other parts of the preindustrial world and had already undergone a long period of growth and expansion.

Kuznets's views on early growth, expressed over twenty years ago, might have been expected to have a big impact on research programmes. Yet although lip service is not infrequently paid to them, they inspired little research and even less teaching apart from the period beginning with the 'industrial revolution' of the eighteenth century. Recency is mistaken for relevance. But the game in town was an older one, and it was leapfrog. Europe had to catch up earlier economic revolutions in China and leap over them; Indian science had to be absorbed and surpassed, and so did that of the brilliant Islamic Middle East. Kuznets himself did not investigate these other episodes of rise and decline in histori-

cal detail. He left the agenda open, and the present book considers it. What it looks at are the conditions conducing to the period
of Europe's rise and the reasons specialist authors may have for
describing Asia and the Middle East as 'frozen' or 'slumbering'
during comparable periods.

CONTROLS

The obvious comparisons or contrasts with nascent Europe are
thus to be found among the other large societies of the long early
modern period, which were in Asia. For this purpose the term
'Asia' is the merest label of convenience, particularly as it is also
used to include the Near and Middle East. Nothing is meant to
be implied along the lines of a universal or immutable 'Asian' behaviour pattern. In the sense meant here, 'Asia' is merely a geographical expression for where the other vast organized populations of the world happened to be located (they still are) during
the long early modern period of Europe's history.

Whether to tackle these other economies via a general model
or one by one depends partly on taste and partly on the space
available. In many ways it might be preferable to do both. A
scheme is certainly required to organize the strings of special
cases that constitute the histories of particular areas. On the
other hand, both writer and reader need to keep a natural curiosity about possibly significant details that may have influenced
economic performance. The three main Asian empires are tackled separately here, though the common theme of the effects of
conquest empires on huge customary agricultures is empha-
sized. Grouping together the Islamic empires, Ottoman and
Mughal, as one category would have made sense too, including
also the smaller Safavid empire in Persia, but the Chinese empire usually needs its own coverage. In any case every individual empire lay across a different indigenous society. Each had its
own ecological setting, though the theme of higher disaster risk
in 'Asian' than European environments can be discerned.

Asian environments were generally far from biologically unproductive. Most of India, in particular, had abundant warmth
and moisture for growing crops – if the monsoon came. When the
rains did come, plant production outstripped anything in Eu-

rope's chilly fields. In the seasons when the monsoon failed there was tragedy. The difference lay not in average productivity, which was higher in south and southeast Asia than in Europe, but in the greater variance about the mean. Large shocks which destroyed capital works as well as numbers of people were commoner than in Europe, although given the nature of historical evidence this is hard to demonstrate statistically (Pryor 1985; Jones 1985). A greater frequency of disasters increased uncertainty as well as risk, and thus militated against long-term investment.

Political risk was even more acute. Economies are politically embedded, and this is decisive for the way they perform. The customary Asian political form, the empire, produced little incentive or an actual disincentive for important groups to engage in productive investment. The largest social group, the peasantry, had low incomes and little surplus. Peasants were without redress against arbitrary taxes, to the point that eating any small surplus that a harvest did provide made more sense to them than hazarding it in new ventures. Merchants were necessarily inferior to warriors in societies where status accrued to military conquerors. Some merchants did grow rich, but unless they themselves became landed officials (which was open to them only in the Chinese case) their wealth remained at risk of confiscation by public officials. Individual merchants might bribe their way to influence, but emperors never needed to rely on them as impecunious European kings did, and they did not gain influence as a class. They never succeeded in hollowing out the Asian empires into bourgeois states.

Land ownership in these empires was not usually hereditary. The *jagirdars* of Mughal India were moved around by the regime; the sons of Chinese scholar-gentry had to sit the classical examinations. They could form little permanent attachment to the land and lacked the incentive of European landowners to invest in the productive capacity of estates for the sake of their offspring. The procedure was to milk the peasantry, without crossing the line of bringing on peasant revolt (though they were not always good judges of that).

The empires did not become service states. Sultans and emperors amassed vast wealth but received incomes that were nevertheless small relative to the immensity of the territories and populations governed. Even with a will, which they did not have, they would have lacked the central government budgets needed for the economic development of their lands. Thus the customary economy of the agricultural sector, the limited market sector, and the command elements of these systems all lacked the makings of sustained advance, despite the burst of productivity that followed each initial establishment of peace and order by the conquerors.

These were vast but brittle systems. Faced with defeat, or an end to the military successes that had brought them into being, they turned inward. Mounting revenue needs tended to crowd out productive investment on the required scale. Tended is a key word. Particularist historians will want to object with counterinstances of the achievements of one empire or another. History is very full. Our aim is to identify the general tendencies, and these simply were not cumulative development and growth on the European plan.

In addition the Islamic empires never fully solved the problems of succession to the throne. Europe's past is besmeared with wars of succession—Austrian, Polish, Spanish—but the struggles of the Orient were endemic and more consistently destructive of internal order. Attempted solutions, such as keeping the heir in a 'cage' until he was needed, virtually guaranteed inexperienced rule and poor economic management. Few men confined since boyhood in a harem, fawned on by eunuchs and concubines, were likely to acquire the expertise or self-discipline needed to preside over empires otherwise barren of checks on arbitrary power.

This view of the prospects of the major Asian economies attaches to the particular Ottoman, Mughal and Manchu dynasties. It is not Wittfogel's view, nor Marx's, nor Engels's, of an endless Asian Mode of Production. Asian economies were not locked forever in an environmentally determined posture where central control over irrigation rights put a permanent stop to progress. Asia *had* changed, long before Europe. Income growth may have become 'frozen' in these centuries, but the freeze has identifiable historical roots in particular invasions from the steppes. The economies then became command hierarchies imposed on customary agricultures. These weakened investment in human and physical capital, slowing and diverting for the duration of the empires much further growth of the market.

Investment and its political determinants may be challenged as the focus of study. The key to the empires may not after all have lain in frustrated investment. (Yet if the system is nothing, systematics is all. History otherwise becomes a chaos of anecdotes and special cases.) Perhaps after all the economic performance of empires centred on less tangible matters like religion, culture, ideas, or law. Marx, certainly, lamented that Asian history seemed to be nothing but the history of religions. He would have preferred to ground it on the materialism he believed to lie beneath (Worsley 1984:104–5, 169, 243–4). Heaven knows, if we may so put it, he deserves some sympathy. Religions are not immutable, and Asia's history from far back is one of recurrent missionizing by one faith after another. Ideas in general are malleable, at least over historical time. The puzzle is, how far do they adapt to the deeper circumstances of natural environment or political incentives? To what extent are they formative? Asian religions were in any case only superficially incompatible with economic growth, and if the Christianity of Europe seems all too comfortable with it we can only remark that Christianity had been around for a long time without producing growth. With regard to religious, cultural, ideational, and legal influences, the issue is what lags, what rachet effects, do they insert in material change? The answer, no doubt, lies somewhere between simple materialism and the undiluted history of ideas. The material ground is however more certain, and in an introductory essay the stress may justifiably be placed on the politics and natural environment that influenced it.

EUROPEAN EMPHASES

The plan of the European section moves from prehistory or *very* long-term environmental matters by overlapping stages through the history of technical change, the stimulus of the Discoveries, and the formation of the market, to the nature, origin and implications of the European states and states-system. What is this, one reviewer of the first edition demanded, but the invisible hand of Adam Smith with a helping hand from the state? The interpretation may indeed be distilled into an argument for the combined and synergetic effect of environment, market and state.

First, the environment: This subdivides into features of site, location, and the disaster profile. Among site characteristics, the resource endowment is not very helpful in explaining change. Resources are a function of the available technology and have no economic meaning until a technology has been invented to employ them. The North American Indians knew about oil but had no conception or means of using it as petroleum. In Europe's case the most relevant aspect of the resource endowment was probably the way it was dispersed across a geologically and climatically varied continent, since this provided an inducement to trade.

Another site feature was the discontinuous distribution of good land for growing grain. Europe possessed a number of so-called core areas of high arable productivity, each the home of a denser and richer population than the area around it. One reason why Europe remained politically decentralised may have been that the larger core areas were much of a muchness, and the occupants of any one of them found it hard to dominate the others.

Site characteristics also include climate. A number of reviewers read an emphasis on climatic change into the first edition. This surprises me, because it is not there. I agree with my colleague John Anderson, who has shown that incremental changes in long-run climatic averages were offset by economic adjustments, and that some of the supposedly depressing climatic effects were more likely the results of other events, such as the fall in population after the Black Death (Anderson 1981). The closest he or I come to attributing major economic consequences to shifts in weather (not climatic) variables or to any other changeable element of the physical or biological environment is in discussing disaster shocks (Anderson and Jones 1983). The central point about these is that they strike hard and fast, and although costs can be spread by insurance devices (themselves not a free good), disasters are an environmental phenomenon that cannot be wholly avoided.

The locational advantages seem to have been twofold. Europe, at any rate western Europe, was a long journey from the central Asian epicentres of the invasions which from time to time captured other parts of the Eurasian periphery, notably India and China. Distance was some protection, as was a forested landscape unsuited to cavalry warfare. On the other hand, once adequate sailing ships were built, the western European seaboard was found to lie conveniently opposite some of the richest seas and most exploitable and least defended lands in the world. The mention of shipping technology, nevertheless, introduces the wild card of the environmental pack. By itself geography explains nothing. Historical events, including specific technological innovations, are needed to put site or location to given uses. Yet geography may not be altogether dismissed. The layout of the world does affect the relative costs of economic activity under any one technology. Europe overall was not as disfavoured with respect to trade, political variety and capital accumulation as its rather chilly northern location and short growing season might suggest. Indeed, from the standpoint of disease a northerly location may have been a positive asset.

The cultural environment of Europe was unique in one deep-seated sense. In a classic paper, Hajnal (1965) has demonstrated that marriage participation rates were lower, and the female age at marriage higher, west of a line from Trieste to Leningrad. Profound consequences for capital accumulation and living standards may have flowed from this, although the questions of how the demographic behaviour related to the natural environment, and why Europeans should have behaved in this special way, remain open.

Capital accumulation may also have been encouraged, though slowly, by an apparent bias of disaster shocks towards the destruction of labour rather than capital. In Europe there were worse epidemics than there were earthquakes. In addition the efficiency of capital was raised by a persistent tendency to bring about technical change. Where this trait came from is hard to make out. A widespread propensity for and success in tinkering, inventing and innovating may have had much to do with the relatively low density and political decentralisation of population; but this still calls for research into early sociology. In this respect those who think Europe's development began early rather than late are surely correct, although it was not early compared with major Asian cultures and did not greatly influence per capita income at first. Much would have depended on the population response and the incidence of taxation.

On the face of it a case can be made for seeing the acceleration of European growth as the effect of the bounty of overseas resources brought by the Discoveries. However, what looks more to the point is the existence of economies that could make good use of what was discovered: a native European rather than an imperialist peculiarity. The bounty might easily have been consumed without changing either the social or economic structure. Cheng Ho's distant voyages had not transformed Ming China, neither had the Malagasays or Polynesians, famous voyagers, transformed their homelands, nor, come to that, had the Vikings transformed an earlier Europe by crossing the North Atlantic. Responsive commercialism had emerged in medieval Europe, and it was that which made the Discoveries effective.

This is one area where I would now be more wary. The Discoveries make a brave tale, but before the nineteenth century their total significance was less obvious than it seemed. A paper by O'Brien (1982) provides some rare and much-needed quantification. Although it might be said that the seven percent share of Europe's continental product, which is all he finds contributed by extra-European trade before 1800, may still have been the critical margin for growth, this proportion is infinitely less than implied by writings on Europe's exploitation of the 'periphery.'

The expansion of Europe's market economy was, as has been noted, significant because it included the freeing of factor markets. As a result of competitive processes internal and external to European political units, resource allocation became more responsive than it had been before, or than it was anywhere else. From the point of view of commodity trade I still see Europe as marked by an early rise of many-sided trade in bulk loads of everyday items. This trade stemmed from and further expanded a broader social participation in the market than was induced by luxury trades.

It is less certain how vital to trade development political and legal security may have been. National loyalties were more diffuse than they have become, and trade continued even in wartime. War in any case created some economic demand to set against its net destructiveness. Alfred Russel Wallace's *The Malay Archipelago* contains a striking passage. At Dobbo in the Aru Islands (Indonesia) he found a great mixture of races: 'This motley, ignorant, bloodthirsty population live here without the shadow of a government, with no police, no courts, and no lawyers' (Wallace 1962 edn.:336). Yet they did not cut each other's throats or steal all the time. 'It puts strange thoughts into one's head,' he remarked, 'about the mountain-load of government under which people exist in Europe.' The most efficient form and 'density' of government may be the point where common opinion is most open to contradiction. Another challenge to our customary view of the value of governmental intervention comes from the following description of the alleyways and shanties of Hangchow at the start of the twentieth century: 'Difficult as it is for the European to realise that such a mixture of filth, slime and squalor constitute a city, it is even more difficult for him to realise that just inside these same shanty-like shops there are hundreds of thousands of dollars worth of merchandise and sleek, well-fed and well-clothed proprietors who count their wealth with no less than six figures' (Cloud 1906:14).

The role of government in economic development is thus more problematical than it seems. A first reaction to the two quotations above – and it is an important rider – may be that the Aru Islands and Hangchow lacked the public health measures devised in Europe. European modes of organisation were sometimes, and rightly, perceived as a benefit. Indian bankers and civil servants for example were quick to shift into the suburb of Hyderabad where, in 1808, the British residence had been built, 'preferring probably our sanitary and police arrangements to their own' according to a British author quoted by Alam (1965:8).

It is easy, in this species of history, to mistake the forms of development for their essential causes. From the narrowly economic standpoint a more important step, taken in much of Europe after a struggle in the Middle Ages, was probably the curtailing of predatory governmental tax behaviour. Beyond that, more problems than we might think could perhaps look after themselves, although disaster management and the provision of other public goods still seem to me great and peculiarly European advances.

Protection from one's own ruler was second in importance only to defence against outside attack. 'Peace and easy taxes' is not an empty first approximation, and Adam Smith was not altogether bigoted when he saw them as preludes to business prosperity, however little flow-on to the average citizen there may have been at first. Political decentralisation and competition did abridge the worst arbitrariness of European princes. There were many exceptions, but gradually they became just that, exceptions. Meanwhile freedom of movement among the nation-states offered opportunities for 'best practices' to diffuse in many spheres, not least the economic.

The nation-states that grew up around the better core areas in Europe were consolidated by the attractions of the king's justice and by the centralising power of the king's cannon, both overawing the disorder of lesser lords. It was more important still that the number of states never shrank to one, to a single dominating empire, despite the ambitions of Charlemagne, the Hapsburg Charles V, or Napoleon. Within many states a long process in the history of economic thought conditioned rulers to listen to academics and other wise men. Writers of the seventeenth and eighteenth centuries in central and western Europe dared to offer advice about how to rule, some of which was taken. Compare this with Honda Toshiaki in Tokugawa Japan, who dared not publish, or Pososhkov in Petrine Russia, who did publish and perished in gaol for his pains.

Humanitarianism and national prudence in much of Europe brought forth the admirable policies of disaster management to which reference has been made, even if other national interests led to many less pretty acts of state. Improvements in welfare or at any rate in the level of risk became matters of national and not merely local concern. At the same time production was being privatised. The enclosure of common fields, dissolution of guilds and abolition of serfdom all seem to express the rise of economic individualism. Yet in the very same breath governments were taking responsibility for fundamental aspects of social provision.

Conditions promoting economic development in Europe

formed long ago. Growth in the sense of a sustained rise in average incomes sprouted out of them, slowly but early, perhaps as early as the high middle ages. Pulling this complex of conditions apart does not find us an 'engine of growth.' The pattern, not a single magic change, was what 'brought down the bird.' A relatively steady environment and above all the limits to arbitrariness set by a competitive political arena do seem to have been the prime conditions of growth and development. Europe escaped the categorical dangers of giant centralised empires as these were revealed in the Asian past. Beyond that, European development was the result of its own indissoluble, historical layering.

E. L. J.

Institute for Advanced Study, Princeton
December 1985

References to the Introduction

Alam, Shah Manzoor. 1965. *Hyderabad Secunderabad (Twin Cities): A Study in Urban Geography*. Bombay: Allied Publishers.

Anderson, J. L. 1981. Climatic Change in European Economic History. *Research in Economic History* 6, 1–34.

Anderson, J. L. and Jones, E. L. 1983. Natural Disasters and the Historical Response. *La Trobe University Economics Discussion Paper* 3/13.

Bairoch, Paul and Levy-Leboyer, Maurice, eds. 1981. *Disparities in Economic Development since the Industrial Revolution*. New York: St. Martin's Press.

Beckerman, Wilfred. 1974. *In Defence of Economic Growth*. London: Jonathan Cape.

Berliner, Joseph. 1966. The Economics of Overtaking and Surpassing. In *Industrialization in Two Systems*, ed. Henry Rosovsky. New York: John Wiley and Sons.

Cloud, Frederick D. 1906. *Hangchow: The 'City of Heaven'*. No place or publisher stated.

Crotty, Raymond. 1983. Review of *The European Miracle*. *Irish Journal of Agricultural Economics* 9, 193–5.

Deane, Phyllis. 1979. *The First Industrial Revolution*. Cambridge: Cambridge University Press, second edition.

Hajnal, J. 1965. European Marriage Patterns in Perspective. In *Population in History*, eds. David Glass and D. E. C. Eversley. London: Edward Arnold.

Issawi, Charles. 1980. Europe, the Middle East and the Shift in Power: Reflections on a Theme by Marshall Hodgson. *Comparative Studies in Society and History* 22, 487–504.

Jones, E. L. 1985. Disasters and Economic Differentiation across Eurasia: A Reply. *Journal of Economic History* 45, 675–82.

Kuznets, Simon. 1964. Underdeveloped Countries and the Pre-Industrial Phase in the Advanced Countries. In *Two Worlds of Change: Readings in Economic Development*, ed. Otto Feinstein. Garden City, New York: Doubleday/Anchor Books.

Maddison, Angus. 1982. *Phases of Capitalist Development*. Oxford: Oxford University Press.

Needham, Joseph. 1967. The Roles of Europe and China in the Evolution of Oecumenical Science. *The Advancement of Science* 24, 83–98.

North, D. C. and Thomas, R. P. 1973. *The Rise of the Western World: A New Economic History*. Cambridge: Cambridge University Press.

O'Brien, Patrick. 1982. European Economic Development: The Contribution of the Periphery. *Economic History Review* 2 ser. 35, 1–18.

Parker, W. H. 1982. *Mackinder: Geography as an Aid to Statecraft*. Oxford: Clarendon Press.

Posner, Richard A. 1981. *The Economics of Justice*. Cambridge, Mass.: Harvard University Press.

Post, John D. 1977. *The Last Great Subsistence Crisis in the Western World*. Baltimore: The Johns Hopkins University Press.

Pryor, Frederic L. 1985. Climatic Fluctuations as a Cause of the Differential Economic Growth of the Orient and Occident: A Comment. *Journal of Economic History* 45, 667–73.

Reynolds, Lloyd. 1983. The Spread of Economic Growth to the Third World. *Journal of Economic Literature* 21, 941–80.

Reynolds, Lloyd. 1985. *Economic Growth in the Third World, 1850–1980*. New Haven, Conn: Yale University Press.

Sunar, Ilkay. 1980. Anthropologie Politique et Economique: L'Empire Ottoman et sa Transformation. *Annales E. S. C.* 35, 551–79.

Van Leur, J. C. 1955. *Indonesian Trade and Society: Essays in Asian Social and Economic History*. The Hague: W. van Hoeve.

Wallace, Alfred Russel. 1962 ed. *The Malay Archipelago*. New York: Dover Publications.

Will, Pierre-Etienne. 1980. *Bureaucratie et famine en Chine au 18e siècle.* Paris: Mouton.

Wong, R. Bin and Perdue, Peter C. 1983. Famine's Foes in Ch'ing China. *Harvard Journal of Asiatic Studies* 43, 291–332.

Worsley, Peter. 1984. *The Three Worlds: Culture and World Development.* London: Weidenfeld and Nicolson.

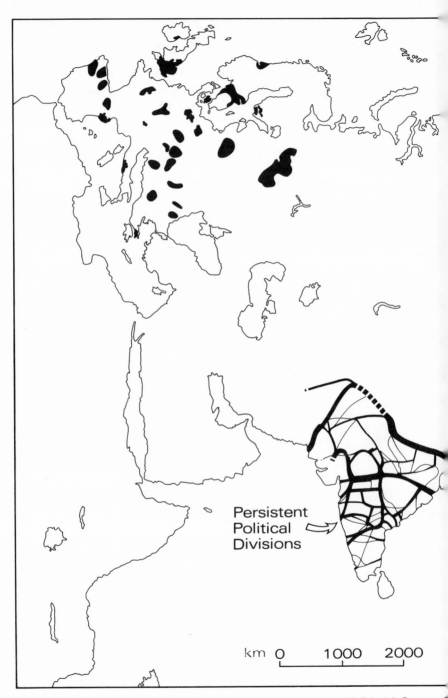

Persistent
Political
Divisions

km 0   1000   2000

Map compiled from regional maps in Buchanan (1967); Pounds and Ball (1964); Spate and

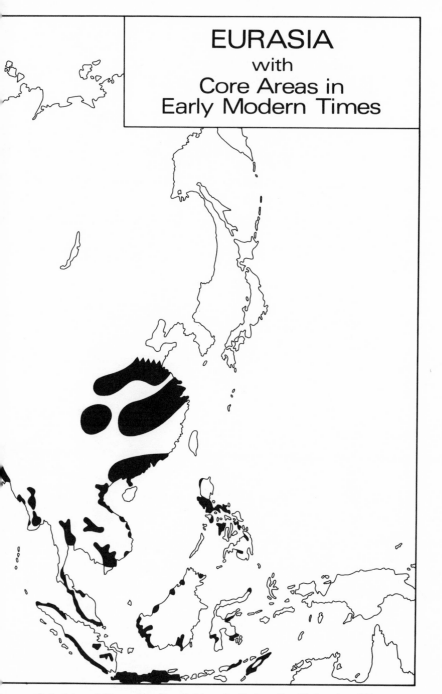

EURASIA
with
Core Areas in
Early Modern Times

earmonth (1967); and Stover (1974); and drawn by Rodney Fry, University of Exeter

Eurasia

Chapter 1

Environmental and social conjectures

We could have left man out, playing the ecological game of 'let's pretend man doesn't exist'. But this seems as unfair as the corresponding game of the economists, 'let's pretend nature doesn't exist'. The economy of nature and the ecology of man are inseparable. . .

Marston Bates

EUROPE did not spend the gifts of its environment 'as rapidly as it got them in a mere insensate multiplication of the common life'. This phrase from H. G. Wells (in *Men Like Gods*) sums up the quality of Europeanness. Nevertheless Europe became successful enough biologically to stand third in population in the world after China and India in 1500 and to do proportionately better than they in the period 1650–1850. In total biomass, that is including the weight of domestic livestock, its rank even in 1500 might have been a very close third indeed. Probably the energy output of its population was above third place. In the *very* long term Europe was economically more successful still. Despite considerable fluctuation, the real wage tended to be high since at least the thirteenth century, compared with India even in the twentieth century (Krause 1973:169). And in its eventual, simultaneous achievement of both biomass gains and real income growth, Europe stood quite alone.

European economic history is a special case of the economic history of all Eurasia, where over three-quarters of the world's population lived and still lives. We may therefore conveniently contrast Europe with the older polities and vaster economies of China and India, the other large societies of the world. Oriental civilisations struck Europeans as monumental and grand. Much of the apparent grandeur was a compound of imposing works of civil engineering and luxury for the court circles. Mechanical engineering lagged. The standard of living of the mass of the people languished. This condition is most easily accounted for by

3

political mechanisms which devoted tax revenues to massive public works and an easy life for the élite. Overall these societies were not rich in the sense of high average real incomes, the dimension in which Europe was to surpass them. Late Manchu China with a population of some 400 million still supported only seven-and-a-half million non-producers, fewer than two per cent of the population (Stover 1974:16). This two per cent élite however consumed in the 1880s twenty-four per cent of the national product (Stover and Stover 1976:110). For comparison, Le Roy Ladurie (1979:87) suggests that almost fifteen per cent of the forty million people in France, Germany and Britain at the start of the fourteenth century had already risen above peasant status and were supported by the peasantry.

Europeans commanded more working capital per head than Asians, mainly in the form of livestock. As a corollary they ate more meat and livestock products, so far as the archaeological or literary evidence can tell us. They brought more draught animals to bear on their fields than the Chinese and stronger, better-fed ones than the Indians. By medieval times Europeans also disposed of more energy in the form of water power. They used more timber per head and were usually able to smelt more charcoal iron. It is true that about A.D. 1100 iron output *per capita* in China had been twenty per cent higher than it was in the Europe of 1700, but that phase had not lasted. The rice region of China, containing two-thirds of her population, became a great clearfelled zone. Further, Europeans came to achieve, by means of international trade, a marked degree of substitution for resources which were becoming scarce in the developing parts of the continent. When the domestic output of charcoal from coppice woodland proved inadequate in late preindustrial times, and the continued expansion of iron production was threatened, 'metropolitan' western Europe, notably Britain, was able to import iron from areas of more extensive forest and abundant ore, such as Sweden, Petrine Russia, and finally the American colonies. By 1750 the Americans were producing fourteen per cent of the world's iron. The coke-smelting of iron on a production scale was then just about to begin, doubling the already massive trade additions to the resource base which had rescued Europe from the scarcities afflicting the remainder of Eurasia. The area that had been acquired in consequence of the Discoveries had actually reduced Europe's man–land ratio, at a time when this ratio was rising elsewhere. China and India both had three times the European population density in 1500, even before the post-Columbian reduction of Europe's effective density. Neither China nor India was in a position to import timber or iron or other raw materials or food.

The distribution of income in Europe was unusually equal, that is to say not equal at all but with a flatter Lorenz curve than obtained in Asia. This was reflected in the sense of dismay with which many early European travellers reported on the depths of poverty among the masses and the heights of prodigality among the rich that they came across in Asia (Lach 1970 vol. II:827). The splendours of Asian courts, the religious and funerary monuments and hydraulic engineering works, the luxury goods and skilled craftsmanship seemed merely to testify that political organisation could squeeze blood out of stones if the stones were numerous enough. 'Century after century', writes Harris (1978:172), 'the standard of living in China, northern India, Mesopotamia and Egypt hovered slightly above or below what might be called the threshold of pauperization', according to fluctuations in population density, while 'western observers have always been astonished by the static or stationary nature of these ancient dynastic systems'.

European travellers in early modern times were aware of the advantages of their own civilisation, though some were too easily thrilled by the magnificence of oriental courts. Commentators in the seventeenth century were clear that a higher standard of living was enjoyed by a majority of Europeans, not simply the rich, who could indeed hardly match their Asian counterparts for conspicuous waste. Ordinary Europeans had better clothing, more varied food, more furniture and more household utensils, above and beyond the requirements of compensating for their chilly climate (Hajnal 1965:131). The gulf between East and West may have been widened by industrialisation but was not caused by it. Preindustrial societies had long been dissimilar, not only culturally but in characteristics of first concern to economic historians and development economists, the structure of investment, and the level of *per capita* income and the mechanisms determining it.

For most of its history Europe had been culturally a backwater of Asia. By late preindustrial times, however, Europe had the edge over other parts of the world in education and literacy, which are both correlates of investment and consumption. Europe experienced ahead of the other continents the prolonged and widespread process of development that eventually blurred into industrialisation. While there is no proven connection between *very* long-term well-being and the final mushrooming of growth, we may assume that, slight though it was by modern standards and distorted by distributional peculiarities, it was not a handicap. We shall need to consider its causes and implications. In this chapter we look at the ecological individuality of Europe for ways in which it may have influenced the special performance of the economy.

Europe was not, by Asian standards, a lush habitat. Large social groupings emerged there much later than in the warmer parts of Eurasia. Civilisations had long been rising and falling in warm latitudes, although they appear to have been springing up farther and farther north. Such explanation as the literature offers for this shift is essentially climatic (Gilfillan 1920; Lambert 1971). On the one hand it correlates mean temperature and the output of human energy, and on the other it claims that in warm regions man was subject to a build-up of endoparasitic infestation which caused each society there to reach a plateau of attainment and then stagnate. Northern winters, in contrast, prune deleterious organisms as they lie in the soil and water. Ploughing also exerted control over soil parasites, while it was the Iron Age plough that first brought up enough soil nutrients to produce a good yield in northern areas where rain occurs throughout the year and there is little evaporation.

Asia was not so favoured. Consider China. During the Southern Sung period, when agriculture and settlement were shifting south, schistosomiasis and other worm infestations were first described, in a text of 1264 for example (Elvin 1973:186). Faeces discharged into water made China the world reservoir of lung, liver and intestinal flukes and the Oriental schistosome, all serious causes of chronic illness (Polunin 1976:127). Human excreta were used as a fertiliser, and soil-transmitted helminth infestation was an occupational hazard for the farmer. According to Han

Suyin (1965:390) there was ninety per cent worm infestation among children in Peking in the early twentieth century and worms were visible everywhere on paths and alongside buildings. A 1948 source ascribed twenty-five per cent of deaths to faecal-borne infections. The aggregate weight of liver parasites in Chinese bodies is estimated as equivalent to the combined weight of two million human beings; in 1960 ninety per cent of the rural population (i.e. eighty per cent of the total) were said to be infected with tapeworms; and one-third of all deaths were reported to be caused by this helminthian worm infestation (Borgstrom 1972a:108). Anti-social customs apart, this was the penalty for a dense population operating irrigation agriculture in a warm climate, with inadequate sources of fertiliser. Endoparasitic infestation on the resultant scale may well have impaired human energy, holding down output in China and in the other Asian and Near Eastern homelands of civilisation. In consequence the gap in effective manpower between Europe and Asia was probably much narrower than population figures would suggest. Combined ill-health, heat and malnutrition in the tropics have been shown to cut labour productivity per man by up to eighty-seven per cent, besides raising absentee rates (Harrison 1979:604).

McNeill (1976) has claimed that Chinese populations learned to live successfully in warm, wet lands and are better adapted to microparasitic infestation than Europeans. The one population moved up a disease gradient, the other, by moving north from the Mediterranean lands, moved down such a gradient. It is not clear that this rules out the debilitating effects of the endemic worm infestation among the Chinese and the peasants of the Ganges valley and the Nile delta, who also worked in warm, standing water and where, at any rate in India, public defecation is prevalent. It is consistent with a vulnerability on the part of Europeans to intermittent epidemic shocks, because of their lack of adjustment to diseases endemic in Asia. McNeill (1976:138–41) finds that epidemics kept the island populations of Britain and Japan low until the Middle Ages, but whether or not this applies to the whole of Europe *vis-à-vis* mainland Asia is uncertain. There were certainly epidemics in Asia too. It is possible that there was a different time-trend, and if so this might be important for the

difference in developmental history. With demographic growth
at the end of the Dark Ages and the northward shift in the centre
of gravity of settlement, medieval Europeans may have first
endured and then adjusted to epidemic disease, whereas India is
said (Davis 1951:42) to have experienced the equivalent phase of
severe epidemics only after 1700 when her trade contacts were
opened.

Comparison in terms of the physical productivity of the soil is
unfavourable to Europe. The oriental alluvial river-basins were
more productive of plant life. In the Middle Ages, and in some
parts into the eighteenth century, seed–yield ratios for the principal cereals of 1:3 or 1:4 were all that Europeans achieved on their
sown arable, which is to say that if the area always being rested
fallow is included the yield would be lower still. Even at remote
periods of prehistory the seed–yield ratios of the oriental river-
basins are reported to have been far higher than this (Herodotus
1954:92, 308; Slicher van Bath 1963:18, 172–7; Russell 1967:96,
179). The great contrast with Asia stands revealed by the difference in population densities. In Egypt in the first century B.C. the
density was around 725 persons per square mile. In China in the
early twentieth century it was 183 persons per square mile in
Shansi province in the north, 554 per square mile in rice-growing
Chekiang in the south. These figures are to be set against those
for the most densely populated part of Europe, the province of
Holland, which in the sixteenth century A.D. still had only
ninety-five persons per square mile. It might seem that different
kinds of social organisation may have been responsible for these
differences in settlement density and hence in available labour,
which in turn accounted for the variation in yields. Nevertheless
the observables of temperature, soil moisture and the deposition
of minerals and silt, all correlates of plant growth, were initially
widely different and seem a major cause of the differences in
population densities. The very impracticability of hydraulic agriculture freed a fraction of European energies for other purposes.
The rainfall farmers of Europe might be fewer in number than the
farmers of China and India, but the former spent less time on all
aspects of farmwork than the latter spent on water control work
alone (Russell 1967:97).

More interesting than the differences in population totals and density was the European persistence in maintaining a relatively high consumption of draught animals, livestock products and woodland products, all of them heavy users of land in competition with the growing of cereals. By sowing every spare acre with grain, as was done in the river-basins of the Orient, a larger population could have been supported. Europe's human crop was not maximised. The political consequences of a society with a huge, manipulated peasant mass were avoided. The customary view of these consequences derives from Karl Wittfogel, *Oriental Despotism* (1957), a study of the long-standing relationship between irrigation agriculture and the political régime in China. The needs of constructing and co-ordinating big hydraulic works are depicted as having given rise to societies of hordes of peasants dragooned by repressive élites. Harris (1978:173–4) cites examples of ruthlessly organised building projects where the numbers of workers were clearly too large to have organised themselves on a voluntary basis, like a village fête. The instances demonstrate a difference in kind between the social control exerted in vast, centralised polities and the social control in the decentralised society of Europe. The latter had no joys to offer like the building of part of the Grand Canal of China around A.D. 600 by a population of five-and-a-half million, guarded by 50,000 police inclined to exert fierce retribution on families who withheld labour. Reportedly more than two million men were 'lost' (Russell 1967:99). Of one million labourers conscripted at the start of the seventh century to build the Great Wall over half are said to have died on the job (Dawson 1972:62). In contrast Stonehenge, Avebury, and Silbury Hill (the largest artificial earthwork in Europe) do not seem overwhelmingly massive. Their construction cannot have required or destroyed labour on anything like the scale of the Great Wall. The debates about the manner of their making do not preclude the use of seasonal task forces over many years, indeed the postulated sledging of the Stonehenge sarsens over frozen land from Fyfield Down positively calls for this.

We ought to beware of accepting too readily that Ancient and Oriental societies permanently exerted the organising rigour of modern command economies. In reality rather little, or at any rate intermittent, coercion may have been needed to cream off what little fat there was on the peasantry and thus clip the margin for investment. The large surviving monuments of Antiquity, which are the touchstone of belief in a draconian past, are not necessarily fair evidence of any particular political organisation. The vision of slaves toiling under the whip to raise the Pyramids may be misleading, or it may refer to only certain régimes of the past. Kaplan (1963) points out that from Egypt to China and beyond, great monuments may have been erected in the slack seasons of the year. There is little evidence that they involved great armies of workers at any one time and they may have taken generations to complete, with labour forces voluntary and motivated by religion. Stover (1974) also paints a much less directly coercive picture of hydraulic agriculture in China than does Wittfogel. Harris's (1978) modification of the Wittfogel thesis derives oriental despotism from the organising of workers to create new irrigation works, but only in times of pressing population growth. Reports from Manchu China suggest that repair work rather seldom required co-ordinating over whole river systems and was often inefficiently carried out by local administrators. This abolishes the need to envisage permanent slave states. Some more subtle means may have been what kept the bulk of the people poor.

Yet whatever modification we make to hypotheses about the origin of the great works of the East, they must reflect societies capable of centralised rallying power above that displayed in the Europe even of the Crusaders. Europe simply never matched the observed examples of the conscription of peasant labour for state projects. Harris (1978:90-1) observes that the six most likely regions of pristine state development (Egypt, Mesopotamia, India, China, Mexico and Peru) all featured circumscribed zones of production which presented 'special difficulties to villages that might have sought to escape from the growing concentration of power in the hands of overly aggressive redistributor war chiefs'. European agricultural society was able to avoid a comparable history of authoritarianism – a kind of political infantilism – by virtue of an open-ended productive environment of forest land and rainfall farming.

On the face of it, the absence of major frontier movements from India or China in search of *Lebensraum* is surprising. For long periods they remained to all intents and purposes closed economies, though in the historic period China undertook a great interior colonisation of southern river valleys and forests. Neither India nor China pushed settlement far into central Asia, admittedly a less productive area than the coastlands. On the contrary they were, as Rome had been, at the receiving end of invasions begun by small populations from the steppes, only five million strong or four per cent of the Asian total at the start of the Christian era. So far from occupying the steppes, the military technology did not exist that, at an acceptable cost, could protect settled zones from nomad attack. Western Europe was reasonably free from that menace.

Initially Europe had been settled from Asia. In Mesolithic times hunters and gatherers had occupied the coasts of Europe while the deciduous forests of the interior remained largely uninhabited (Clark and Piggott 1965; Waterbolk 1968: 1100–1). The Mesolithic communities were unable to switch from hunting and fishing to farming because suitable ruminants to domesticate did not occur in the continent. Agriculture had its beginnings in western Asia, where domesticable ruminants and suitable pasture grasses for them did exist, and was brought to Europe by Neolithic arrivals during the sixth millennium B.C. These immigrants created an environment around themselves in which farming might take place by clearing woodland, particularly light woods on ridge tops, and transporting with them livestock, cereal crops, pasture grasses and a whole living entourage, not all of it intentional or desirable. They brought for example the weed species of open, beaten ground.

This early Neolithic settlement was based on communal systems of full villages. House types and ethnographic parallels suggest that, from the end of the fifth millennium B.C., there was a shift away from communal villages to a system based on the extended family. The new arrangement was better adapted to settling a frontier in virgin forests which became less and less like the steppes as one moved north-west. House plans changed again at the end of the third millennium. They went from long rectangular buildings 100 feet long to less than half that length. Ethnographic comparisons suggest that this was the archaeological expression of a shift (completed by the middle of the second millennium) from a society of extended families to one of nuclear families. Long houses hardly occurred west of the Rhine. The western Neolithic had rectangular or circular houses appropriate to nuclear families and presumably deriving directly from Mesolithic hunting units. The significant trait was the nuclear family, which unlike the extended family is usually considered to offer incentive and opportunity to limit family size and which might therefore play a large part in explaining the European preference at the margin for goods rather than for children. We need to see what explanation is put forward for the persistence of a social system in Europe based on the nuclear family rather than the extended family of Asia.

European society of the second millennium B.C. was on the Celtic or Germanic pattern. Oriental in its origins, spreading out into the cold forests had transformed it. Patrilinear nuclear families met in free assemblies with a council and an elected chief. The economy was agricultural and pastoral with a landscape of farmsteads, villages and the courts of rustic princelings in open country or in assarts in the forest. Society was stratified, with farmers and field labourers, a priesthood, a warrior élite, perhaps a rudimentary class of merchants. Mutual obligations resembling those of feudalism bound society together. The culture was barbarous and insecure, with ceaseless movements of population. With no towns there was no true civilisation and the culture was therefore the antithesis of the corporate civic life that developed around the Aegean from the same Oriental roots and which became the other strand of the European heritage.

Pastoralism, which had probably been represented since early in the second millennium, appears to have developed further in later La Tène times. The scale and nature of livestock husbandry is a valuable indicator of an economy's wealth and production and consumption habits. By La Tène times enough forest had been cleared to permit a considerable growth of flocks and herds, hence perhaps the numerous Iron Age hill forts built as defended compounds for stock. It is significant that there was never a ubiquitous scavenger animal, only chicken. Pigs did scavenge in European towns, for instance in Sir Walter Scott's Edinburgh, but in the countryside there was usually enough woodland to provide a more adequate pannage than refuse and droppings. This is in contrast to China, where pigs were the main livestock, and scavengers at that, and India where in Mughal times there may have been more cattle than in Europe of the same period, but they were miserably thin scavengers with a lower milk yield (Maddison 1971:20).

'It may not be extravagant', Clark and Piggott (1965:309) conclude, 'to see an origin for much of medieval Europe in the prehistoric societies which developed in the second millennium B.C.' They consider that this was the form that persisted into the early Middle Ages and which found the rule of Rome a passing intrusion. Only when plough husbandry improved during the Dark Ages did the population grow enough to generate towns and civilisation and lift society above its old frontier status. Not only the vaunted heritage of Greece and Rome but also the cellular, high-energy, high-consumption life-style and individualist preferences of the Celtic and Germanic tribes were carried forward to become early medieval society. The once-nomadic peasantry remained bellicose. McNeill (1964:27–34) suggests that this was because they were thin enough on the ground to have to combine soldiering with their farming. The *levées en masse* of the Asian peasantry were not at all the same thing. On this archaeological perspective, therefore, Europeanness lies in the form of the original settlement history. What it amounted to was a decentralised, aggressive, part-pastoral offshoot and variant of western Asian agricultural society, moulded by the forest.

Does the establishment of a cultural form in remote prehistory *ipso facto* explain the special behaviour of later European society? The tendency among archaeologists, and anthropologists, seems to be to think that it does – to see cultures setting early and persisting inertially through thick and thin (e.g. Stover 1974:26–7). One authority, Ishida (quoted by Stover and Stover 1976:13), claims that 'the lasting character of each people has its roots in the basic culture of the time when the people first came into being'. He goes on, astonishingly, to find the emphasis on cereal-eating in eastern Eurasia, as opposed to the meat-eating of the West, in a divergence between graminivorous and carnivorous populations of *Australopithecus*. At best *Australopithecus* is a doubtful ancestor of *Homo sapiens*. Man's competition probably extinguished it. Another authority, Harris (1978:39, 168–70), sees much in culture descending directly from the range of animal species available for domestication in a given region at the very first development of agriculture. (We noted a similar emphasis in Clark and Piggott's (1965) discussion of Mesolithic and Neolithic Europe.) Harris claims, for example, that the greater depletion of large mammals in the New World than in the Old World 'set the two hemispheres on divergent trajectories and imparted to each of them a different pace of development'. This is a kind of mammalian determinism, and it encapsulates a strong methodological predilection: 'after a society has made its commitment to a particular technological and ecological strategy for solving the problem of declining efficiency, it may not be possible to do anything about the consequences of unintelligent choice for a long time to come' (Harris 1978:182).

There is an old gibe that economics is about choices, while sociology (and anthropology too on this showing) is about how people do not have any choices to make. Where a pattern of behaviour is maintained over a long span, the methodological preference of the economist is certainly to look for evidence that the short-run payoffs are stable. The assumption is that if incentives shift, behaviour will adjust rapidly. This distinction between economics and anthropology stems from studying market and non-market societies respectively (sociologists have less excuse) and the orientation has sunk deep into the mind-set of each discipline. Our concern is to account for Europeans persistently holding population growth a little below its maximum and keeping land back for livestock husbandry and woodland uses, thereby holding their consumption levels a little above those of Asia. If we find that short-term cost/benefit considerations constantly favoured the observed *very* long-term pattern of each continent, we shall have no need to rely on the postulate of cultural persistence, over unspecified periods, changeable by no predicted shift of incentives, and therefore incapable of explaining change when it did come. To investigate these matters we need to compare the calculus of forces influencing past demographic behaviour in Europe and Asia.

We might suggest, for instance, that because their initial resource endowment had permitted Europeans to consume ample livestock products and energy from draught animals, and ample wood-fuel and timber, they were unwilling to give up this standard of living. They were prepared to trade-off, at the margin, children for goods, to maintain a given target income or pattern of consumption. For the patriarchies of the past it would have been as manageable as it was attractive to marry off each and every girl as soon as she became nubile, but unlike their counterparts in the major Asian cultures European males did not practise this immediate division of the spoils of love. By that restraint they were able to hold down the growth of population. But this only rephrases the question. Why were they the ones to make that choice? After all, the initial forested landscapes of China or India would have permitted smaller populations to enjoy high material consumption, by early standards that is. Instead, population was permitted to grow without such deliberate restraint. Seemingly, copulation was preferred above commodities.

Hajnal (1965) has shown in a cautious but stimulating essay that Europe west of a line from Leningrad to Trieste was distinguished from non-European civilisations by a high age at marriage and a high proportion of people who never married at all. Birth-rates were rarely above 38/1,000 even before the adoption of artificial means of birth control, compared with rates of over 40/1,000 and often over 45/1,000 in less-developed countries today. Late marriages also allowed a spell for saving before the family was formed. These savings would be spent on mundane goods such as the family required, not luxuries, and might generate a demand for utilitarian goods on a scale not seen elsewhere. European men thus tended to defer marriage until they were able to support a family. In the 'stem family' system whereby the holding descends to a single heir, marriage was put off until the couple acquired the land. They were not encouraged to marry as soon as they were physically able by having the support of an extended family system such as existed outside Europe. What they would form was a nuclear family, closed off from their own siblings. This pattern must of course go back much further than the sixteenth century A.D. if it is to explain a persistent preference at the margin for goods over children. The demographic literature skirts the issue, but one authority does note that the nuclear family goes back 'probably to the Germanic tribes described by Tacitus' (Meyer Fortes in Hawthorn (ed.) 1978:124). We may indeed suspect that the European marriage pattern was a feature of the social order described as descending from the second millennium B.C.

The peculiarity of the European pattern is taken up by Schofield (1976). He points out that all populations are kept in balance with resources – deliberately or willy-nilly – by variations in nuptiality and fertility rates. 'What is remarkable about the populations of pre-industrial western Europe', Schofield concludes, 'is that they not only evolved a set of social rules, which effectively linked their rate of family formation with changes in their environment, but also managed to secure such low fertility that they achieved both a demographically efficient replacement of their population, and an age-structure which was economically more advantageous than the age-structures generally to be found amongst non-industrial societies today.' An essentially similar point was made by Krause (1973). Langer (1972) further urged that population growth in Europe in the eighteenth century was restrained not only by delayed marriage but by the stronger controls of widespread celibacy and infanticide. Regions where population growth threatened to swamp economic development supplemented these cultural devices with actual regulations governing marriage. Thus Wurttemberg issued decrees from 1712 requiring official approval of every marriage, effectively banning pauper weddings, and after the breakdown of regulation during the Napoleonic wars a number of Swiss cantons and all the German states except Prussia and Saxony reintroduced similar restrictions.

Studies comparing the historical demography of Europe and Asia are scarce. Among the few comparative investigations, Goody (1976) contrasts Africa with an undifferentiated Eurasia, while Macfarlane (1978) is really concerned to distinguish English experience from the remainder of Eurasia. The nearest we can find is Krause's (1973) contrast of European trends in the past with modern trends in less-developed countries, especially India, which yields the figures shown in Table 1.1.

According to Narain (1929:338), in India, 'marriage is universal. . . . Economic conditions are not taken into account by people intending to marry, or by parents when marrying their children. The proportion of the married to the total population would remain practically unchanged from decade to decade but

TABLE 1.1 *Married women as percentage of female population*

	Married (aged 15–19 years)	Married or widowed (15 years or older)
Sweden 1750	4.4	65.4
Finland 1751	(Not available)	69.3
India 1931	83.9	96.4

Source: derived from Krause 1973:171.

for calamities which cause a change in this proportion by altering the age constitution of the people.

The usual explanation for this state of affairs is that Indians, and Asians generally, wished to insure against their old age by producing sons to keep them, and to produce as many sons as possible they had to have the maximum number of children. This seems an unconvincing motive. Old age can have been contemplated with equanimity nowhere in the preindustrial world and the greater life expectancies of Europe (comparative data are given by Narain 1929:332–3) would surely have meant that old age would have been a greater consideration there. A more plausible reason for maximising family size may have been to command as much labour as possible to help recover from the effects of recurrent disaster. The background of disasters was such that Davis (1951:24) noted that the population of the Indian subcontinent moved in cycles during 2,000 years: 'The population would tend to grow slightly in "normal" times, because the customs governing fertility would provide a birth rate slightly higher than the usual death rate. This would build up a population surplus as a sort of demographic insurance against catastrophe. Inevitably, however, the catastrophe would come in the form of warfare, famine, or epidemic, and the increase of population would suddenly be wiped out.' McEvedy and Jones (1978:182–4) have recently made estimates showing a slowly and smoothly rising trend of population in the sub-continent for 1,500 years from 500 B.C., but they add that 'presumably the vicissitudes of empires, the onslaughts of epidemics and the fluctuations of food supply kinked the graph on many occasions, but of these we know almost nothing. . . . The comparison with China's graph, so often notched by catastrophe, is striking but could easily be due to China's better records.' As Russell (1979:28) observed of the McEvedy and Jones graphs, 'the assumption of fluctuations is actually far more plausible than that of smoothly upward growth'. The point is well taken in that with both India and China we are dealing with societies with an abundant environment *on average*, where there were nevertheless very frequent shocks.

The need to sow again quickly after a drought-induced famine or an epidemic was the crucial phase (Davis 1951:41), the hungry gap of the system as it were. At the end of a European winter the plough animals sometimes had to be carried, weak and trembling, from the barns to the fields, to recoup their strength on the new shoots of grass. After a monsoon failure the inhabitants of an Indian village might be in much the same state. After an epidemic it was vital that enough members of a family be left, and left fit enough to work the land. This was a motive for having as many sons as possible. Post-disaster recovery was the *pons asinorum* that Asian society had to cross.

Compare the strategy of breeding children, or sons, with the attitude to cattle in the Hindu world. At first sight it seems odd that cows were venerated above oxen, for oxen were the plough animals, just as men were the prime field labour. Venerating cows ought, *ceteris paribus*, to have had as its counterpart the better treatment of girls and women than boys and men. But just as boys were more numerous and better looked after than girls, so it was the oxen that were more numerous and ordinarily better cared for than the cows. When it came to drought or famine, however, it was the cows that were preserved at all costs. The reason was that the family's future depended on owning a cow from which stocks could be bred. As Harris (1978:163) remarks, what counted most was performance during abnormal rather than normal agricultural cycles. In an emergency cows could be used at the plough and since they were also the strategic resource for livestock breeding, they were the animals most safeguarded despite the agonising temptation to consume them. The future breeding of sons was taken care of not by venerating women but by marrying off even physically and mentally defective girls as soon as they reached twelve years of age. This conduced to a high level of fertility. Marrying off all the girls seems to have been a response to the numerical imbalance of the sexes at adulthood. In turn this was the result of disfavouring girl children so that fewer of them survived than boys. Disfavouring female children was presumably the behaviour of societies too poor to raise all children equally well and where the ordinary utility of males was higher. A similar calculus therefore underlay human demographic strategy and veneration of the cow: the goal was to scrabble through periods of disaster with breeding potential unimpaired and a supply of labour and draught power for cultivation during the recovery phase. We may add that if Europeans did not discriminate against female infants, this was surely because they were rich enough to afford the luxury of more equal survival rates.

The stringencies of the Asian environment made play-safe behaviour all too necessary. Although there is a fertility conservation problem in India, the overmastering agricultural characteristic is the climatic risk (Hutchinson 1966:249). In China there was a drought- or flood-induced famine in at least one province almost every year from 108 B.C. to A.D. 1911 (Mallory 1926). Although double or even treble cropping may be possible and in an average year a large population may be supported, the acid test is the frequent below-average season which comes as abruptly as the ice-hockey playoff of 'sudden death'. One response in India was to sow large areas with low-quality grains like *bajra* or *jowar* which resist drought better than the preferred wheat or rice. Another was to protect the short- and long-term supply of cattle in the form of cows rather than the oxen preferred for field work. Yet another was the bias in childhood care and attention that maximised the size and strength of the (male) labour force for short-run recovery, while securing the long-run supply by the obligatory, early-age marriage of all possible girls. These were not fixed and immutable cultural features, as has been shown by the shift in demographic preferences once famines became fewer in the present century (Cassen 1978:45, 54–5). They were responses to recurrent problems, whose rewards and penalties constantly reinforced them.

We may adopt the evolutionists' terms to distinguish the broad Asian and European demographic strategies (although in evolution these terms are normally used to categorise different organisms instead of populations of one and the same species). Asians would have been *r*-strategists, maximising numbers as an adaptation to frequent mortality peaks, so that some might hope to survive catastrophes. Neither nuptial age nor marriage participation rate was altered in response to adverse circumstances. Instead they tried to roll over the effects of disaster by maximal breeding. Since disasters killed disproportionate numbers of children and old people, the standard of living of adults of working age actually rose in their wake, but the birth-rate rose and high dependency ratios and low standards of living were soon restored (Davis 1951:41–2).

Europeans on the other hand would have been K-strategists ('K' referring here to the environmental carrying capacity, not to capital). Living in a more stable environment they had less to gain from producing the maximum number of progeny. They could afford to control fertility by marriage restrictions. This subtly improved the quality of the human capital, since the family could put a little more investment into upbringing and mothers were not so young and inexperienced, nor were all the women under such pressure to marry. Placed in an Asian situation, a European peasantry would have faced the same risks and would have adjusted its breeding strategy accordingly. As it was, slender though the margin above subsistence may have been for many European peasants, they remained in the *very* long term slightly but significantly better off than their Asian counterparts.

This places the explanation of the difference in Asian and European levels of breeding and income squarely in the fertility response to different risk environments. It is not quite the same as saying that marriage and fertility behaviour were the dominant influences in either environment. However, even the chief critics of the view that age-at-marriage changes played a major rôle in accounting for population change (in England) agree that a rise in the mean age at marriage of three years, say, could have at least halved the growth-rate during the eighteenth century (Crafts and Ireland 1976:510). Indications in the literature are that the gap was greater than that between Europe and Asia, or at any rate India. Our account is highly aggregative, certainly, and not all European societies were adept at coping with harvest failure or economic débâcle, as Wrigley (1966:109) points out. He compares the thin resilience of the Beauvaisis in the seventeenth century explicitly with the vulnerability of parts of (modern) South-east Asia. In the absence of technological change, populations come to rough equilibria with their resources but the resultant living-standards are not all the same. In one limiting case, proposed by Malthus and approximately equivalent to India and China in the *very* long term, living-standards will be minimised and numbers maximised. In the European case we have a model in which family size was allowed to rise with the waves of good times but to sink down in the troughs of tight resources, and numbers were kept below the maximum and incomes were kept above the minimum. Higher real incomes may have had a physiological feed-back effect in that diets high in protein and low in carbohydrate are thought to reduce fertility (Harris 1978:26–7). Underlying the European response pattern was an adjustment to a more favourable risk profile than in the remainder of Eurasia. The options were simply a little broader.

Chapter 2

Disasters and capital accumulation

The old tropical civilizations had to struggle with innumerable difficulties unknown to the temperate zone, where European civilization has long flourished. The devastations of animals hostile to man, the ravages of hurricanes, tempests, earthquakes, and similar perils, constantly pressed upon them

Henry Buckle

DISASTERS may be looked on as abrupt shocks to the economic system. Whether they arise naturally, from sudden instabilities of the earth's crust or atmosphere, or from outbreaks of disease in humans, animals, or crops, or as social disasters such as wars and accidents, there seems no practical alternative to an osmotic definition, for the effects are in any case functions of the technological specifications in which they occur and the social and economic systems which play host to them. They are not, in truth, completely exogenous acts of God divorced from the choices made by man. For example, the density of human populations, their income level and social organisation, the crops they grow and the animals they keep, all affect the degree of vulnerability to particular shocks, and the impact they will have.

Historically there is a further complication in the paucity of hard evidence on the frequency and severity of disasters which prevents us from drawing up a firm balance sheet, while even with a full record of physical losses the economic consequences would be difficult to calculate. With certain exceptions, such as early modern famines, some outstanding epidemics like the Black Death, wars (and then with little systematic concern for the effects), and the Great Fire of London (as if it were the unique urban conflagration), few types of shock to the economy are discussed by historians. Asian disasters are particularly neglected, at least in the available English-language histories. Shocks as a class of phenomena are virtually ignored; they are treated as individual, transient events of no general significance. The omission seems to reflect a stylised approach to the study of the past. Perhaps this may be passed off as resulting from a conviction that such events are outside human history and cannot be accounted for in its terms. We might have expected that narrative demands and sheer dramatic quality would have guaranteed disasters a better billing. The sum of the evidence and the real influence of disasters do not warrant such neglect.

Economists equally treat the subject as one of little interest. They tend to look on disasters, that is negative shocks which cause a fall in aggregate income, as wholly exogenous to the economic system. This can be most misleading. Economics abstracts from 'external' events that cannot be predicted on the basis of initial conditions and behavioural equations. Shocks are assumed to be mere interruptions of smoothly changing functions. Yet the past in reality was not a mill-pond occasionally ruffled by the breeze. It was made up of a ceaseless succession of adjustments to disturbances, big and little. Thus while it may be true the shifts of supply and demand curves and the movements of relative prices as an outcome of disasters are in principle no different from the merest everyday adjustment within the economy, there is as a result a descriptive neglect of disaster economics and the aggregate effect is overlooked. Most disaster history has indeed been written by natural scientists with interests in particular physical events or classes of phenomena. Their ultimate professional concern is with prediction, not with retrospective measurement of economic damage. Their scientific affiliations mean that the classifications are physical orderings and where the impact on man receives a mention, it is usually only the death toll.

Three issues especially concern us. Firstly, there is the general question of the relationship between patterns of disaster and the timing and form of economic development in Europe. Second, did disasters cause more or less damage in total in Europe than in mainland Asia? Third, was there a difference in the bias of shocks between these regions: that is, was more labour than capital destroyed in one than in the other? Given the nature of the sources, we shall follow the straightforward procedure of working through a classification of disasters and discussing their incidence and effects on Europe and Asia, concentrating on the period 1400–1800. Where possible an attempt will be made to scale the impact by putting disaster deaths on a population basis, using the population figure for the previous half-century date given in McEvedy and Jones (1978). A physical classification, as opposed to one in terms of value of loss, might be four-fold: (1) geophysical (earthquakes, volcanic eruptions, tsunamai); (2) climatic (hurricanes, typhoons, hailstorms, floods, droughts); (3) biological (epidemics, epizootics, outbreaks of crop disease, locust invasions); (4) social (warfare, settlement fires, collapse of man-made structures). These categories might be refined, but they are sufficiently comprehensive given the available evidence and the weight of argument it will bear.

Geophysically and climatically Europe is quieter than most other parts of the earth. It is therefore a little unfortunate that the type of natural disaster about which we possess most information is the earthquake. Presumably the reason for this is that earthquakes are well-defined and often spectacular occurrences. They came, however, only third in the league table of loss of life in world natural disasters between 1947 and 1967, well behind floods and atmospheric storms (Cornell 1979:5). A recent investigator (Ambraseys 1971) claims that, unlike wars and epidemics, the numerous earthquakes of the past twenty-five centuries have had little if any serious influence over historical developments in the Near and Middle East. They have never ruined a culturally advanced state, far less terminated a whole civilisation, contrary to suggestions in the older literature. According to Latter (1968–9:378), although earthquake casualties are eight to ten times greater than those in volcanic eruptions, the latter have had the more profound effect on human affairs. He instances the destructions of Minoan Crete about 1400 B.C. and the Hindu–Javanese state of Mataram in A.D. 1006 (see also van Beemelen 1956).

This interpretation of historical significance is far too narrow. Civilisation-wide cataclysms may never have happened. They are a tall order, best left to the movie makers. Nevertheless disasters have burdened certain economies more than others with overhead costs in terms of loss, damage and disorganisation. For the sake of illustration we shall start with the earthquake record in general. Next we shall look at its effect during the crucial years for European preindustrial development, 1400–1800, when the industrial stage was being set, and go on to examine the effects of the other main categories of disaster during that period.

A belt of latitude within $35° \pm 10°N$, including Japan, Central Asia, the Middle East and the Mediterranean lands, contained ninety-one per cent of all loss of life in the earthquakes studied by Båth (1967:422), some of them being remote historical events. Seventy-eight per cent of the total loss of life took place within a narrower belt at $35° \pm 5°N$. According to Båth this was due to the zone's high seismicity operating in conjunction with densely populated areas and old cultures with buildings in poor condition, itself an interesting sidelight on the state of the capital stock of these areas. European sub-totals cannot be extracted from the data, nor usefully from historical catalogues such as that by Milne (1911). Catalogue data have been severely criticised by Ambraseys (1971) for implying that the most seismic parts of the Near and Middle East are the cities. If what we are interested in is the distribution of seismicity, such scepticism may be justified. There is a disjunction between seismic scale of earthquake and level of destruction. The physically largest earthquake of the period 1948–68 occurred in Alaska in 1964, but it led to only 126 casualties, whereas that at Agadir, Morocco, in 1960, which had been several hundred times smaller in terms of energy released, caused about 10,000 deaths (Latter 1968–9:362). If however what we are interested in are the economic effects, the human tendency to report deaths, damage to major structures and to any very large number of houses makes historical catalogues of some value. Ambraseys's (1979:56) later judgement that earthquakes in the Near and Middle East have caused no significant economic loss is doubtful and seems to rely on the relatively small loss of life there in modern times.

From Latter's figures we can calculate that fewer than two per cent of earthquake deaths in the world between 1948 and 1968 happened in Europe. Will this stand proxy for the historical periods in which we are interested? Historically reported death tolls seem often to be mere conventions, or they vary, and even when the totals may be reconciled they seldom permit comparison between Europe and Asia as a whole. Davison (1936:4)

specifically notes that bodies were removed after the Lisbon earthquake of 1755 without having been counted. Estimates of deaths
in that instance vary from 30,000 to 70,000, most authorities citing
60,000 including some 10,000 due to a forty-foot seismic wave
along the valley of the River Tagus and deaths in burning buildings, but excluding 3,000 deaths in Faro (Shepard 1977:54). This
should warn us of the slipperiness of the estimates. With this
proviso in mind, the following cumulative totals are drawn from
Latter's work:

TABLE 2.1   *Cumulative deaths between 1400 and 1799 in 'earthquakes
in which the number of deaths equalled or exceeded the total in all
earthquakes between 1949 and 1968'*

China	1,230,000
India	300,000
Europe	110,000
Near East	77,000

Source: derived from Latter 1968–9: table 4.

An alternative table may be composed from the work of various
authorities (see Table 2.2). In this table the deaths at Calcutta
included a proportion as the result of a tsunamai or storm surge
in the mouth of the Hooghly river, and possibly also some
hurricane fatalities. As we have noted, some of the Lisbon
deaths were also attributable to a seismic wave, and to fires.
Property damage, as well as the death toll, is specified in
the reports for the Lisbon and Calabrian earthquakes, and for
Calabria its value is stated, but the figure hangs in the air –
we have nothing with which to compare it. The detail available about the destruction of towns and buildings in Calabria
is exceptional for the period. The earthquake literature contains almost no historical information on property damage in
Asia, only an occasional item such as that in the well-attested
Shensi earthquake (until recently the worst on record) vast numbers of cave dwellings as well as entire towns were destroyed. As
regards loss of life, China and India were more severely affected
than Europe. With Europeans comprising some 21 per cent of the
total population of Eurasia, only 0.7 per cent of the deaths in

TABLE 2.2 *Deaths in major earthquakes, 1400–1799*

Date	Location	Deaths	% of continental population
	CHINA (total 1,250,000)		
1556	Shensi	830,000	0.3
1622		20,000	0.005
1662	Not stated	300,000	0.08
1730–1		100,000	0.02
	INDIA (total 300,000)		
1737	Calcutta	300,000	0.07
	EUROPE (total 273,000)		
1693	Naples	93,000	0.09
1693	Catania, Sicily	60,000	0.05
1755	Lisbon	60,000	0.04
1783–6	Calabria	60,000	0.04
	NEAR EAST/NORTH AFRICA (total 70,000)		
1716	Algiers	20,000	
1759	Syria	30,000	
1759	Baalbek, Lebanon	20,000	

Source: Båth 1967; Cornell 1979; Davison 1936; Editors of *Encyclopaedia Britannica* 1978; Hamilton 1783; Tazieff 1962.

major earthquakes were recorded in Europe. Put another way, an Asian was thirty times more likely to die in a major earthquake than was a European.

As far as their relative incidence in Europe and Asia is concerned, climatic disasters may be grouped with the geophysical category. River flood damage, for example, has been frequent in Europe and the damage to farming and sometimes to structures has often been serious enough at the local or even the national level, but scarcely at the level of the whole continent (cf. e.g. McCloy 1938:528–9). From the seventeenth century coastal engineering has reduced the number of sea-floods (Lamb 1977:128). Europe has nothing to compare with the massive flooding along the Yellow River in China, to mention only one of the Asian flood zones. The Yellow River constantly silts up its bed and has to be confined between dykes so that the waters of 'China's Sorrow', 'The Ungovernable', or 'The Scourge of the Sons of Han' can make their way across the plain from ten to forty feet above the surrounding countryside. The river has broken out and completely shifted course several times, and a single break in the dykes may spread flood water over hundreds of square miles and cut off millions of farmers from working on their land. The land may be unfit to cultivate for years afterwards. The situation is the same on the Yangtze (Fairbank *et al.* 1973:9–10). The adoption of American dryland crops, following the post-Columbian exchange of plant species about the world, caused massive deforestation and soil erosion in the south-western plateau of China, with consequent silting of the Yangtze drainage system and large-scale flooding of the central lake region (Stover and Stover 1976:115). Lamb (1977:142) however claims fewer floods occurred from the fifteenth century.

At the other extreme, the problem of drought was also more severe in Asia than in Europe. A study cited by Mallory (1926:38) found that in 610 seasons between A.D. 620 and 1619 one or more Chinese provinces received too little rain for growing crops, and of these, there were 203 years when a 'great' or a 'very severe' drought was recorded, probably severe enough to cause a famine. Climatic disasters have a propensity to turn into famines: rainstorm breaches of the dykes of paddy fields often flood adjacent dryland crops, leaving the paddies too dry for the rice to grow.

TABLE 2.3 *Death toll for the largest individual natural disaster, by categories of disaster, Eurasia, 1400–1799*

Date	Type of event	Location	Death toll
1556	Earthquake (and landslide)	Shensi, Honan and Shansi provinces, China	830,000
1642	Flood (inland)	Kaifeng, Honan province, China	300,000+
1737	Hurricane, tsunamai and earthquake	Calcutta and mouth of Hooghly River, Bengal, India	300,000
1618	Avalanche	Plurs, Switzerland	1,496

Source: Barton 1974; Cornell 1979; Editors of *Encyclopaedia Britannica* 1978; Lane 1965; Latter 1968–9; Tannehill 1956.

Other types of biological and social disaster, ranging from
locust swarms to war, frequently produced famines, which are
not 'pure' disasters in themselves but economic summations of
other disorders. The sources tend unfortunately to note no more
than the bare fact of famine in many cases, and are not full
enough to permit exact continental comparison of the incidence,
let alone the severity. Examining lists by authorities including
Walford (1878 and 1879), Keys *et al.* (1950), Mallory (1926), and
Moreland (1972), we may see nevertheless that the frequency of
famines was greater in India and China than in Europe. China
was called the 'land of famines'. Mallory cites a study which
reports for the period 108 B.C. to A.D. 1911 a total of 1,828 famines,
or one almost every year in at least one province. According to
Buck's (1937:124–8; cf. May 1961:26–7) study, most famines between 1850 and 1932 were caused by unfavourable weather,
drought more often than flood or any other cause. Buck estimated that over all the reported famines, twenty-four per cent of
the population in the areas affected were reduced to eating bark
and grass, thirteen per cent emigrated, and five per cent starved
to death. In the worst-affected region cannibalism occurred on
average in twenty-eight per cent of famines.

Hollingsworth (n.d.:9–10) argues that cannibalism on any scale
would usually be reported and is an indication of truly severe
famine. It does not seem possible to distinguish on this basis
between locally severe and more widespread famines, but certainly the European record nowhere approaches the Chinese for
overall frequency of cannibalism (cf. Mallory 1926:40). Nor on the
face of it can we find any single European famine as severe as that
in Bengal in 1769–70, when about ten million people died,
amounting to one-third of the population (Berg 1973:211). In
some individual regions of Europe there were a few bigger losses
in proportion to population, but no single famine in which the
proportion lost of the whole continental population equalled the
Asian proportion lost in the Bengal famine. Taking the lower of
possibly conflicting estimates in Rich and Wilson (1977:555, 604,
614), East Prussia lost 250,000 people or forty-one per cent of its
population to starvation and disease in 1708–11; but comparing at
the European and Asian levels we find that the Prussian shock
was an order of magnitude less than that of Bengal (0.2 per cent,

cf. 2.02 per cent of the respective continental population totals). A higher estimate of 'half' the Prussian population lost does not alter this conclusion, since it would raise the European loss only to 0.3 per cent. Nor would an alternative guess that only three million died in Bengal in 1770 reduce the Asian proportion (0.6 per cent) below the European. At the minimum the effective demographic shock in Asia was double that in Europe, and the best of the estimates suggest that it was an order of magnitude greater. Obscurely reported death tolls for famine and disease in Louis XIV's France begin to approach the most likely level of the Bengal shock, the peak being two million in 1692–4 (Rich and Wilson 1977:597), or 1.9 per cent of the European population. This was however the European exception to prove the rule. There are no real counterparts to the constant background of severe Asian famines (Keys et al. 1950; Moreland 1923; Tinker 1966; Cornell 1979).

These famines were food-famines and not the work-famines that began in mid-nineteenth-century India when the Raj recognised the existence of unemployment on a scale necessitating special relief (Moreland 1972:205ff.). The earlier problem was that of physically finding food to eat, not the problem of securing the means to pay for it. There were insufficient carry-over stocks to provide against years when the monsoon failed over a wide region. Transport and communications were too primitive to bring in food on a mass scale. Relief measures in Mughal India were trifling and more than offset by engrossing on the part of the powerful – although in true food-famines affecting a wide area there was nothing adequate that could have been done. A solution awaited not only better social organisation but the improvement of agricultural productivity and of communications.

The options, when the monsoon rains and hence the supply of food failed, were mass emigration which took the form of aimless wandering, cannibalism, suicide or starvation. Voluntary enslavement, which often took place when there were some men who had stocks of food left, was not a real solution when there really was too little food for all to survive. Neither was expropriation of the fortunate. Yet all these things happened on a scale and with a frequency that caused a Dutch chronicler in 1650 to burst out, may the Almighty protect all Christian lands from such terrible calamities'. Recovery was a slow and tedious business. Survivors of those who had wandered away returned only slowly. Among the effects was the periodic destruction of capital, notably when the working animals died, and the lowering of levels of skill because of the deaths of expert peasants and workmen. Gujarat cotton and other goods suffered in reputation for years after the famine of 1630, certainly as late as 1639. The Deccan was still impoverished from that famine in 1653. One harvest failure could cause serious mortality; two, closely spaced as they might be when exogenous changes in the weather were acting on agriculture, could bring catastrophe. One lost crop every decade requires saving over ten per cent of gross output and thirteen to fourteen per cent of annual net output, which are stocks as large as producers care to carry even now in relatively rich countries (Kahan 1968:361). The fragility of economies that could scarcely manage this and might in any case lose more than one crop in succession is all too obvious.

Turning now to disasters with more narrowly biological causes, we come first to famines as a result of crop disease, that is the rusts and smuts which are fungal diseases of cereals. Unfortunately the main sources (Large 1940; Carefoot and Sprott 1969; Parris 1968) are primarily western in scope and do not permit comparisons between Europe and Asia, though both Europe and India are noted as suffering some particularly bad rust years.

The predominant direction of spread of human and animal diseases has been out of the Orient, across Russia or the Near East, and into Europe. These were the routes taken by cattle plagues, the bubonic plague, and in the nineteenth century by cholera. The implication may be that the vast, densely packed and poor populations of Asia were the primary breeding grounds or reservoirs of organisms parasitic on man and his livestock (cf. Polunin 1976:124). China, with its huge human population living cheek by jowl with an army of pigs, which are not unlike man as a host to micro-organisms, may have been the epicentre of virus outbreaks. Although we know of many major epidemics in Asian history (Dunstan 1975; Elvin 1973; Ho 1964; McNeill 1976; Polunin 1976), it also appears that many of the worst intermittent scourges of Europe were endemic in Asia, though spread about from time to time when pilgrimages, wanderings during famines, and military invasions mixed up populations. Although any non-historian would be astonished at the neglect of systematic study of events of such plain historical importance, this is a relatively new area of research, and we cannot yet justify definite statements. It does seem that Europe may have been at greater risk of the epidemic form of several diseases, while remaining healthier during the interludes than tropical regions where there are so many debilitating diseases and endemic killers (Lauwerys 1969:152–3). Perhaps there was also a difference in the time-pattern. Davis (1951:42) considers that whereas Europe suffered her major bout of epidemics during the Middle Ages, when she was filling up with people, India only did so when her trade contacts increased after 1700, by which period of course Europe was experiencing profound economic development. Some of the plague losses in Europe nevertheless almost rival the great disasters of Asia, although those that took place during the more recent past steered away from the developed regions of Europe:

TABLE 2.4   *Some major European plague losses, 1400–1799*

Date	Location	Death toll	% of continental population
1656	Naples	300,000	0.29
1703	Prussia and Lithuania	280,000	0.23
1711	Brandenburg	215,000	0.18
1770	Moldavia	300,000	0.21

Source: Cornell 1979:184; see also Kahan 1979:256.

Epizootics among farm animals were also spread during social disruptions like wars. The chief outbreaks of rinderpest, which was the main affliction of cattle, were definitely associated with wars. Herds driven to provision armies carried it across Europe. From the Don in Russia in 1709 it reached Switzerland and Italy by 1711, and France, the southern Netherlands, England and Ireland by 1714. One-and-a-half million cattle are said to have succumbed. From 1742 to 1748, during the War of the Austrian Succession, it was again taken across the continent and three million beasts were lost. Whatever the accuracy of these loss figures, contemporary writers make it clear that the loss of working capital represented by cattle deaths (and horses which perished during simultaneous outbreaks of a second disease, possibly anthrax) was very heavy. Governments took them seriously since losses of draught animals vital to the harvest were at stake, as well as the direct loss of livestock products. Once again we lack comparable data from India or China.

Material for exact comparison is also unavailable with respect to locust invasions, though Europe escaped lightly. Occasional swarms did make their way into southern and central Europe, but there was nothing remotely akin to the frequent and endless infestations in warmer parts of the world, such as those covering two hundred square miles or more which, having bred in India during the monsoon, move to southern Iran or Arabia to breed again and pass on to the Sudan or East Africa (Thesiger 1964:42).

Coming to the fourth 'real world' category of disasters, social disasters, we must first consider settlement fires. There were astonishingly frequent fires which destroyed entire towns and villages (Jones 1968; Jones and Falkus 1979). Scandinavian towns were particularly affected. In medieval England fires were so common that houses could be leased *'usque ad primam combustionem'* to enable landlords to recover the plot from tenants whose losses rendered them unable to keep up the rent. No compendium exists from which world-wide comparisons may be drawn and data from Asia are as usual scarce in western sources, though there are occasional references to the ever-present danger of fire in thatched, wood-built towns and villages in India (Nath 1929:162), just as there are in Europe. Accounts of town burnings are scattered through descriptions of invasions. When the Mongols cut their way across into Poland and Hungary in the thirteenth century they ruined more towns in Asia than in eastern Europe (Chambers 1979). There is also some evidence from the Ottoman empire which indicates that major fires persisted late. In Constantinople 7,000 people died in a fire in 1729, 20,000 houses were burned down in 1750, 15,000 in 1756, 10,000 in 1782, and 10,000 again in 1784. In Smyrna in 1772 3,000 houses and 4,000 shops were destroyed (Cornell 1979:313, 319). We know that over this period fires of comparable severity were decreasing in Europe. The main cause was rebuilding in non-flammable materials and will probably be found to relate to the advance across the lands of seaboard Europe of a brick frontier, or more precisely of the tile roof frontier that slightly preceded it. Gothic brickwork had appeared between 1200 and 1500 along the coast from Prussia to Flanders, Aragon and Old Castile. Warsaw had become a city of brick as early as 1431 when it was rebuilt after a fire (Wyrobisz 1978:77; Morris 1972:179). The seventeenth and eighteenth centuries saw brick more extensively used for ordinary housing, and tiles for the roofs, especially within parts of this belt of brick. In England and almost certainly elsewhere in Europe this greatly reduced the frequency of fires. Rebuilding in non-flammable materials was a function of rising incomes (while boosting them through the greater efficiency of capital) and of the precautions insisted on by central and local authorities. It is not surprising that Asia did not share in the advance. Since buildings represented a large share of fixed capital, Europe's gain from the reduction of fire loss was a sizeable one.

War was an even more serious social disaster. Did it become more or less destructive? In Europe, between the Thirty Years War and the wars of the French Revolution, destruction does seem to have fallen away. Between 1494 and 1559 Italy had been wasted by war; between 1618 and 1648 Germany was martyred. This was partly because governments were hiring larger mercenary armies than before and were incapable of supplying them properly, so that looting and plundering became their vocations. Yet with the continued growth in the size of armies, looting was reduced. The figures for the size of armies and accompanying non-combatants during the Thirty Years War and the War of the Spanish Succession show an almost fourfold increase. With no fast growth in the total population and little improvement in agriculture or transport outside England and the Netherlands, this growth was so large that there was an essential requirement for an efficient commissariat (Perjés 1970:1). Adequate provisioning stopped the worst of the looting. War of course continued to interfere with production in those areas near the fighting. Studies of tithe data for the Low Countries show that in the period 1660–1740 war years cut cereal output by fifteen to fifty per cent, a similar proportion to the shortfall in the harvest caused by a bad season. 'Peace was actually an *exceptional and abnormal* condition for a major portion of the seventeenth century' in the southern Netherlands, and indeed until the Treaty of Utrecht in 1713 (see van der Wee and van Cauwenberghe, eds., 1978: 65–75, 103–4, 113).

As regards loss of life in war, John Donne in 1621 was premature in his optimism: 'They have found out *Artillery* by which warres come to quicker ends than heretofore, and the great expense of bloud is avoyded.' But once the loss of one-sixth of the German population as a result of the Thirty Years War was over, there were moves that added up to economising on the lives of troops – until the French Revolutionaries deliberately overturned 'the rules of war' (an interesting concept) and even forbade the exchange of prisoners in attempts to deny troops to the enemy (Vagts 1959:113–14).

The literature contains several suggestions that a declining rate of population growth in Europe between the mid-seventeenth and mid-eighteenth centuries had made labour the scarce factor, and prompted economies in using it. Carnot said of the military engineer Vauban (1633–1707) that his 'principal care was always the preservation of his men' (Speaight 1975:119). Warfare became stylised, with marchings and countermarchings after the fashion of the Grand Old Duke of York. The first volley was to settle the issue. Soldiers were outfitted in bright colours, such as scarlet, with crossed bandoliers of white. This was good for cohesion and for an element of ritual amidst the blood and sick of war. It also made for excellent targets, but only the American guerillas would take advantage of that. What may have placed these play-acting limitations on all-out slaughter was the expense of hiring mercenaries when armies were growing faster than populations. Mercenary losses were thought exceptionally high when during the eighteenth century Switzerland, the recruiting ground *par excellence*, lost half-a-million men on foreign battlefields. But out of a population of one-and-a-half million this was only a loss of 0.3 per cent per annum, and of reproductively expendable males. It was in any case a substitute for losses by the hiring states, France, Spain, the Netherlands and various Italian states, which in this way externalised their costs. Out of the total of Europe's population the Swiss losses must be accounted trivial.

Losses due to disease far exceeded those of the battlefield. A

typhus epidemic killed 17,000 of the 20,000 men lost by the
Spanish army besieging Granada in 1490 (Lauwerys 1969:157),
and there are many similar cases. Eleven Frenchmen died of
deprivation and exposure between Moscow and the Beresina for
every one who died in combat. Gneisenau twice saw half his men
die in cantonments after surviving campaigns and he died in a
cholera epidemic himself. One-third of the Prussian army in
Poland died in hospital in 1794–5 (Vagts 1959:127). Attempts
were being made to reduce such losses. The French set up medical hospitals and training schools early in the eighteenth century
and founded a medical corps in the 1770s. Medical and health
routines were employed by France, Prussia and Britain to
improve the health of their armies, which as McNeill (1976:269)
observes 'were both too valuable in the eyes of authority and too
amenable to control from above not to benefit from a growing
corpus of sanitary regulations'. The feeble state of the healing art
however impeded these efforts to save military lives.

   In Asia there seems to have been no comparable incentive or
effort to economise on human life in war. Indian, Burmese and
Siamese armies were virtually *levées en masse* stiffened with mercenaries, and prone to leave an utterly devastated countryside
where they passed (Lach 1970 vol. 2:832). The Manchu invasion
of China in the 1660s cost that vast land seventeen per cent of its
population. That was a loss of twenty-five million people compared with two million lost in Germany during the Thirty Years
War. Landes (1969:34) is satisfied that the time-trend of destruction was in favour of Europe, especially its north-western parts.
On this view, Timur, who celebrated his victories by piling up
pyramids of skulls, was only the worst of a long line of Turkoman
warlords, all bad, with no equivalently murderous European
counterparts. The Muslim world, certainly, was ravaged by war
between the Ottoman Turks and the Safavid Persians for over 200
years from the early sixteenth century, with campaigns, sieges,
and massacres passing in unending succession. Iraq had never
recovered from the Mongol destruction of her irrigation dykes.
Asian bloodbaths like the sack of Delhi had no European equal.
Historians of south-east Asia emphasise the ceaselessness of
warfare there. Moreland (1972:2–4) states that if war were not the
normal condition in India and over much of south-east Asia and

the Middle East, it was at least sufficiently probable to dominate production and exchange. In Arakan, Pegu, Siam, Indo-China and the Indonesian kingdoms, there were constant local wars, at any rate in the sixteenth and seventeenth centuries. Fortunately, so Moreland believed, 'the economist can pass lightly over the details of such conflicts. . .'. The economist must nevertheless take into account the implications of nearly perpetual warfare for economic stability, and its rôle in checking development without succeeding in stemming the long-run growth of population.

Europe probably lost fewer men per 1,000 to warfare than did Asia, but it is likely that the ratio of capital equipment she lost was much less still. A salient difference may have been that there was no hydraulic agriculture with its long lines of dykes vulnerable to being breached. European capital goods were atomistic: cleared land, hedges, roadways, houses, farm buildings, livestock, small-scale manufacturing plant, stocks of goods behind the houses. There is no doubt that it was a strategy of medieval war to destroy such items and to lay waste the enemy's countryside rather than to plunge into headlong combat (Hewitt 1966:115, 117, 127, 135; Genicot 1966:section iii). What may have been the first national, or international, war, the Hundred Years War, plundered France for four generations. In Froissart's account, the English in 1346, 'brent, exiled, robbed, wasted and pilled the good plentiful country of Normandy' (Trevelyan 1942:224 n.1). After a century of these ministrations much of the farmland was grown over with brambles, thorn thickets, bracken and broom, plants which metaphorically 'came to France with the English' (Lewis 1972:26). So war continued. In the sixteenth century Ambroise Paré wrote of a campaign in France, 'we went and burned several villages, and the barns were all full of grain, to my very great regret' (n.d.:23).

Distressing as these accounts are, recovery could begin as soon as hostilities ceased, in a cellular fashion. Each little unit of farmland could be cleared and sown and harvested independently of the next. J. S. Mill (1965 vol. II:74) made the point that disasters were quickly overcome because what they represented was only the equivalent of a very fast consumption of goods that would in any case have been used up or worn out. Mill was glossing European experience. The threshold of organisational

effort that had to be crossed to put irrigation agriculture back in
working order was much greater. In Europe, recovery, however
painful, could be achieved by local initiative, piecemeal. In thirty
years the one-third of France supposedly put out of cultivation by
the Hundred Years War was all brought back (Darby 1961). This
recovery was aided by measures to reduce tax and rent burdens
and generally expand the economy (Lewis 1972:39–51), but
governmental involvement was not essential to the recuperation
of a decentralised agriculture. In European history, once peace
was restored, it is striking how quickly recovery took place; and
not only recovery of the status quo but the start of new building,
as if war were a temporary interruption to normal progress. One
of the best indicators of the stop–go economy is the war–peace
cycle of church-building (Hoskins 1950:36–41). Utilitarian structures were built too, and we should in any case remember that
churches themselves had uses as meeting-houses and school
rooms.

Referring to France between 1330 and 1730 Le Roy Ladurie
(1979:12) comments on 'its incredible capacity for recovery', and
he draws on studies of the aftermath of the Hundred Years War
for the conclusion that 'the last trooper and the last Englishman
had hardly left before the peasants of the Ile-de-France were
beginning to reconstruct their parishes, their landscapes and
their population, in an exact replica of the time-honoured patterns which had flourished a century and a half before'. There
was probably a little more than just replication, and we know that
later there were moves made to conserve capital as well as labour.
Carnot reported that Vauban's carefulness in designing fortifications arose because he 'could not bear buildings to be destroyed,
or the house of a besieged town to be fired upon' (yet his *principal*
care was to preserve his men). The Austrians abstained as late as
the Napoleonic wars from throwing up field fortifications lest
they damage agricultural land in the Low Countries (Vagts
1959:113).

Indeterminate though the available record may be of the frequency and level of disaster damage, and the constituent capital–labour ratios, we are now a little nearer some conclusions.
Europe's overall losses seem markedly less serious than those of
Asia. They certainly were, according to the careful maps of the

disaster-prone areas of the world drawn for the International Red Cross in 1923 (Montandon 1923), although of course by that date medicine and public health had gone a long way to protect Europe from epidemics, further than they had so far gone in Asia. Historically, Europe offered, in its own environment, better protection for capital goods than for labour. The shape or bias of its shocks leaned this way. Geophysical and climatic disasters were few, while wars, epidemics and famines persisted, though a combination of stylised militarism, quarantining, and the introduction of new crops like maize and potatoes began to exert an influence by the eighteenth century.

In Asia, within the context of higher overall disaster damage, shocks seem to have been more even-handed in destroying labour and capital. In China, for example, Perkins (1969:24) suggests that working capital in the form of implements and draught animals did no more than keep pace with population growth. The absolute, but not the proportionate, fixed capital in the form of farm land grew. There is little sign of the qualitative improvement in capital equipment which technological change was bringing about in Europe and which further decreased vulnerability to capital-destroying shocks there. Chinese building materials continued to be wood and pisé (rammed earth), though stone and brick did make a little headway in Ming and Manchu times. A price had to be paid for the sluggish rate of technological advance. For instance until shipping improvements, made only in the eighteenth century, China's northern seas remained distinctly unsafe and there was a continued high rate of loss of coastal shipping (Elvin 1973:139).

On the other hand Europe was developing technologically far back in the Middle Ages. The advance was asymmetric in that labour-saving changes lagged. Eventually the organisational change of the quarantine, which deserves to be included under the general technological heading, had a considerable impact, but most technological change was capital-conserving. This was particularly true in earlier periods, when medicine and public health measures lagged. Kuznets (1965:15–53) supplies an interesting view of the central but usually underrated rôle of inferior materials. Net capital formation was held down in the preindustrial world, he urges, not merely by lower average incomes and lower savings propensities but by a weaker capacity to control and recover from social and natural calamity. A large annual effort was needed to maintain or replace the slender stock of productive capital goods. Physical deterioration dictated a short economic life for assets, unlike the present day when industrial products such as motor cars, made of improved metals and plastics, physically outlast their acceptable or planned economic life. Now that the rate of technological change is high this may not matter. New technologies are not held up even briefly while goods wear out. In medieval Europe, examined closely, technological change appears unceasing, but no one could call it fast by these standards. There was in general a treadmill replacement of worn-out capital equipment.

European society in the Middle Ages and far later had two building strategies, one born of ignorance, the other of poverty. Public works and structures erected for the rich tended to be over-designed. Surviving stone bridges and the like reveal this, though the sample must be biased towards the massive. The embarrassment when magnificent buildings such as cathedrals came tumbling down, as occasionally they did, was an induce-ment to have safety factors to withstand up to twenty times the expected stress. Nowadays better computations and the testing of scale models give us bridges designed to carry only 1.4 or 1.5 times the heaviest expected load. Before theoretical work on stress analysis in the nineteenth century only experience could reduce the sizes thought safe and so raise the efficiency of capital. As the late Jacob Bronowski observed, it is only in the modern world that materials can be designed for given structural tasks rather than structures for the materials available (Pannell 1964; Knoop and Jones 1967:70–1; Taylor 1975; Timoshenko 1953). The alternative strategy was used for most buildings. They were constructed of weak and flammable materials and wore out quickly or were burned down. Excavations of deserted medieval village sites show that peasant houses lasted only a generation. The wall bases of frequent rebuildings on slightly different alignments are to be found.

These defects of construction and materials were slowly cor-rected. As we have already noted, a brick frontier did spread across Europe in early modern times, greatly reducing vulnerability to fire, as well as simple wear and tear. More capital became available for building purposes. Interest rates were already low in the Middle Ages, compared with the Islamic world, or ancient Rome (Heers 1974:623). According to Homer (1963:139–42) interest rates on commercial loans in England and Holland fell decisively during the seventeenth century, down to five, four, even two per cent. In China on the other hand, where in any case most borrowing was for private consumption and loans for productive purposes were rather rare, interest rates stayed at around thirty-six per cent. Interest rates sum up the supply and demand for loanable funds. There is no sign that European demand for funds fell off in early modern times, quite the reverse, and to Cipolla (quoted by Gould 1972:156–7) the fall in interest rates was therefore the 'true economic revolution'. Our knowledge of the rates comes from slender samples, the dispersion makes averaging an arbitrary enough exercise, and it is not always certain to what types of loan the rates refer. There is however some corroboration. According to Gregory King (cited by Deane 1960–1:352–68) capital was accumulating in England between 1600 and 1688 at an average annual rate of 1–1.5 per cent whereas population was growing at only 0.2 per cent per annum. This is consistent with a labour-destroying bias of shocks, though that would not be the entire explanation. There were shocks enough. Adam Smith (1937:328–9) marvelled that 'in the happiest and most fortunate period of them all' between 1660 and 1760, seven wars, three rebellions, the Great Fire and the Plague had not been able to stop 'the progress of England towards opulence'. Progress in Europe as a whole came a little later, but it was definitely in a similar direction. Severe disasters were less frequent than in Asia. Technological and organisational change was already reinforcing the accumulation of capital which the bias of shocks favoured. The decisive gap between Europe and Asia was widening before industrialisation.

Europe

Chapter 3

Technological drift

The progress of knowledge and industry is accelerated by the emulation
of so many active rivals

Edward Gibbon

EUROPE was a mutant civilisation in its uninterrupted amassing of
knowledge about technology. Described sometimes as a small
promontory of Asia, in its formative stages it borrowed ideas
through Islam from as far afield as India and China. In Europe,
within even the advanced quadrant of the north-west, the resultant growth was admittedly regionalised; but unlike Asia there
was, in essentials, one technological community, a system where
change in one cell tended to communicate to the remainder.
Cultural connections and the competitive nature of the states
system encouraged continual borrowing and the 'stimulus diffusion' which meant that if a problem were solved in one country it
was assumed it could be solved in another.

Nothing is clearer than that the fires of modernisation and
industrialisation, once lighted in Britain and Belgium and the
Rhineland, burned quickly to the fringes of this European system. Even Russia and the Christian colonies of the Ottoman
empire smouldered. But at the asbestos edge of the Muslim
sphere the fires abruptly died. They never took light over most of
the non-European world, Europe's overseas annexes excepted.
Deliberate European policies, such as the unequal tariffs of the
Anglo-Ottoman treaties of 1818 and 1838, sometimes helped to
dowse the flames, but this is far from being the whole explanation. Areas unaffected by Europe showed no sign of responding
or of spontaneous combustion. Japan was the only successful
non-European industrialiser. Thus Europe was a distinctive,
long-developing ecosystem. Despite internal differences in the
timing of change, it shared the fact of change and must be treated

45

as an interconnected whole. The differential progress within Europe is not our concern here.

The improvement of the means and context of production by gradual steps from ancient times is a puzzling feature of the European record. The widening of the market and swings in relative factor prices do not seem to account powerfully for the steady onward drift of technology, one of the pointers being that advanced techniques were retained and others actually emerged during periods of demographic and price recession or slow-down such as the later Middle Ages and the 'General Crisis' of the seventeenth century. Neither does any gross deficiency in raw materials seem to provide more than background encouragement to the search for substitutes. Some solutions to problems of rising prices for materials are technically impossible until the state of the art is far advanced, meaning until underlying scientific concepts are refined and fed back into the production process. For instance, it was difficult to save on land-using raw materials for the textile industries before the arrival of factory-made synthetics, but if it was not easy to save on land it did prove possible to save on labour by substituting capital in the form of machinery. This may have imparted a bias to the course of technological change but hardly explains its genesis, and neither does the intriguing fact that Europe became a continent where the fundamental scientific work went regularly forward, neither too much stimulated by the industrial needs of the moment, nor too aloof from the practitioners of the industrial arts to be unnoticed and unused by them.

With invention the inspiration was not necessarily financial. Particular scientific enquiries or technical problems attracted work by men whose elasticity of effort was low with respect to material reward, although economic growth would have had a positive effect by expanding the number of individuals who could take such an attitude and still make a living of sorts. The explanation of the underlying European propensity does not seem directly economic, however, and we would be well advised to look at the nature of the society to try to grasp the backgrounds of inventive individuals and the toleration with which, by and large, they were regarded. What we do in this chapter is to examine the record of technological change in order to emphasise how far back and how persistently it runs, and to stress the accumulation and significance of an underbrush of technical lore.

We begin at the Roman domination over western Europe. For four hundred years and more barbarian expansion was kept in check. During that time, in order to support a growing population which could no longer flow into fresh lands, the Germanic peoples were given an incentive to turn to technological invention and innovation, to the extent of improving their ploughs and extending the use of improved types (Wailes 1972:173–7). From the retreat of Rome until about A.D. 800 much of the continued increase of population was the result of the immigration of these peoples from further east. Between 800 and 1100 there is evidence of a renewed intensification of production in the shape of assarting and land reclamation. The population had settled; it was still growing; but whether that renewed growth was really the cause of the intensification of agriculture or one of its effects is not established.

As late as the sixth or seventh century, Europe north of the Loire was so thinly peopled still that the bubonic plague pandemic administered much less of a shock there than in the older-settled Mediterranean lands (Biraben and Le Goff 1969). A recent find of remains of the black rat, *Rattus rattus*, in a filled-in Roman well in York, several centuries before the previously accepted date of its arrival in Britain, raises the possibility that plague was in fact recurrent in Anglo-Saxon England, and even that it occurred in fifth- and sixth-century towns ('S.B.' *Nature*, 13 Sept. 1979). Nevertheless an asymmetry in the effects of the pandemic is a reasonable inference from the lower concentration of population in northern Europe than in the urbanised hinterlands of the Mediterranean. Because it was, and could be, less shocked, the suggestion has been made that the north-west was subsequently able to advance relative to the south. The population in the former overtook the latter about A.D. 800 (McEvedy and Jones 1978: fig. 1.10).

High, even rainfall and passable summers made much of north-western Europe suitable for growing the small grains, wheat, barley, oats and rye, and for grazing animals on the vigorously growing grass. A varied diet comprising a thin mess of cereals in the form of gruel, together with the products of food-gathering, hunting and animal husbandry may have become more heavily dominated by bread during the Dark Ages. The argument is that the waste, which was in reality low-intensity grazing land with scrub, together with hunting territory, retreated before the plough. Increases in the number of water-driven flour mills and flour merchants on inland waterways, even in the heart of barbarian Europe, and in the numbers of bread ovens are all said to reflect the greater proportion of bread grains entering the diet (Duby 1974:188). On the other hand scarcer grazing may have inspired more care in managing livestock.

Nutritional advantages over the cereal diets of the older civilisations probably remained in the continued supply of a relative abundance of livestock products. A claim has also been made for the special vitality imparted to Europeans by the beans in the wheat/beans/fallow rotations established on heavy land. 'I realized', wrote White (1962:159), 'that an enlarged supply of proteins might have something to do with the abounding vitality of Europe in the later tenth century.' The chronology of this development is perhaps more doubtful than its general outline. The diets of agricultural Europe, adjusting to the filling up of the land with people, may have retained advantages compared with purely cereal diets if they included beans, livestock products and a residual supply of hunting products.

Dark Age agricultural advances based on the 'new' heavy plough with wheels, mouldboard and coulter, the horseshoe, the horse collar, and above all the transition from a two-field to a three-field system in Carolingian times have been the subject of doubts. Little improvement in methods or in rotations has been demonstrated from the time of Charlemagne to the twelfth century (Duby 1974:189). This implies that the main changes were in the area cultivated, which squeezed the area for permanent grazing and may have altered the mix of output. Conceivably it was only in the eleventh, twelfth and thirteenth centuries that most farmers were able to afford the new technology; the changes historians have detected did occur, but were patchy and very slow. It was after the ninth or tenth century that horses replaced oxen, and then slowly. They were still rare in Germany and at the southern and northern extremities of Europe as the Middle Ages closed, though by then they had colonised the territory between. Since horses were not usually used or sold for meat and cost more to feed than did oxen, their adoption does presuppose an adequate production of fodder and a degree of specialisation within the livestock industry (Le Roy Ladurie 1979:85–6; Lewis 1958: 490–1; Grigg 1974:161).

There is an identification problem. Were these technological diffusions a response to population growth or its cause? Thus the better utilisation of the horse's strength by means of the horseshoe and collar saw two-wheeled carts replaced by four-wheeled ones by about 1250 (Chaunu 1979:233). But this might equally have been a new ability to transport larger loads of crops, helping to make demographic expansion possible, or a response to the need to provide for an already growing population. The notion that there was an agricultural revolution which permitted and encouraged population growth and economic expansion in the tenth and eleventh centuries has seemed to fill the requirement of an explanation for that growth. A felt need does not however guarantee a correct explanation. The whole topic is shadowy. It may even be the case that historians of the early medieval period have exaggerated the degree of economic revival. Bridbury (1969) has urged that the roots of the revival stretch way back into the Dark Ages and were not the result of renewed Italian maritime trade and urbanisation during the eleventh century. Metcalf (1967:357) argues that north-western Europe was already wealthy by the end of the eighth century, as witnessed by a bustling exchange of goods and coin. The level of development tempted the Norsemen and permitted them to cause more widespread dislocation than a purely subsistence farming population might have felt. Other authorities are inclined to push the centre of gravity of agricultural change (the extensive adoption of new methods) in the other direction – later into the Middle Ages. One obvious danger is that what historians observe is what is recorded and that what we are being shown is a growth in recording rather than in the economy. Perhaps we exaggerate the real as opposed to the symbolic ending of external aggression, but surely only in part. The reality of demographic growth in the tenth century is generally accepted.

The explanation of expansion may be agricultural, as in most of the accounts cited, or political, or the two combined. Consider the 'political' case. The westward folk migrations of the fourth to the seventh centuries settled down, giving rise to considerable ethnic and linguistic diversity because they lapped over older settlers in a topographically fragmented Europe. Stable states closed quite rapidly around the feudal hierarchies. External pressure from Vikings, Magyars, and Moors was contained, though the invasions had bitten deeply enough into western consciousness to leave a recognisable Magyar and Islamic imprint today on ceremonial horse equipment in Britain and the United States (Jankovitch 1971). With the end of the assaults trade revived, especially trade initiated by the Scandinavians, and trade in the Mediterranean. A belt of new states in Poland, Hungary and Bohemia represented an eastward extension of settled government of a kind conducive to commercial revival. As trade expanded so towns grew, and the urban demand for food stimulated agricultural revival (Barraclough 1976), though one may doubt the power of tiny towns to make much difference. Mere peace and the end of invasion did permit a rise in population, in turn requiring more intensive cultivation, more reclamation and more internal colonisation. This demographic pressure, with its political causes, may have impelled the diffusion of the better methods of farming. One writer goes so far as to observe that the boom from the eleventh to the thirteenth centuries in building, commerce and urbanisation may have derived from a more efficient squeeze on agricultural producers and not from any inherent rise in their productivity (Hilton, in Hilton and Sawyer 1963:95–100).

It is indeed not clear that any test has been proposed to discriminate between the political and technological explanations of this progress in Europe. The best clue, which seems to make new farming techniques a dependent variable, is their very slow diffusion. The capital formation needed to extend animal-drawn plough husbandry on the existing cultivated acreage and on marginal land, mostly former forest, was not easy. Although for the period up to the eleventh century there are no reports of severe population pressure, such as relate to the early fourteenth century, the alacrity with which men joined the Crusades at the end of the eleventh century may show that Europe was filling up.

Although there was still room, clearing the forest and tilling the waste may have seemed harder than the time-honoured practice of seizing resources from someone else that now presented itself again in the guise of a march on the Holy Land.

At first Europe was not well placed to capitalise on the gains in either farm productivity or political stability. Politically, western Europe was fragmented into originally defensive feudal units bristling like hedgehogs against the onslaughts of the Magyar horsemen (who once reached the mouth of the Loire in the tenth century); the Moors (whose pirates destroyed Barcelona in 985, pillaged Pisa as late as 1004, and established an outpost in the Alps which compelled coastal bishoprics in southern France to move inland); and the Vikings. Feudal units were arranged like nests of boxes, as John Aubrey put it. But as feudalism evolved into, or found itself encased within, emergent states, its energies may have been projected outwards into conflicts between the larger polities. A king who could in this way externalise the aggression of his barons was safer from revolt at home. Internal disorder fell off as kings did begin to arbitrate and police conflicts among their subordinates. The change was faint at first and there were still armed clashes between the retainers of landowners in sixteenth-century England, but it was change for the better.

The approximately contemporaneous ending of external shocks, and the waning of the worst of feudal strife, seem to calibrate European history. There was a new beginning in the tenth century, whether or not political events are sufficient to account for the economic upswing. The Vikings were repulsed at the siege of Paris in 885 and heartily defeated on their return in 896. Soon afterwards they were converted to Christianity and the French recognised their settlements in the 'Duchy of Normandy'. In England they were confined to the Danelaw by Alfred after 886. They became traders of Flemish woollens to the Baltic, and they settled down. Canute in 1017–35 united England, Denmark and Norway. As to the Magyars, they were beaten at Lechfield near Augsburg in 955, Christianised, and settled to form the Hungarian state. Islam had been contained since her defeat by Charles Martel near Tours and in any case the forests of central France reduced the manoeuvrability of the horses of such invaders and put them at a disadvantage. Islam's own political divisions were to Christendom's advantage. By the end of the tenth century Islamic countries were importing slaves, metal goods and timber from Europe in exchange for gold (Homer 1963:86). The trade was indeed older, but repeatedly broken in war by prohibitions on the export of strategic materials (arms, iron, timber, occasionally food) to Islam, mainly in attempts to keep down her navy. Now the trade became more regular (Strayer 1974:403–4).

In the east, Russian and Byzantine resistance to the central Asian hordes made a buffer for Europe. Gradually the balance swung the other way and Europeans took their turn at being the aggressors. Pisans and Genoese took the offensive against weakening Arab power, conquering Sardinia, assaulting Arab Sicily and the coast of North Africa, freeing the Tyrrhenian Sea, and in 1091 recapturing Corsica. The Norman invasions destroyed Arab power in Sicily and established the principality of Antioch in Syria. The First Crusade of 1096 gave control over the Mediterranean to the Italian cities and made it possible to open orderly trade with the East. It was not only the ending of the shocks as Europe went on the offensive that was significant, but the political growth implied by the alliances that made large-scale resistance and a shift to the attack possible. For example, France was welded together at this time by Franks, Goths and Roman provincials combined to fight the Magyars, while Austria was consciously founded as a frontier March (Mackinder 1962:247–9, 254).

In the tenth and eleventh centuries there were signs of distinct expansion. Land was reclaimed along the North Sea estuaries. Towns grew and in the High Middle Ages a great wave of new ones (Bastides) were founded, laid out on a grid plan, often on wasteland at the junction of two parishes, inserted between existing market centres by lords and bishops and kings seeking to cash in on the expansion of market activity. Church-building increased greatly in the tenth century. Population began to thicken up the continent away from the Mediterranean (McEvedy and Jones 1978; Usher 1930). Economic and cultural development quickly followed the demographic flag. Between A.D. 1 and 1000 the wave of high-density population (by the standards of the day) advanced from the Lombardy Plain on a rather narrow front through France to the Channel coast and the line of the modern Franco-Belgian border. Western France was not yet affected. By 1200 the area that is now Belgium, and parts of Germany and central Europe west of a line from Ostend to Trieste, lay within the wave front. This meant that a dense rural population with a degree of urbanisation had come into being, representing a market or markets large enough to dissolve the tighter non-market ties of feudalism. As McEvedy and Jones (1978:29–30) guardedly remark, 'societies which have (1) a high density of population for their time and (2) a high rate of increase seem to be better at innovating than most'. This seems to accord with the vigour of high medieval western Europe.

To younger sons the continent may quite swiftly have come to seem crowded. The Crusades may have been examples of would-be mass outmigration. Between 1098 and 1250 five Crusades took place, the first involving 300,000 people in setting out for the Holy Land on marches of up to 2,500 miles. By the Second Crusade of 1101 the shipping capacity was available for combined land-sea operations. About 1095 Pope Urban spoke of crusading in frontier terms. In 1108 at a mass meeting at Merseburg in Germany similar words were used to whip up an assault across the Elbe into the lands of the pagan Slavs. Men were invited to win at one stroke salvation and a land of milk and honey: 'the country is excellent, rich in meat, honey, feathered game and flour' (Trevor-Roper 1965:129). Despite all this brave activity there was a surplus now for investment at home, non-material though its goals often were, suggesting that sources of rising productivity had been tapped – or creamed off. Thus, almost at the same moment as the Crusades, there occurred ecclesiastical building on a scale sufficient to be labelled the 'Cathedral Crusade' (Gimpel 1977:43). Between the years 1150 and 1280 some eighty cathedrals were erected in France alone. Many of them were in the cloth towns of the north, witnessing a big and profitable expansion of trade and industry. In England between 1100 and 1400 twenty-five or thirty cathedrals equivalent in size and design to Westminster Abbey were built or substantially altered, together with a great many abbeys and parish churches (Johnson 1967:203).

Eventually the medieval economy may have run into a problem

of declining yields, though the case for believing that this must have been so has been questioned by a modern ecologist (Loomis 1978). By the early fourteenth century the evidence is consistent with an erosion of income gains by the continued growth of population. To this society, caught without defences, the Black Death came as a massive shock. Yet all along there was an accumulation of organisational and technological skill, accompanied by a physical accumulation of buildings and other structures some of which, and not only religious edifices, remain in use. In other words, neither population pressure nor the Black Death wiped out the gains of the High Middle Ages as regards technological knowledge or stocks of fixed capital.

There had been definite and lasting extensions of control over some aspects of the environment. There was a diffusion of water-mills over northern parts of Europe which represented a tapping of inanimate energy sources. Water-mills supplied more generous and reliable power, first for milling grain, in the ninth century for making mash for beer, in the tenth century for fulling cloth, and in the twelfth century for the metal trades. This was more ample power than was available before (grain-mills were a real advance on pestle and mortar) or than was to be had around the Mediterranean or in Asia. Thousands of water-mills were in use by the tenth century. Whereas 40 had been constructed in Picardy between the middle of the ninth century and 1080, 50 were added by 1125 and 165 more before 1200. In England, too, the numbers continued to rise after Domesday, especially in 'under-developed' areas like Devon (Duby 1974:187). Some tide-mills were added during the eleventh century and in the thirteenth century there was a rapid spread of windmills (White 1962:84, 87). The complex machinery and gearing found in mills presumably caught the attention of all who sought solutions to mechanical problems.

Environmental control was exercised in the household. No doubt this primarily represented welfare gains, but there was a feedback on work efficiency. Clothes made of wool spread in England from the end of the twelfth century. The Normans brought the use of masonry in place of earthen and wooden dwellings. More efficient domestic heating was made possible in the lower rooms of castles by moving the hearth from the centre to the side and putting a broad flue through the wall, which avoided smoke pouring into the upper chambers. The invention of the fire-grate and the chimney, the use of coal, and the making of glass with which to glaze windows all made for greater indoor climatic control (Markham 1947). Slowly these devices trickled down from the rich man in his castle towards the poor man at the gate. The first chimney in the world, or perhaps the claim is that it is the oldest dated survival, is probably in the King's House, Southampton, and is of the twelfth century. The earliest glass windows in north-west Europe are in the twelfth-century church of St Denis, Paris. Henry III, having married a southerner, Eleanor of Provence, in 1236, may on her account have issued his orders for improvements to his castles up and down England. These changes included glazing the windows, making porches, wainscoting walls, lining the roofs, and building fireplaces and chimneys. A century or two later these innovations had spread more widely. In the mid-fourteenth century fireplaces were introduced into Lombardy and Tuscany, but in those regions there was no satisfactory means of controlling the heat of summer. It was in north-western Europe when the chimney, the hearth and the glazed window had tempered the worst of the winter chill, and where the summer was seldom hot, that dwellings first became adequate all-year living and working environments. A controlled microclimate was a generalising of that comfort of caves, furs and fires which had softened the rigours of man's first entry into the misnamed temperate latitudes but which could not be provided on the scale of an agricultural society. This was not a matter of health and welfare alone; it offered a gain in productive efficiency for the mother and the housewife, the scribe and the worker in domestic industry. The real spread of such improvements into the dwellings of the yeoman class (in England) did not come until the sixteenth century. At that period upper storeys were inserted in hall-type houses, proper chimneys were built, windows were glazed, and more and better furnishings were acquired. 'Individual distance' was respected when chairs replaced medieval benches (such as survive for low table meals in Oxford and Cambridge colleges). Great effects have been attributed to these improvements, in particular the survival rate for mothers lying-in is thought to have been favourably affected.

The Dark Ages and the Middle Ages thus saw slow improvements in dietary standards, available inanimate energy, the human habitat, technological know-how, the stock of capital and the size of political groupings. Europe was like a nestling cuckoo flexing its back muscles among the older civilisations which were its siblings. By the start of the fourteenth century, population growth was reducing the gains in diet as men and their livestock came into competition for the food output of the limited supply of land. Technological change in agriculture was not fast enough to offset this. But other advances were not much eroded. Equipment, know-how and organisation all survived the Black Death. To that extent there was a ratchet effect in European development. The fall in population as a result of the bubonic plague has been described as a kind of Marshall Plan. Thereafter, according to Herlihy (1971:164), Europeans were psychologically prepared by the better diet that a reduced population could afford, and 'perhaps' by the greater energy that came from being better fed, to enter a renewed age of expansion. As Chaunu (1979:286) points out, the shift towards meat and wine consumption in fifteenth-century Europe tended in terms of available human energy to counteract the effect of a shrunken population. We may wish to speculate that in a largely agricultural society there were inverse movements of population and *per capita* protein consumption. Adjusted for quality and energy the input of labour may have fluctuated less than the big demographic cycles suggest. Together with accumulating technical skills this may imply that the pace of economic development was steadier than first appears. The danger of a *very* long-term approach is that lags in development may be brushed aside as transient pauses in an irresistible forward momentum, as if the economy must solve its problems, given only time. There is no certainty that technological or scientific problems will yield solutions. And yet on the technological front, the history of Europe does begin to look like a persistent drifting advance in which, compared with the sluggish nature of other civilisations, the lags seem relatively minor.

Studies of technology transfer have concentrated on intercountry movements. Cultural similarities and frequent migrations of skilled workers did provide a basis for successive and overlapping diffusions among the countries of the European (and American) orbit. Treatment of technology transfer between whole civilisations has been more cursory. Usually it is confined to mentioning borrowings at the interface of two pairs of systems, China and Europe or Islam and Europe. The sequences were obviously more complicated than that. There were significant flows from China to India and Islam, and from India to Islam. As Taagepera (1978:124) has observed, western history has a pronounced but largely buried cultural bias and has been skilfully pruned of some of its roots as well as some of the branches: 'The term Renaissance itself is suggestive. It is as if the scientific–technological phoenix flew from the Middle East to Greece, then to Rome, and then died, only to arise from the same Italian ashes a thousand years later.' In reality the phoenix had gone back to Byzantium, travelled all over the Arab world, picked up some feathers from India and China, and only then returned to Italy.

Europe certainly assimilated technologies that had originated as far east as China. The prior existence of intellectually advanced civilisations created important external economies for Europe, externalities unavailable to late-comers outside the Eurasian land mass, such as the cultures of Meso-America. Some of the borrowed techniques were directly useful in the European voyages of discovery: navigational aids,' the compass and astrolabe; improvements in rigging (a fusion of Atlantic and Red Sea modes); gunpowder for cannon to subdue the unwelcoming. Other technologies were borrowed too. Or they were stolen (sericulture is a case in point). In most instances the'origins of these techniques are misty; elaborations and even independent discoveries within Europe need to be considered. When individual inventions are looked at closely they often prove not to have been single formative events, blinding flashes on the road to Damascus, but accretions and improvements on a good idea. The dating of invention and innovation, still more the assessment of economic impact, dissolves into less precise and longer periods than are the units of conventional historical discourse.

European society could generate novelties and it was capable of borrowing effectively. What Bacon could label in Jacobean times as the three greatest inventions known to man – compass,

gunpowder and printing – all derived from China. Yet it was
Europe that brought them to a high pitch, employed them pro-
ductively on a wide scale, and generally in technology and science came to surpass its mentors. Europe's achievements
stretched back to the horse-collar, horseshoe, water-wheel,
crossbow, and barrel, all introduced in the Dark Ages (Wesson
1978:154–5). The boom in cathedral-building necessitated and
bred immense skill in design and construction, which by itself
might have paralleled the leaning towards civil rather than
mechanical engineering that characterised the ancient and oriental civilisations. But it did not stand alone. Progress in other
directions, such as the application of inanimate power to productive ends in the water-mill, was adding a mechanical dimension.

The Middle Ages have been described by a popular work as
technologically 'the lull that never was'. The eleventh century
saw ships built by the cheaper skeleton-first method instead of
hull first (White 1972:167; Chaunu 1979). The twelfth century saw
sericulture (as distinct from the weaving of imported eastern silk)
spread first to Sicily, then to Italy. The thirteenth century saw
ships powered by sails instead of oars, and steered by the hinged
rudder. The compass was taken into widespread use between
1270 and 1300 and broke down the old seasonality of sailing since
it made safer voyages possible in the Mediterranean in winter
and made voyages from the Straits of Gibraltar to the English
Channel safer at all seasons (Lane 1965:331–44). As White
(1972:167) mentions, this raised the efficiency of capital. Bernard
(1972:318) adds that the fall in insurance rates by the mid-
fifteenth century down to five-and-a-half per cent for ships and
cargo on the Genoa–London run reflects the improvements taking place in navigation as well as in the writing of risk insurance
itself. Other developments – wheelbarrows, spectacles, mechanical clocks, the spinning-wheel, all of them appearing in the
thirteenth century – leave no doubt concerning the technological
vitality of the Middle Ages. The social savings associated with
them are scarcely to be measured but may be conceived by the
mental exercise of imagining the world without them. The production of armour with separate joints to be fitted together suggests that a factory-like division of labour was already starting to
emerge (even though in principle a single armourer could build

up each suit of armour by that method); certainly it was emerging in the disarticulated factories of cottage industry, with the concentration here on one process, there on another.

Despite difficulties in measurement and dating, the fifteenth century turns out, on examination, to have been a period of distinct technological advance. Vilar (in Landes 1966:37) goes so far as to cite a United States government report which counted 50 'important' inventions for the period 1450–1525 compared with only 43 during the eighteenth century. A count of this kind, which I have failed to find in the report cited, usually involves treating as homogenous units inventions that were quite diverse in character. Even so, the point is probably established that the fifteenth century saw vigorous inventive activity. The industrial inventions of the eighteenth century, three hundred years later, cannot sensibly be treated as though they burst onto the stage of history and suddenly galvanised a frozen set of actors. Some key inventions of the eighteenth century are easily enough picked out, *sine qua non* of the machine age, but they distract too much attention from the traditionally inventive economy in which they appeared.

The middle years of the fifteenth century witnessed quick developments in the making of cannon which became capable of laying waste castles. By the early years of the sixteenth century, in an institutional change of great military significance, the permanent army replaced the forty-day feudal levy (Bean 1973). In only fifty years sea-going sailing vessels progressed from single-masters into three-masters carrying five or six sails (Toynbee 1957:296). The easily handled caravel then produced was indispensable during the voyages of discovery. Parry sums up his meticulous discussion of the evolution of boat-building by reporting that 'the vital marriage between square-rig and lateen, between Atlantic and Mediterranean, occurred in the short space of about twenty years in the middle of the fifteenth century' (Parry 1964:63). Ships became sturdier, better at catching the wind, easier to steer. Navigation became easier and by 1500 good portolan maps (sailing directions) were to be had.

Developments were wider and went deeper than even these fundamental examples show. In one direction they succeeded in affecting the productive basis of the economy in food production.

This was by the takeover of originally Indian crops which Islam had brought westwards to Spain (Watson 1974) and the insertion of forage crops like clover into rotations in the Low Countries. The crops of the earlier Arab Agricultural Revolution were tropical in origin and their potential in northern Europe was mostly nil. But as Europeans began to farm transatlantic colonies from Brazil to Virginia these crops came as effectively onto European markets as if they had been sown in the fields around London or Amsterdam. Similarly there were mysterious but profound improvements in the methods of fishing and fish processing which the Dutch, the northern Netherlanders as they were then, raised to real arts at the very beginning of the fifteenth century. And in an institutional change conducive to a high rate of technological change in the future, Florence issued the first known patent in 1421, for a canal boat equipped with heavy-duty cranes, and Venice in 1474 enacted the first formal patent law (Sprague de Camp 1974:393). In still another direction the development of the printing press began to push down the price of information.

The German, Gutenberg (d. 1468), synthesised a number of known devices to produce movable type, and the printing press itself, and hence the replicated book. Block printing had long been used in China and so had paper-making, which Islam learned from Chinese prisoners in the eighth century, and Europe learned from Islam. A press to flatten the paper was derived from the winepress. Gutenberg added the use of cast-metal print and a system of interchangeable parts by fitting shanks to individual letters so that they might be picked out and slotted in again to compose different words (Steinberg 1961). The prospective multiplication of the printed word was at once evident, though the initial advantage over hand-copying was not quite such a foregone conclusion as may now appear. Hand-copying was an established trade with an organised market for its products. There was one entrepreneur who carried out crash commissions to copy manuscripts by employing 45 copyists. In a single 22 month period he was responsible for turning out two hundred works in an unreported number of copies (Wightman 1972:59). The copyist gilds were so strong in France that the effort to undercut them was at first mostly made in the feudal units of Germany where central control was lacking (Innis

1972:141). Within fifteen years of Gutenberg's death, however, the effort was sufficiently successful for there to be printing presses in every European country except Russia. By 1500 there were 1,700 at work in a total of 300 towns (Febvre 1976:178–9, 184–5). The number of titles being printed annually was over 2,000 by 1600 and by 1815 had risen to about 20,000. Spectacles had already prolonged the reading life of the old and now cheaper books brought that life forwards, to wider and wider groups of children. Cheap stores of technical knowledge moved outwards to the men of action and affairs, the military, the administration, the landowners. The habit of having resort to the written word was much extended when it became available in printed form and although printed contracts and law may seem to represent conservative precedent, they could also be mulled over, argued about and changed by the force of the minds of men who, without multiple copies of ever more numerous books to consult, would never have come into contact at all with the precisely stated ideas of others (cf. Eisenstein 1970).

Knowledge has been remarked as a curious factor of production, for it is not diminished by being used as physical resources are. The stock of knowledge now began to build up in books and libraries. The main market for printed books was secular, not ecclesiastical. An international network of trade routes and fairs was used to sell books, for, despite the hardening of national languages at just this time, scholars still spoke, wrote and read Latin and books in that language had international currency. The rise of national languages did not in any case mean an infinite fragmentation of the market because it was at the expense of lesser regional languages like Cornish. The comparatively high degree of literacy and wide distribution of middle-level incomes in Europe helped the book market, as did the openness of society attested by incomplete and haphazard censorship now that the church was no longer universal and the rulers of the various nations took different views of what it was permissible to print. This openness of society, together with its inventiveness, becomes what is to be explained. The economic consequences were enormous. The contrast with China is marked. Although as many as one-third of the books in the Imperial palace library were printed volumes by the start of the fifteenth century (Dawson

1972:261), the printing technique used was not as flexible as Gutenberg's so that, even had more Chinese been literate, mass production would have been difficult.

The parallels in form and timing between the breakthroughs in European printing and exploration are striking. Both had respectable prior records, the big increase in manuscript production and the secularisation of subject matter from the twelfth century in the one case, the big extension of experience of the world outside Europe acquired by such travellers as the Vikings and Marco Polo in the other. Both leapt forward in the late fifteenth century, with the effects of Gutenberg, with Columbus and da Gama. There had already been an increase in the extra-somatic information available to western man with the writing and copying of texts by hand. These stores of data could be replicated and they did not die with the biological individual. Facilitating this process by means of printing meant a quantum jump of an order comparable with that made geographically by the explorers. The ratchet effect so evident in western progress owed much to the superior means of storing and disseminating information.

The history of such major advances, though they were compounds of minor improvements, still gives by itself too discontinuous and dramatic an impression of the manner of technological change. Ceaseless tinkering is a defining characteristic of the culture. Gilfillan (1935:275), who studied the developments in ship-building, noted the error in separately labelling what were merely stages in a continual evolution: 'what is called an important invention is a perpetual secretion of little details . . . somewhat arbitrarily defined by a word or phrase in the English language, and by our standardising habits in thought'. In his view the process was more akin to a biological unfolding than a series of acts of creation. Myriad small changes in technical design diffused themselves through many industries, though not so fast before the nineteenth century as to engender the expectation that there would be much real advance in a man's lifetime. From the point of view of the economy there is the further problem that what needs to be charted is innovation rather than invention, with the insuperable difficulty of measuring the contribution of endless little waves and eddies of change.

This version of events implies that there was no single dramatic phase of cost reduction. Instead progress was always being made in some sector, stimulated by the increase of trade, the widening of the market, and regional specialisation. Rostow (1975) has argued that this momentum was incapable of sustaining itself. As the benefits worked themselves through the economy, so the effects would run down. There was no breakthrough to self-renewing techniques that could go on cutting manufacturing costs before the inanimately powered machines of the eighteenth century. This is a misconception about the dynamic of earlier technical change and the vast remaining scope for it. To support his view Rostow twice quotes Perkins (1967) to the effect that Chinese experience demonstrates there to be no 'natural or irre-sistible' movement from commercial development to manufactur-ing. Rostow adds that this is borne out by the histories of Greece, Rome, India and the ancient empires, and he quotes an observa-tion that an Athenian citizen of the time of Pericles could dine off food and lounge on furnishings from points in a trading world spaced as far apart as the Black Sea, Persia and Carthage, without that world having generated significant technological change in the manufacturing industries. Curiously, Rostow admits that there was slow technical change in pre-eighteenth-century Europe but only in the two industries where he is also prepared to concede that there was substantial trade, i.e. food and textile production. This slights the extent of trade in timber, salt and metals. Technological change was much wider than the agricul-tural and textile sectors and only by the febrile standards of the last two hundred years can it be called slow. By the pertinent measures – Europe's own past or the standards of the ancient or oriental societies – technological change in late preindustrial Europe was not slow at all. The fact that it was unchecked was unique.

A proper conception of European technology throughout the medieval and early modern period is of remorselessly creeping change, partly by trial and error, increasingly as the result of more abstract speculation. Given the long-standing mechanical background of even benighted rural areas, where there were water-mills with complicated gearing, and given the inquisitive practicality of many who in other societies seem to have spent their leisure single-mindedly in pursuit of pleasure or at best in impractical philosophising, the persistent advance is not so surprising. Looking back and thereby telescoping time, the interpretative danger is surely of being surprised that progress was as slow at it was. Unspectacular though individual changes were, the cumulative impact was solid. 'Human felicity is produc'd not so much by great pieces of good fortune that seldom happen', remarked that observer of the late preindustrial scene, Benjamin Franklin, 'as by little advantages that occur every day' (Leary 1962:121). Franklin was, it is true, partly speaking about a seemingly trivial improvement, street lighting; but there is evidence that this was not trivial and had wide economic repercussions (Jones and Falkus 1979).

If we consider more closely the example of China, from which the lack of a 'natural or irresistible' follow-up from trade to manufacturing is generalised, we find two flaws in the assertion. The first is that the substantial trading economy of Sung times, without experiencing the West's scientific revolution, was most inventive technically, and did develop and disseminate a water-driven spinning-machine for hemp of an elaborateness that did not surface in Europe until very much later (Elvin 1973). That China actually abandoned the use of this machine and regressed in terms of industrial technology is an interesting puzzle, but one that speaks of quite other changes in her economic context and does not deny the original achievement. The second difficulty with generalising from the Chinese example is that the different population response there did not face manufacturers with the challenge of an inelastic supply of labour like that experienced in the middle of the eighteenth century by a crucial handful of textile entrepreneurs in Lancashire, Derbyshire and Nottinghamshire. This is not intended to imply that a simple difference in factor ratios explains European industrialisation. Technological responses were too various for that, some being biased for instance towards resource-saving, like the several reductions in the width of saw blades which greatly economised on Scandinavian timber. It does suggest that the 'no natural or irresistible' axiom has no universal application. In certain social, political and economic situations, trade expansion might well 'naturally' spark a manufacturing response.

Rostow's view is that 'Smithian growth' – the benefits of trade, the widening of the market, the specialisation by regions – was certain to wear itself out. Ultimately this must be true, but that the limits were anywhere near being approached in eighteenth-century Europe is quite implausible. Small but productive technical changes were constantly being made in the more advanced regions, though many are scarcely discernible in the documentary sources and are individually too minor to figure among the stylised facts of technical change during the Industrial Revolution, which rears up like a cliff face in the textbooks where it should emerge instead from swelling foothills. The less advanced parts of Europe clearly offered a field for the constant diffusion of 'best practice'. New ways were arising to organise and administer and even mechanise the economy of the continent and the individual countries within it. Economic integration was proceeding voluntarily despite the distance it still had to go.

Technological change was diffuse, bound up with activity at the roots of society, involving a large class of mechanical tinkerers, sometimes in association with enquiring natural philosophers. The gains from organisational improvement, almost a species of technological change in itself, were considerable too, but even more likely to steal unnoticed across the face of the historical record. A society capable of innovating in the one might be expected to have been able to do so in the other. North (1968; cf. Shepherd and Walton 1972) has computed the sources of productivity gain in ocean shipping over the period 1600–1850 and shown that organisational rather than technological change was the primary agent. He cites the positive externalities produced by suppressing piracy, which enabled shipowners to effect cost savings through employing smaller crews and carrying less armament per ton of cargo. A nice example of the simple savings possible in this sphere was described in 1769 by Benjamin Franklin when he was Postmaster General for the American colonies. Franklin had received complaints from the Boston Chamber of Commerce about the slowness of the transatlantic mail packets. On enquiry he learned that the English skippers of the packet boats were sailing the direct route, which was a kind of duffer's route since it meant breasting the Gulf Stream. As Franklin discovered from Captain Timothy Folger of Nantucket, American whalemen knew a better way. In crossing the Gulf Stream in pursuit of whales, Folger reported, the packets were sometimes met and spoken with: 'we have informed them that they were stemming a current that was against them to the value of 3 miles an hour and advised them to cross it, but they were too wise to be councelled by simple American fishermen' (Chapin and Walton Smith 1953:111). With light winds the packets were carried back by the current further than they were forwarded by the wind, and as Folger noted, even with stronger winds behind them, 'the subtraction of 70 miles a day from their course is of some importance'. Franklin began investigations of the Gulf Stream, using a thermometer to locate it. His grandnephew was co-author of *Thermometrical Navigation* (1799) at a time when savings in Atlantic sailing times were being realised by a spate of such pilot books and nautical compilations. In the late preindustrial world good plain observation of a natural history sort was capable of giving a commercial payoff.

Organisational improvements like a quicker turn-around time for ships in port could raise productivity as surely as narrowly technological changes. It is unusual to find an attempt to separate the two such as North has supplied for ocean shipping. Nevertheless, reflecting on the complexity of economic life and the multitudinous aspects of its working, the endless variety of opportunities for minor advances in its efficiency may be sensed. Most of the smaller advances will have gone unrecorded, but if we take the case of agriculture, which as late as the eighteenth century employed eighty per cent of the total occupied population of Europe, we can see that a host of small changes in cropping routines and farm business practices were under way. In this sector the great significance of widely diffused minor improvements, rather than single transforming inventions, is obvious.

Another illustration of an under-emphasised source of productivity gain is the increase of efficiency during the late seventeenth and eighteenth centuries in the marketing operations of hundreds of market towns in England. Slow-growing urban populations were coming to handle a fast-growing inland trade. This was the result of physical improvements to the streets, market houses and other facilities and of obscure developments in business practices (Jones and Falkus 1979), kinds of unremarked change that we could anticipate finding in a number of sectors in a number of countries. These same small towns in turn nurtured a society more creative than they now possess, with a social structure and provision of grammar schools that kept them intellectually alive. They were the background shared by William Shakespeare, Thomas Hobbes, and a crowd of less high-flown, more pragmatic thinkers. Preindustrial European society, especially in the West, offered considerable scope for individual and local solutions to scientific and administrative problems.

While there may have been no compulsion for a society engaged in wide organisational and technological change of a mundane kind to arrive at the particular burst of cost-reducing processes at the heart of industrialisation, there is surely no need for astonishment that it did arrive there. The gross differences from other civilisations show up. The record of Chinese exploration which was halted in 1430 and prevented by fiat from resuming in 1480 shows what could happen in a centralised empire that could not happen, or be enforced, in a decentralised system of states like Europe. Progress might be sluggish and frustrating but it was less likely to be permanently baulked; to pursue the example, Columbus did eventually find a sponsor. The other large societies of Eurasia that might potentially have developed as Europe did develop, tended to suffer from various disabilities including political centralism and whimsicality. Their earlier and perhaps greater intellectual promise was always stultified. Consider the record of the neighbouring Ottoman empire with respect to the printing press. Constantinople acquired a press in 1726 but closed it down from 1730 to 1780 and again in 1800. Between 1726 and 1815 that press brought out only sixty-three titles. As McEvedy (1972:4) has commented, the literacy gap between Europe and Turkey was the difference between fifty per cent and five per cent, a tenfold difference, while the difference between publication rates was a factor of 10,000. Religious intolerance and a steeper social pyramid meant that there was an authority able to impose censorship and not enough centres of resistance to it. Balkan merchants had to defy their Turkish rulers to have books and journals printed in European cities and shipped in.

Censorship was all too common in the countries of Europe but it was seldom absolute and there was enough resistance to place restrictions on the censors and finally to clear them away from all except the cobwebby corners of pornography. Social and political decentralisation in this as in other respects was fundamental to economic and technological progress. With extensive trade and the modernising nation-states jockeying for position, change and productivity gains were already built in. Looking back at this, instead of looking back from it or across from contemporary societies, is a bad perspective. By fair comparisons, significant and systematic change was to be expected. Once there were expectations of scientific solutions, the practical significance of the magical beliefs held even by great scientists of the past was going to shrink away. The fatalism of the Middle Ages, which was not fatalism at all but a desperate scrabble for a living against apparently rigid parameters, would fade. Only its appearance remains in the horoscopes of the newspapers, like the grin of the Cheshire cat. We might even entertain the counterfactual speculation that a recognisable and prosperous modern Europe might have evolved without the drama of an Industrial Revolution (cf. van Klaveren 1969:253). If the elasticity of the population response with respect to real wages stayed low, perhaps it really was possible.

Technological lags may seem to damage the idea of a permanent forward march. Despite the 'Renaissance' discovery of how to discover, lags could amount to virtual vacua. There was a long, long lull, after all, between the attempt by Eilmer the monk to fly from the tower of Malmesbury Abbey about 1010 – though he was not entirely forgotten and Milton is said to have mentioned him – and the launching of the steam-powered model aeroplane by John Stringfellow at Chard, Somerset, in the 1840s. No urgency was felt. Not in that particular direction. In others, by 1700 surely, technology was in constant forward drift.

This implies a conception of a late preindustrial Europe, or at any rate western Europe, that was already decisively ahead of its medieval past in terms of productivity, business methods, the quality and quantity of goods and of much of the urban housing and milieu. It recognises the extent of the modernisation that had taken place and was taking place in such visible spheres as the unification of communications, weights and measures and coinage, and in the intangibles like public order and the predictability of government actions. Montesquieu and other writers before Adam Smith fully realised the scope of this transition and gave it even more emphasis than did Smith (himself an analyst of the preindustrial world). Much recent writing on social history has missed all this and has beamed the full blaze of its own discontents on the malfunctions of that world, lighting up the bubbling froth of, say, the food riot as indicating deep currents of social dislocation. Of course society was poor and changing it had a price. But the pot was half-full as well as half-empty and there were stars to be seen as well as mud. There were productivity improvements, especially in agriculture, before the full onset of industrialisation. In terms of fundamental services and security there was distinct progress. We have become too mesmerised by the task of explaining industrialisation as if it would teach us a specific for the ills of the Third World today and too affronted by the obvious inequities of the industrial world to get the historical record straight. Doing so means giving credit to just those dull, everyday, pragmatic, honest betterments in simple technology, routine services, law, and administration that were taking place in Europe before the Industrial Revolution and doses of which would wash away much of the misery in the world today.

Chapter 4

The Discoveries and ghost acreage

I sing of dews, of rains, and, piece by piece,
Of balm, of oil, of spice, and ambergris.
I sing of time's trans-shifting. . .
Robert Herrick

FROM THE FIFTEENTH CENTURY, Europe added to its physical resource base and potential market in a great ballooning expansion overseas. The story of the Discoveries is a familiar one which, however, is properly seen as the European culmination of Eurasian technological advances and earlier European probing, and the outcome of which was a major impetus to Europe's development. The conventional starting point is the 1490s, with Columbus's voyage across the Atlantic and Vasco da Gama's visit to India. This is too simple. Both events were stages – long jumps certainly – in an old endeavour to pierce the void apparently surrounding Europe. The Portuguese in particular had been systematically ranging out to the Atlantic islands and down the west coast of Africa since very early in the century. Close examination shows that European society had been pulsating and probing at its bounds for a long time before that, at least since the tenth-century turning of the tables on her invaders, or earlier still if the Viking crossing of the North Atlantic be included.

The expansion following the last years of the fifteenth century is also less straightforward than at first seems to be the case. Leap-frogging movements of people continued to take place within Europe and on its eastern, landward margins. They are often overlooked in accounts of the transoceanic voyages and the Atlantic economy. Welshmen moved east after the Act of Union (1536) in an attempt to civilise the English. A steppe frontier was pushed outwards into grasslands wrested from Muslim herders in the Great Hungarian Plain and the Ukraine. Frenchmen sidled eastwards into Lorraine. A surprising number of Scots migrated to eastern Germany and Poland in the seventeenth century. The naturalist Forster and his son, who sailed with Captain Cook, were returned descendants.

Pre-Columbian frontiers indicate just how energetically Europeans had sought release from what has been portrayed as their encircled continent (Mackinder 1962:48). Europe had to its south, the desert; to its west, the ocean, with steady offshore winds down the African coast making a passage almost impossible for ships that could not sail close-hauled; to its north, the ice; and to the north-east, a boundless forest of pines through which the rivers flowed only to the Arctic or down to the landlocked Caspian Sea. To the east lay a vast desert and mountain emptiness of 35,000,000 square kilometres whose nomadic inhabitants were capable of keeping the civilisations of China, India, the Near East and Europe at arm's reach from one another (Chaunu 1979:53). Only to its south-east were there routes between Europe and the old Asian civilisations over which, the nomads of the steppes permitting, spices, silk, saffron, quicksilver and other luxuries could come. Between the seventh and the nineteenth centuries the Arabs or the Turks kept these routes closed more often than not. The fifteenth century was a time of closure. In the sixteenth century the rulers of Egypt were willing to let the spice trade pass again, but they did so with every attention to the price that the market would bear and did not undermine the new sea-borne trade.

The preceding expansionary endeavours denote the kind of society that eventually broke out westwards from this near-isolation. The Norsemen, who were not solely Viking raiders but traders as well, if one counts as trade the hawking on the Russian rivers of goods stolen on the North Sea coasts, early settled as far east as Kiev. In the westerly direction they settled Iceland, Greenland, and briefly Vinland on the coast of North America. It is ironic that fifteenth-century Europe permitted the Greenland settlements, that had once paid tithe to Rome, to perish. The Normans in the eleventh century had conquered Sicily and Italy and settled these former Muslim areas with settlers from northern and central Italy, actually under written contract. The Germans in the period from the tenth to the thirteenth century undertook a prolonged *Drang nach Osten* across the river Elbe to the Vistula and Vienna, leading to the settlement and Germanic-isation of Slav lands. The Crusaders in the eleventh and twelfth centuries made supreme efforts to force their way south-eastwards and secure the holy places. Although there were demographic currents sweeping men into those ventures, they were not really the start of a would-be conquest of the Orient. Colonies were however founded in the Holy Land in the twelfth century, though lost again at the end of the next century (Parkinson 1963:149).

Richard the Lionheart seized Cyprus in 1190 and from then until the mid-fourteenth century westerners replaced Greeks in the islands between Cyprus, Crete and the Aegean coast. They established a number of states on the mainland and a concession, which was first Venetian, later Genoese, in the Byzantine empire. Venice and Genoa indeed founded armed commercial networks one thousand miles eastwards, connecting up outposts in the Levant, the Aegean and the Black Sea, joining up with trade routes across Asia and the profitable carrying trade be-tween Egypt and Russia. All this was truncated by the advance of the Ottoman Turks in the third quarter of the fifteenth century, but by that time, and during the final quarter, the Atlantic sea-board on the other side of the European system was alive with gossip about the outer world. Cabot is said to have made an early visit to the New World. Bristolians are said to have discovered 'Brasil' (Sauer 1973:20, 32–5), and when Cabot received his pen-sion from the hands of Richard Ameryk, collector of customs at Bristol, the name America was presumably born, rather than originating later and so improbably from the Christian name of the Italian, Vespucci (Hudd 1957). The Atlantic islands were bustling with activity by that period, with Italian settlers in Madeira, the Spanish in the Canaries, and the Azores so peopled with men from Flanders that they were called the Flemish Isles. Seamen's knowledge may well have exceeded what was written down. Illiterates can be superb seamen. It was a Polynesian navigator, Tupaia, who told Captain Cook about fifty per cent of the islands Cook went on to 'discover' (Gatty 1958:42–3), point-ing up Stefansson's ironical definition of discovery as the first time a white man, preferably an Englishman, sets foot somewhere. On the other hand, as Chaunu (1979) several times observes, the *sigillo* or secrecy policy of the chief exploring nation, Portugal, has enabled some historians to write about pre-Columbian discoveries quite without evidence.

Europe's location had long facilitated the acquisition of background knowledge. The truly isolated civilisations of the world outside Eurasia had no chance of the common stock of knowledge filtering through. Medieval Europe rediscovered the classics of Greece and Rome at her doorstep, though perhaps only when there had been sufficient growth to make a body of political and legal precedents worth having. The education of Achilles and the rape of Ganymede are shown on the capitals of pillars in Vézelay cathedral, denoting the return to the classics in the final years of the eleventh century. Juxtaposition with Islam was at least as important. When the Muslims were expelled from Sicily in 1090 Christian rulers surprisingly viewed the libraries as booty and encouraged the translation of numbers of Arabic works. Following the fall of Toledo in 1085, Cordova in 1236, and Seville in 1248, Muslim libraries were thrown open. In 1126 Adelard of Bath translated Arabic trigonometrical tables and Evendeath (1090–1165) made the Arabic numerical notation available (Innis 1972:129). As a result of the Crusades, Europe came under a variety of religious, architectural, and cultural influences, obtaining the veil, the four-poster bed designed to drape mosquito nets, the conical hat draped in muslin that became the thirteenth-century fashion, besides the more utilitarian compass, astrolabe, chain-mail, crossbow, gunpowder, methods of rigging, paper-making and printing, several of these items having first been received by Islam from China. 'The Crusades brought the Christian rulers and their men into close touch with the civilised East', as Parkinson (1963:149) has correctly pointed out; 'the culture of the Middle Ages is to a large extent what they brought back with them.'

Armed with what they had learned and acquired, Europeans set about the conquest of the seas. What must not be forgotten is that they also set about the conquest of land distance, for the north-eastern boreal forests proved less formidable than they had once seemed. Novgorod, the main inland depot of the Baltic trade, constructed a network of trading posts and river routes in the land of the Finns, across to the Arctic, and eventually over the northern Urals to the river Ob. Russian monasteries were also agents of the expansion of settlement. The Urals were crossed in 1480, once Muscovy had freed herself from the Mongols. The eastward journey towards the northern Pacific began. In distance terms this was more formidable, and its completion more impressive, than its twin, the crossing of North America at the end of the eighteenth century. Yermak and his cossacks began to conquer Siberia in the 1580s. The Yenisei river was reached by 1620 and Yakutsk on the Lena 1,200 miles further east was attained only twelve years later. The Sea of Okhotsk was reached in 1638, representing a total journey one-third as long again as the crossing of North America. By 1649 the Bering Straits had been reached and an expansion of the fur trade and the colonisation of Russian America followed. 'They are more like a leather bag filled with oil, than like an animal', wrote the German naturalist Pallas in 1778 about Caspian seals, when he was in Russian employ (Urness 1967:31), for this was how the faunal resources of the world were appraised even as they were being scientifically inventoried. The outward pressure of the Russians was also felt to the south and south-east, where scarcely a season passed during the sixteenth and seventeenth centuries without fighting against the Turkic and Mongol tribes of the steppes. During the seventeenth and eighteenth centuries over two million settlers moved south into the wooded steppes and the steppes proper, and 400,000 moved into Siberia, though far to the east the Russians were deflected north from the Amur river by the Manchu Chinese. 'The history of Russia is the history of a country which colonises itself' (Kliuchevskii, quoted by Pipes 1974:14) but it only seems like that because the area that was made Russian was a contiguous land space.

The Slavic movement was part of a wide process in which Europeans were expanding at the expense of less organised, less well armed and less densely settled peoples. Thus the Swedes were moving in early modern times into the territory of the Lapps and Finns and the English and Lowland Scots were extending into Ireland and the Scottish Highlands. Ireland and the Hebrides were the nurseries of the techniques used in New England and Virginia against the Red Indians (MacLeod 1967). In addition to these frontiers of settlement there were fishing, plantation and mining frontiers. One of the features of the fishing industries in late medieval times was an outward shift of French and English fleets to take cod off Iceland. A sugar plantation frontier was already on the move. The Arabs had raised cane sugar as far west as southern Spain in the ninth and tenth centuries. Copying them, Europeans were running slave plantations in Cyprus during the thirteenth century (Reynolds 1965). The slave trade was partly an outgrowth of this. Venetians, Genoese and others from northern Italy financed sugar and indigo cultivation in Sicily. Then, in the fifteenth century, the Portuguese and Spanish carried the sugar frontier to the Cape Verde islands, the Canaries, and Madeira (where Henry the Navigator put up the capital for a water-mill to crush cane), and on to Brazil, whence in the seventeenth century it reached the British West Indies and became the pivot of the Atlantic economy. As to mining, there was an advance guard of activity in silver and lead across Sardinia, Sicily, and the coasts of Asia Minor. Genoese prospectors had been busy in interior Sardinia in the twelfth century, and a Genoese entrepreneur with mines and a company town in Asia Minor was selling alum widely through Europe by 1300.

Seen against these various backcloths, the Discoveries and the opening of extra-European trade appear as a continuum of expansion. A recurrent theme is that the directions and activity of the fifteenth century were the results of a displacement at the hands of Islam. Conflicts with Islam were a formative influence which has definitely been underemphasised in English-language historiography relative to maritime ventures. The two spheres were in reality linked. When the Christian *Reconquista* in Iberia came to its close, having taken seven centuries to recover what had fallen to Islam in seven years, the impetus was carried on over the seas. The Portuguese pursued the Moors to Ceuta in Morocco in 1415, but when they realised that they were not capable of overrunning the whole of Morocco they began to think of outflanking it. Similarly when Spain recaptured Granada in 1492 she diverted her armies to Mexico, apparently to forestall the disruption that might follow disbanding them at home.

Islam was on the retreat only in Iberia. The differences were not between a vital, expansionist European culture and a static, hostile Islamic world. Both systems were expansionary. They collided, came to rest, scraped against one another at intervals, and came to uneasy rest again like two tectonic plates meeting in continental drift. The effects on their civilisations differed because the zones into which they did expand were quite distinct in resource endowment, and because they had structures which dictated quite different exploitation of their acquisitions. In the sixteenth century the Mughals invaded India; early that century Moorish colonies had been established in Indonesia; in 1517 the Ottomans captured Egypt from the Mamelukes and in 1551 they took Tripoli. The sixteenth century also saw a struggle between the Turks as they captured North Africa and the southern Europeans who would have liked to do so. The Moors, though expelled from Iberia, defeated the Portuguese at Al-Ksar al-Kabir in 1578 and were able to penetrate southwards in 1582 to capture the Songhay salt deposits and in 1591 to move against the Songhay empire across the Sahara. This strength enabled them to divert trans-Saharan trade and West African gold eastwards (Davidson *et al.* 1966:126ff.), so that the Europeans no longer tapped part of it at the Mediterranean shore.

With Islam glowering to the south and south-east, western ambitions to sidestep, even in a counter-intuitive westerly direction, become more understandable. The cutting of the overland spice trade was not primarily responsible. A better case may be made for the cutting of Black Sea trade. The fall of Constantinople in 1453, usually portrayed as an afterthought of Ottoman Turkish expansion, was of some importance because it meant that the Bosporus could be blocked. The Ottomans could divert Black Sea grain, fish and timber to their own swiftly growing capital at Constantinople and deny them to the Italians. Genoese Kaffa in the Crimea, a city as big as Genoa itself, was afterwards only reachable overland, through Hungary and Poland, and combined Turkish and Tartar pressure in any case eliminated Kaffa in 1475.

Because the Italian cities were dependent on imported food and raw materials these events were significant. Italy was soon to become an important market for Baltic grain and Newfoundland cod. Genoa, with over 100,000 people by 1450 and no agricultural hinterland to speak of, became a buyer of wheat from Moorish

North Africa (van Klaveren 1969:50). The Genoese turned somewhat from freighting to finance as their Black Sea colonies collapsed. Venice's shipping also disintegrated under corsair attacks
and prolonged sixteenth-century naval operations against the
Turks (Coles 1968:111). The Italian cities were thus inclined to
invest in other peoples' shipping, and Genoa in particular
already had appropriate links with the Atlantic. Two Genoese
ships had tried to sail westwards to India in 1291, passing out of
the Straits of Gibraltar, and vanishing (White 1962:168). The
Genoese, who held Corsica and Sardinia and bases along the
Barbary coast in the western basin of the Mediterranean, had
established the earliest direct sea links with Flanders and England (Bernard 1972:294). They had communities of merchants
living in Iberian towns, and early on in the Portuguese colony of
Madeira, an island first discovered in 1341 by a Genoese and
Florentine expedition which had called en route at Lisbon. It had
been a Genoese who rediscovered óne of the Canary Islands
between 1325 and 1339. Genoese investment in Portuguese and
Spanish maritime ventures is therefore not surprising and was
particularly influential in Seville, backing Spanish treasure hunting (Verlinden 1953; 1972; Pike 1962). It was soon joined by other
free investment funds, especially from Germany (Samhaber
1963).

The more we realise that treasure was not the sole or even the
earliest goal of maritime exploration, the better we can understand the shift in attention from the Black Sea to the Atlantic.
What Europeans actually obtained outside Europe, and to a large
degree what they sought, were fish, whale oil, seal oil, timber,
and land on which to grow grain, sugar, or grapes. 'Let not the
word fish distaste you', wrote Captain John Smith, 'for it will
afford as good gold as the mines of Guiana or Potossie' (Barback
1967). Vasco da Gama's famous reply of gold, Christians and
spices, when he was asked in Calicut what he wanted, obscures
half the reality. Historians have been more lastingly diverted by
the glitter of gold than history was. The Portuguese inhabited an
infertile little kingdom at the south-western tip of Europe. They
were fishermen, interested in finding new grounds. When they
settled Madeira what they did was to clear-fell the forests for
which it is named and send the timber back to make furniture in

Lisbon, and then sow cereals and sugar and Malvoisie grapes from Cyprus. They fished out of the Atlantic islands and hunted the seal colonies there, and eventually right down to the Cape of Good Hope, to the brink of extinction. They did trade for the miscellaneous products of West Africa; they were pleased to find gold where they could; they entered the spice trade as soon as they reached the East. All these things were among their aims too. Their motives, says Chaunu (1979:104, 150), were on the part of the bourgeoisie to find land to grow sugar cane; on the part of the aristocracy simply to find land; and on the part of the state to find supplies of grain, since Portugal's harvest fell short one year in three and she had become more and more dependent on Moroccan sources. There were motives of curiosity, mission-ising, crusading, and seeking gold, but the interest in real resources was a central one.

This is not quite the same as arguing that it was actual resource depletion that impelled the Europeans outwards. There was no sharp or sustained rise in food or raw material prices in fifteenth-century Europe in general. There were a few German forest conservation laws, other than those to preserve hunting-grounds, but they are inadequate to establish a general scarcity of timber. Nor was exploration the concerted effort that pressing need could quite well have caused. Europe's expansion came about, in Adam Smith's famous phrase, from 'no necessity'. The possible exception where there may have been a close nexus between real resource depletion and transatlantic exploration is the supposed discovery of the Newfoundland fishery and the Gulf of St Lawrence whale fishery by the Basques. The medieval Basque whalemen are said to have virtually exterminated the European population of migratory right whales which followed a tongue of deep water close inshore in the Bay of Biscay each season. The Basques are then supposed to have pursued the right whale into distant northern waters and by about 1372 as far as Greenland and the St Lawrence (Sauer 1973:6–7). Some support seems to be given by the fact that the Basque name for codfish was apparently known to the Newfoundland Indians when the next explorers arrived. Were the Basques really the first to know that Finisterre was not the end of the earth? Unfortunately for a good story, De Loture (1949) examined French and local Basque histories and found none that offered proof. The first French fishing boats bound for the Grand Banks left Rouen in 1508 and the first certain evidence of the Basques as such off Newfoundland dates from 1528.

The genius of Henry the Navigator shaped Portuguese endeavours into a systematic progression of voyages into the Atlantic, discovering and settling island groups, making in from them to the coast of Africa, pushing ever further down towards the Cape, round it with Bartholomew Diaz, and with a quickening tempo up the east coast with Vasco da Gama to Malindi. At that point the Portuguese had rejoined the known, if alien, world of Islam, and da Gama was able to take an Arab pilot for the crossing to Calicut in India (Bell 1974; Chaunu 1979:308–9). At Calicut a Jewish trader who was already there put the question to da Gama that elicited his echoing reply. Indeed, since they knew that the Arabs had penetrated a long way south down the east coast of Africa the Portuguese had sent messengers (mostly Jews who might find help in Jewish communities along old trade routes) to Hormuz and other places, to try to find out where the southern tip of Africa was said to lie (van Klaveren 1969:123).

Informing all the voyages was Henry the Navigator's School of Navigation at Sagres on Cape St Vincent, with its international staff examining the classics and codifying eastern and western lore. Initially a rebound on Henry's part from the battle of Ceuta in 1415 and the evident impossibility of taking Morocco head-on, exploration grew out of a reconnaissance of the Moroccan coast and the chance discovery of Porto Santo. But Henry gave these exercises the form of a space programme and it was this that his successors continued to finance. His own easternmost goal was probably Ethiopia. Henry the Navigator was a remarkable man, but nothing is known of his personality that would throw light on his extraordinary historical rôle. Nor can we deduce the missing facts with any amount of theory. As Arrow (1969:35) has commented, 'this is one place where theory should not take the place of history'. That is not to say that economic theory is irrelevant, only that it has limitations. Economic factors presumably influence the magnitude of 'technological' progress but have little to do with what may actually be devised or is there to be discovered. Thus, as Arrow says, spices may have motivated European voyages, 'but the brute, though unknown, facts of geography determined what in fact was their economic result'.

The facts of geography worked in Europe's favour. The ocean proved less dangerous than feared, the resources on the far side proved rich. Although the African coast was hazardous for the ships of the day, the Atlantic, once Columbus had made the first brave leap in the dark, was less harrowing to cross than expected. 'Who would have thought', asked the seventeenth-century Prague mathematician, Johannes Kepler (quoted by Mason 1978:33), 'that navigation across the vast ocean is less dangerous and quieter than in the narrow threatening gulf of the Adriatic, or the Baltic or the British Straits.' There is a reason for this, in that while ships may topple over down the steepest waves in mid-ocean, upset or damaged vessels are more likely to founder near the coast where they can be blown onto the rocks. Europe was thus surrounded by a more dangerous belt of water than the open ocean, and it was this that sailors knew and which in their minds they projected into the infinite distance. The far shore was dangerous again, but the total danger was not a linear function of distance. Nor was the oceanic world as devoid of resources as it may have seemed. Provided the dangers of a landing were braved, provisioning stations were providentially dotted about the seas like stepping stones, offering colonies of marine animals and seabirds and flightless island species of birds: seals, green turtles, great auks, the dodo.

Once that first leap had been made, the continents were reoriented to face the sea and the world could never look the same again. 'The Discoveries turned the continents inside out' (Whittlesey 1944:59). Astonishingly soon (in the sixteenth century) the Portuguese appear to have been exploring a coast as remote from Europe as that of Victoria, Australia, making their way secretly so that the Spanish should not discover the trespass on their sphere of influence (McIntyre 1977). This was all quite remarkable, and yet, given the distances covered by other sea-farers, the Polynesians for example, the voyages are less impressive than Europe's ability to rationalise them and to develop the resources they brought within her reach.

Extra-European resources were vast, varied, and cheap. Most European trade continued to be intra-European, but the extra-

European share grew into a towering significance. 'The Golden Age hitherto put into the past', as Walter Prescott Webb (1952:10 n.13) quoted from a book reviewer, 'is now placed overseas.' Leaving aside precious metals and the later importance of colonial American iron, four main ecological zones contributed. Firstly, ocean fisheries and whale and seal fisheries were of prime importance for the additional protein they made available to southern Europe, as well as oil for lamps, softening leather and fabrics, and until the sinking of Drake's well in Pennsylvania in 1859, for lubricating machinery. Europe was fortunate in being positioned opposite the Grand Banks, where the shoals of cod formed the best fishery in the world. The cod grew to 20 lb or more. They were easy to split and clean and because they were not fatty they dried and kept well (Sauer 1973:63). The costs of working a single-species fishery like this were relatively low.

Second, the boreal woods. In the sixteenth century the commodities exported from Russia to western Europe included furs, beeswax, honey, tallow, hides, train oil (seal oil), sturgeon, flax and hemp, salt and tar (Pipes and Fine 1966). From what was in practice a resource frontier around the Baltic and in Scandinavia, which Hanseatic merchants had penetrated in the Middle Ages, similar products were obtained. Land along the south of the Baltic supplied western Europe with grain during the early modern period. This trade may have been enough to feed only three-quarters of a million people per annum (Glamann 1974:43), but its value was beyond such head-counting in that given the low elasticity of demand for grain the additional supply was able to dampen price fluctuations and no doubt reduce mortality.

Third, land in the tropics and subtropics enabled sugar, tobacco, cotton, indigo and rice to be grown. Among this list the beneficial rôle of tobacco is hard to grasp, since it raises mortality rates; however it will serve to make the general point that production and trade in all the imported commodities had an enormously stimulating effect on European shipping, port handling and warehousing facilities, processing and packaging, and business activity as a whole. We tend to forget that transhipping, handling and transporting goods was immensely labour-intensive. Tropical and subtropical produce figured large in the stream of imports and in influencing consumption habits (Jones

1973), and in attracting investment away from land into the impersonal world of commerce. Various parts of the tropical world were tapped and Meinig (1969) subdivides them according to their products.

Fourth, grain could be grown in temperate North America, at first along the forested eastern seaboard, later in the interior, as well as on grassland in South America, South Africa, Australia, and the steppes of southern Russia. It is not too portentous to claim that the store of energy in grasslands and cleared forest in the thinly populated parts of the globe was broken into once and for all on behalf of European civilisation. Much of this awaited the late nineteenth century. An unparalleled share of the earth's biological resources was acquired for this one culture, on a scale that was unprecedented and is unrepeatable.

Not every European country shared at once in reaping the harvest. Portugal, Spain, Holland, and England became successively the leading nation in overseas ventures. France and to a minor degree Denmark, Sweden and one or two German states were also involved. Their competition with one another is of less moment than the fact that trade spread the benefits widely. The Discoveries were the first positive economic shock, or stimulant in Leibenstein's (1957) terminology, of a magnitude capable of promoting system-wide growth.

The 'general advantages which, considered as a great country, Europe has derived', to use Adam Smith's (1884:243) conceptualisation, were staggering. The average area of land available *per capita* in western Europe in 1500 had been 24 acres, and the Discoveries raised this to 148 acres *per capita*, a six-fold gain. Full utilisation of the resource potential was deferred, partly by the seductions of precious metal. But even in the preindustrial period the 'fall-out' of raw materials and the capital investment and technology generated to exploit them was a boost to the development impulses already being released by the growth of trade within Europe's borders. Commodities came in that could never have been produced at home at anything less than an infinite cost. A range of climates was effectively coupled to Europe's own. New crop plants were added to the rather depauperate cultivated flora of medieval Europe, a half-tone world that is hard to envisage now, though a glimpse may be caught at Lytes Cary in Somerset, where the National Trust maintains a garden restricted to plants mentioned in Sir Henry Lyte's translation of a *Niewe Herball* (1578). Maize and potatoes were the most important field crop introductions. Few species of domestic animals came in, except for turkeys which replaced the peacocks of medieval feasts. Instead European horses, cattle and sheep went out to make productive the other continents where the larger fauna was limited.

Webb (1952) conceived of the whole process as the 'Great Frontier', giving Europe before 1700 primary windfalls of gold and silver, forest products, furs, and ambergris, and secondary windfalls of cattle and plantation crops. The population of Europe in 1500, which Webb put at 100 million (the effect is heightened if we take the McEvedy and Jones (1978:26) estimate of eighty million), had occupied an area of 3,750,000 square miles. That was not to start with an Indian or Chinese density. Now the Europeans found opening before them an under-defended overseas territory totalling 20,000,000 square miles, generally rather rich. Webb drew attention to the remarkable impact on late preindustrial western Europe in terms of the alteration in the effective man–land ratio:

TABLE 4.1 *Persons per square mile in western Europe plus the 'Great Frontier'*

1500	26.7
1650	4.8
1750	6.5
1800	9.0

Source: Webb 1952:18 n. 18.

The entire expansion of the Great Frontier may be looked on as an extension of Europe's 'Ghost Acreage'. This is a concept introduced by Borgstrom (1972a; 1972b:753–7). Ghost acreage measures the tilled land that would be needed to supply, with given techniques, food of equivalent value to that brought from outside into the system. It may be subdivided into fish acreage, that required to raise a supply of animal protein equivalent to that derived from the fisheries; and trade acreage, that required to supply the equivalent of the net import of grown foodstuffs. No statistics exist with which these notional areas may be computed for the period under discussion, but the point is conveyed by Webb's figures.

The emphasis here is on real resources and the physical extension of the market (cf. Jones 1979). Some scholars are disposed to argue that this misses the rôle of treasure and plunder. The real impetus came from outside the market, so it is said (Frank 1978:44–50, 156–66), notably from the Spanish coercion of South American Indians to dig precious metals and the profits of virtually confiscatory trade by the British in Bengal. The scale of these flows is however unknown. The figures cited are transparent guesses. There is not even the frame of a notional calculation like Webb's man–land ratios, while the idea that Indian plunder had an instantaneous effect on the inventions and innovations of the British Industrial Revolution is as unlikely as it is undocumented. Real resources, of undeniable productive use, are much more likely to have had the major influence. The accumulating gains changed the resource structure of the continent, with profound consequences for the size and incomes of populations of European stock and for the distribution of development activity within Europe. When Europe went on to extend its resource frontier vertically downwards – by mining coal – it gave itself another massive boost (Landes 1969; Wrigley 1962). Conceptually the increment of ghost acreage thus obtained might be calculated, the 'coal acreage', stated as the additional acreage that would have been needed, with given techniques, to produce the charcoal and firewood energy and organic chemicals for which coal provided a substitute. But the first big boost had come from overseas; the cotton and much of the food needed by the industrialising economy had only become available as the result of the Discoveries. It would be ludicrous to assert that development came about because Europeans were uniquely predisposed to manipulate and abuse the environment. The history of deforestation and soil erosion in Asia demonstrates that plainly enough. What had happened was that the Europeans had discovered an unprecedented ecological windfall. Europe was sufficiently decentralised and flexible to develop in response, and not merely content to consume the raw gains. This conjunction of windfall and entrepreneurship happened only once in history.

Chapter 5

The market economy

A man will not risk what he has in trade, except for the prospect of very large gains, if he is likely to be robbed by pirates, or to be oppressed by the government if he is successful in business

William Cunningham

FROM ECOLOGICAL PROCESSES WITH AN ECONOMIC COMPONENT we turn to economic processes with an ecological component. We need to examine how the economy, which under feudalism was virtually embraced within the political system, achieved autonomy. Economic development in its European form required above all freedom from arbitrary political acts concerning private property. Goods and factors of production had to be free to be traded. Prices had to be set by unconditional exchange if they were to be undistorted signals of what goods and services really were in demand, where and in what quantities.

Power in the Dark Ages was in the hands of those who commanded the means of coercion. A market economy was an improbable child to be fathered by men who held their position by the assertion of will backed when the need arose by personal victory in combat. A strategic question of economic history concerns the conditions under which power came instead to be exercised by the purse, with police powers mostly a latent threat and physical force on any scale in the control of the central government. Several centuries of change and experiment, recurrent rather than wholly cumulative, were needed to establish that shift in the distribution of power.

Adam Smith (1884:169–70) sketched a solution in *The Wealth of Nations* which we may call his 'bauble thesis'. This depended on the corrosive efficiency of selfishness to dissolve feudal power. He was perhaps generalising the behaviour of the Highland chiefs around the time of the Forty-five rebellion, for several of their sons were among his pupils. He perceived the initial condition of society as one in which rulers and chieftains thought of their comfort, prestige and security as resting on the number of armed retainers who lounged at their call and ate at their table. He saw the moment of change as when some pedlar tempted these rulers with jewellery or silk. No doubt, though Smith did not develop the point, the rulers wanted trinkets to adorn their women, or were pressed to buy them for their womenfolk. This was the thin end of what has turned into the thick wedge of fashion change in ornamentation, dress and furnishings.

Rulers were faced with a dilemma. If they seized his goods the trader would not come back. But in a feudal society based on a subsistence economy they had little cash to spend. The manoeuvre that came to them with a heart-lurch was to require their followers to pay them cash rents for the land they held, instead of continuing to render personal service. In theory there was no such system of rights over the disposal of land – but since the chief was by definition the wielder of the most power he could enforce the change. Ironically, therefore, power was the lever that prised society out of its non-market bed. Retainers were obliged to take their produce to market to get the cash to pay rent. Eventually the surplus produced by the energies they expended on the land instead of idling in the lord's hall or at his table permitted some men to leave agriculture. Towns were able to grow. The system used its under-employed resources and became more productive. It could support a larger population. At last the rulers found that they had commuted so many personal services that they had divested themselves of retainers and no longer felt obliged to seek violent diversions for them. Having usurped title to the land, rulers and chiefs had become less feudal lords than proprietors of estates. They now spent less time fighting, hunting and carousing, took on a little cultural polish, and consumed ever more varied goods. Some of their one-time retainers had become hired servants. Most had become farm tenants.

There is apparently no reason why this 'bauble thesis' (which glosses Adam Smith's exact version of it but is in the same spirit) should not have been an instrument for pacifying society and making it more materialistic since organised society began. The tiniest trade in luxuries should have been sufficient to bring about what Adam Smith implied. After all, luxury trade had existed in remote antiquity. In Edward Gibbon's tart phrase, the commerce that linked Greece and Rome with India, China and Indonesia in the first century A.D. was 'splendid and trifling' (quoted by Grant 1967:4). But it took place, and rulers were able to engage in it, without the structural consequences envisaged by Adam Smith. Where there was any considerable trade in necessities in early times, goods changed hands and were exchanged without the freedoms of the market economy. Often that trade constituted what Karl Polanyi called 'administered trade'. Polanyi looked on self-regulating markets, outside political intervention or control, as late arrivals in a world where traditional authorities were too afraid of riot and rebellion to play with their double-edged logic: freedom to profit and freedom to starve. As he wrote of the Egyptian–Athenian grain trade of the fourth century B.C., 'supplies moved in accordance with price ratios as a result of administrative decisions that took prices into account, [but] *not* as the "automatic" response of large numbers of profit-seeking entrepreneurs' (quoted by Pearson 1977:250). The authorities knew that as far as grain was concerned they might have a revolt on their hands among those who could not meet a free market price in times of scarcity. They made sure they intervened in the grain trade and administered it. Alternatively, in Polanyi's view, trade might be reciprocal exchange, an outgrowth of the stylised exchanges of small groups, or redistributive trade, as a result of the insurance or brokerage function of rulers who contrived to see their subjects fed. Security and even a measure of equity were prized above the productive efficiency of the invisible hand.

North (1977) has pointed out that price-forming markets required a condition not universally met even in the nineteenth century. This was that individual property rights be enforced. Without that, transactions costs were too high, in a disorderly world, for much trade to take place at all. North suggests that the change from non-market to market allocative systems may have been caused by a reduction in transactions costs because of technological advance or population growth. Such developments may have cut information and other costs and thus extended the market; or population growth may have done so simply by

increasing the numbers of potential buyers and sellers and raising the chances of appropriate pairs coming into contact.

A third possibility is that rulers were converted to the advantages of commerce, not necessarily through the seduction of its
baubles but perhaps through the prospect of taxing it. Ironically
enough this taxation was likely to be for the means to pay for that
classic mode of non-market redistribution, war. In Pirenne's
(1913–14) discussion of Dark Age Europe the first traders are
envisaged as pirates or landless wanderers. When does a pirate
become a trader? When he sells his booty to a community too
strong for him to attack, or to his own folk, as the Vikings did with
the proceeds of their North Sea pillaging. Landless men became
traders by peddling goods acquired any-old-how, in one
reported case by beachcombing. For there to be landless men in
the first place, of course, agricultural productivity must have
risen enough to support them. And for landless men to become
traders instead of bandits may require a society strong enough to
protect itself and to offer good legitimate profits. Unexpectedly it
may follow that a tightly organised feudalism was a suitable
setting for the rise of commerce.

The securing of the King's Peace or its local lordly equivalent in
the Dark Ages or early Middle Ages was therefore an important
condition. (Restraining the arbitrariness of kings was for later ages
to manage.) Peace led to dishoarding for investment. Herlihy
(1957) has shown that Italian society, which had displayed a
high liquidity preference and risk aversion in asset holding like
other societies reeling from invasion and turmoil, began in the
tenth century to release treasure hoards for investment in land.
Powerful men were busy facilitating trade just as soon as wars
came to their end. Truces of God were called to permit safe
mingling in the market place. Abbeys took fairs under their wing.
Princes set about putting down piracy and banditry. When
Alfred and Guthrum made their treaty in 886 they negotiated for
an exchange of hostages whenever the English and the Danes
met to trade. Early in the tenth century Edward the Elder enacted
that goods should be bought and sold only in market towns in the
presence of the town reeve. This permitted the conditions in the
market place to be kept under scrutiny. For kings to have gone to
the trouble of ensuring that this was done suggests that they saw

it as a means of obtaining and securing revenues greater than might be acquired from feudal dues and various forms of land tax. Witnesses were indeed required for any transaction small enough to be exempt from the market town rule (Blair 1959:294–6). Rulers surely needed little imagination to see the benefits of definite levies on transactions rather than random, disruptive confiscations. The expansion of trade would have its own demonstration effect. And yet, world-wide, powerful men were slow to accept this, or to allow longer-term considerations to outweigh the short run. Large and complex societies did tend to establish market systems, subject to some degree of intervention (perhaps less than Polanyi claimed), but while the ruler was himself the law, fears of confiscations by him placed limits on the extension of the market.

Medieval authorities performed best at protecting trade by their subjects from internal disorder and external interference. They held back reprisals against foreign merchants in favour of legal procedures. They restricted rights to wreck and flotsam. They began to guarantee trade agreements under the public seals of papal, imperial, royal, episcopal or municipal authority. The backing of a lord or ruler reduced some of the risks of trading abroad. At first it was actually necessary for kings to take action, as in 1315 when Edward II ordered the bailiffs of the Abbot of Ramsey at the fair of St Ives to seize the goods of men of the lordship of the Court of Flanders, which had failed to entertain complaints about a seizure of goods belonging to the king's cousin (Bland, Brown and Tawney 1914:188–90). But gradually the lesson was learned and a body of international trade law was built up, *Lex Mercatoria*, *Jus Mercatorum*, Law Merchant, regulations for traffic by sea, and all manner of courts to adjudicate on matters concerning itinerant traders and required to act within 'the space of three tides' (Bernard 1972:314–15). As in other spheres there was an advantage in the rediscovery of classical lore. The sea law of Rhodes in the first century B.C., for example, was the basis of European maritime law fifteen hundred years later (Wesson 1978:31).

European princes were generally able to impose sufficient order for the prosecution of trade. So were rulers elsewhere. More distinctive in the European scene was the ability of the market to free itself from the worst interferences by the authorities themselves. Part of the explanation may lie in the special volume of bulk, utilitarian, long-distance, multi-lateral trade that Europe's physical circumstances encouraged. Where trade passed beyond the 'splendid and trifling' to the commonplace, sheer volume and low unit values of individual loads elicited different treatment. Bulk trade could be halted more easily than a trickle of luxuries, but sumptuary laws could restrict luxury consumption which is always conspicuous. There is little to choose between trade in luxury or utilitarian goods on the grounds that one might be more easily stopped than the other. If there were to be significant yields of taxes or duties from trade in items of low unit value, bulk trade had to be permitted and even encouraged.

The peculiarities of European trade arose because of the opportunities of the environment. Climate, geology and soils varied greatly from place to place. The portfolio of resources was extensive, but not everything was found in the same place. Sweden for example had no salt, which it vitally needed to preserve fish, meat and butter for the winter; on the other hand Sweden did possess the monopoly of European copper throughout the Middle Ages. Great complementarities therefore existed. Transport costs were low relative to those obtaining in the great continental land masses, since Europe was a peninsula of peninsulas with an exceptionally long, indented coastline relative to its area and with good navigable rivers, often tidal enough in their lower reaches to allow ships to penetrate some distance inland. The conditions were satisfied for multiple exchanges of commodities like salt and wine from the south against timber and minerals from the north, or wool from England, fish from the North Sea and cereals from the Baltic plain. The extent of the market was governed by environmental trading prospects. Only after 1800 does it become clear that demand in 'metropolitan' north-western Europe was strong enough to efface local environmental influences and determine the distribution of production in a series of von Thünen rings of decreasing intensity around the market (Dodgshon 1977). Until then production possibilities rooted in environmental circumstances decisively influenced the choice of regional specialism.

The large-scale, long-distance, multi-lateral trade that came easily to a variegated continent required its own big labour force and a large merchant class. This was eventually to become an independent force for growth. Because trade was heavily in prosaic commodities, it seldom tempted the confiscatory ambitions of princes. They were more alert to the yield of regular dues and taxes. Nevertheless the political setting was not wholly malleable. The economic and political maps of Europe begin to diverge in the later Middle Ages. Market activity was greatest in areas of half-hearted control such as borderlands between feudal units or pairs of political authorities, and in the countryside away from the urban gilds. The patterning of rural domestic industry set up an elaborate trade network between regions and across frontiers, penetrating the more autarkic agricultural economy of former times. The Rhine valley, parts of the southern Netherlands, northern France, and south and central Germany were zones of weak political control between the mid-thirteenth century and the Reformation. Some of the same characteristics were shared by the northern Netherlands, Westphalia, the London area and Bohemia: the rise of a landless proletariat, fast population growth and in-migration, upsets of family life, frequent unemployment for men in the weaving trade, millenarian movements, Lollardry, and general social disturbance (Cohn 1970:53; Macfarlane 1972:153–61). Here in the interstices between stronger states emerged an independent, mobile labour force alien to the feudal order and the Church of Rome. Only in the eighteenth century did the economic and political maps merge again, as the absolutist states began to think in terms of growth programmes. By then independent entrepreneurs, rootless workforces, and their Protestant ideologies were facts of life.

The rapid growth of printing in Germany away from the central control and strong copyist gilds of France is an example of the benefits of slipping the political leash. Playing two authorities against one another was a ploy made commoner by the many and overlapping jurisdictions in Europe. Maastricht, which for centuries had both the Bishop of Liège and the Duke of Brabant as lords, avoided wrangles about precedence by building a town hall with two stairways, and coined the saying, 'One Lord, oh Lord! Two lords – good!' (Hillaby 1972:69). A more important illustration is the way Venice developed her trade with the Muslim world despite Papal opposition, by obtaining concessions instead from the Emperor at Constantinople (Homer 1963:86–7). One authority could always be implored or bribed to intercede with the next. The Pope secured exemption for merchants of Astia crossing the Ile de France from the taxes Philip I proposed to levy on them. The Abbot of Cluny took a neighbouring castellan to task for detaining a merchant caravan from Langres and trying to exact protection money from it (Duby 1974:179).

Political representation of commercial interests was a later development. Direct access to the ruler was easier. The medieval prince who was willing to substitute regular taxation for irregular levies had a problem in doing so without a bureaucracy. The solution was to permit merchants to 'farm' taxes. Those who depended on royal favour were definitely playing with fire. Put not your trust in princes. They are subject to pressures on revenue varying from dull aches to agonising pains, and in societies of poor peasants any man with conspicuous assets is putting temptation in their way. Thus the Order of the Knights Templar, having become largely a banking operation, was destroyed by Philip the Fair of France (1285–1314), who repudiated his debts by the expedient of banishing his bankers. Edward III of England similarly ruined his Florentine bankers by repudiating his debts (Homer 1963:99). Greater security was won, very slowly. The different fortunes of two men of affairs in France may symbolise it. In the fifteenth century Jacques Coeur, the richest merchant in the country, was arrested on a trumped-up charge and, in what amounted to a royal debt repudiation, his properties were taken and he was forced to flee the country. In the eighteenth century by way of contrast the banker Samuel Bernard was able to place his family in high society and leave a vast fortune despite having once been bankrupted by accepting part of the crown's debts (Nef 1960:216–17). Royal and state credit was becoming gradually more secure. After 1671, when with the Stop of the Exchequer the payment of interest and repayment of loans to the Treasury was suspended, there was no further great difficulty on this score in England. The adventurer who tried to pawn his kingdom of Corsica in the eighteenth century was living in a past where the interests of state and ruler had once been assumed to be identical.

Arbitrary behaviour includes irregular levies, confiscations, forced loans, debt repudiation, debasements, expulsions, and judicial murder, all of them productive of uncertainty, to say the least. 'The chief condition which favours the development of enterprise is security for persons and property' (Cunningham 1896:x). We now take this condition so much for granted that we seldom trace out how it was first satisfied. The line of reasoning suggested is that we should examine the abolition or withering away of impediments to economic development. It suggests that economic history cannot be only applied economics jobbed back, but has also to account for the parameter shifts which brought the market system of modern economic analysis into being. Political insecurity and institutional rigidity in feudal and medieval times so obviously held back productive investment that the course of their reduction is virtually a history of development. Explaining the way in which risk was cut and custom eroded is as important for understanding early economic growth as raking the embers of the past for new emergent institutions. Many novelties seem less the causes of development than adaptations to change and expansion in their particular spheres, for example many practices that appear in banking, accountancy, insurance and finance, even the Weberian 'new man' himself.

There are three sorts of indications of the progress in bringing political arbitrariness to heel. Firstly, there is a diminution over time in reports of violence against inferiors. Kings made the pacification of their realms a goal. The law was increasingly resorted to for settling disputes between nobles, as an effect of the transformation of feudal units into centralised states (Strayer 1970:30–3). Churchmen who codified practice into law, and by 1300 specialist lay lawyers too, emerged as a vested interest in the peaceful settlement of disputes. In this case a categorical distinction between the histories of the old arbitrarinesses, on the wane, and the new institutions, on the rise, is not possible. They are two blades of the same pair of scissors. With upheaval and development proceeding in certain sectors of the economy new institutions would be needed, both 'embodied' institutions (like banks) or institutions broadly defined (like rules of commercial conduct). It is not strictly possible to separate these and their causes from the erosion or abolition of old customs or inconvenient practices.

At any rate, violence by the nobility was slowly restricted everywhere, though faster in England than on the continent (Woolf 1970:529). When John Aubrey looked back to the time of Henry VIII he saw great lords reigning like petty kings, able to hang and draw those they had tried and found guilty. Under Elizabeth, feuding by landowners was driven back to the border areas. The Marquis of Newcastle still rode to the Civil War at the head of his tenants like a baron of old, and even in the eighteenth century Beau Nash had to shame the rustic gentry out of wearing their boots and swords to balls in Bath. By its nature non-market power was slow to tame, but the costs of its more serious manifestations must have been seen to be rising and this curtailed excesses. There was little point in killing the goose that laid the golden egg and none at all in prompting open resistance, like the riots that followed attempts by French administrations to raise taxes and increase their share of the national cake (Le Roy Ladurie 1979:13). Signs of an effective popular temper that sought to protect itself against all comers appeared during the English Civil War when the Clubmen of Wiltshire and Dorset held large gatherings to league against plunderers from both sides. In one of the more heartening engagements of military history they severely hacked marauding Royalist troops (Anon. 1645).

Second, a slowly falling liquidity preference shows that overall risks were declining. The reduction of thoughtless behaviour by those in authority was part and parcel of this. Policy became more constructive – intermittently no doubt, but always laying down useful precedents. Thus for the common good of a kingdom trying to recover from war, Charles VII of France ordered a reversion in 1455 to the prewar policy of exempting from taxes goods brought to fairs, including goods belonging to foreign merchants. A memorandum writer in 1465 advised Louis XI to open up trade with England, for England was rich and trading with her would make Bordeaux rich again. The king took this advice, recognising that the late 'divisions' might otherwise make merchants hesitate to visit Bordeaux, for fear of arrest or molestation. He even invited ships from rebel areas, subject to certain restrictions on their stay (Allmand 1973:83, 181–4).

Third, the Physiocrats and Adam Smith were able to insist on the purely economic benefits of the commercial economy, whereas previous writers had expatiated on the political benefits, the value of trade as an instrument of predictability, regularity and order. At the point of change the market economy's full virtue had become accepted. A study by Hirschman (1977) elaborates on the political consequences stressed by earlier writers, such as John Locke, who saw freedom as 'not to be subject to the inconstant, uncertain, unknown, Arbitrary Will of another man'. Montesquieu had discussed in *Esprit des lois*, 'How Commerce Emerged in Europe from Barbarism', and concluded that the Jews, who suffered constant extortions at the hands of kings and nobles, invented the bill of exchange and so made it possible to send investments gliding silently about without rulers being able to catch hold of them by 'great and sudden arbitrary actions'. A writer of Napoleon's time could look back and exclaim that in the history of commerce the invention of the bill of exchange was 'an event almost comparable to the discovery of the compass and of America'. Capital had thus been made mobile and free. Sudden debasements of the coinage were rendered useless or counterproductive because extensive foreign exchange dealings and arbitrage would follow at once, more swiftly than when traders had been obliged to denote debts in kind in order to escape using debased coin. In this brave new world only good government could bring prosperity to the prince. The stage was set for a still newer world in which the market economy could be taken for granted and permitted to operate relatively undisturbed.

We should exaggerate neither the pace nor the permanency with which a risk-free environment was supplied, nor yet the demand for it. An indication that spells of great riskiness recurred is the burying of emergency hoards of treasure (as distinct from the savings hoards typical of times when investment outlets were at best uncertain). Samuel Pepys buried £1,300 in gold in a Huntingdonshire orchard when the Dutch came up the Medway in 1667. A hoard was buried at Bristol when William III was marching up from Torbay in 1688. Continental conflicts produced altogether more frequent uncertainty and finds of buried coin in southern Sweden are a barograph of troop movements during the Swedish–Danish war of 1562–9 (Grierson 1975:124, 132–3). What the merchant class, who had money to hide like this, sought was an end to unpredictable and arbitrary politics affecting them. They did not want war at home, but some kinds of war overseas offered profitable pickings. They did not hanker for democracy or equity. Where traders and merchant oligarchs found themselves in a position to do so they were as quick as any monarchy to abridge free competition. Foreign interlopers were often boycotted, Norwegians in Lübeck by the Hanse, Flemings in Cologne, and in later times foreigners in general in Amsterdam (van Klaveren 1969:64). It is noticeable that among Asian countries the merchants of Europe preferred those with strong central authorities, who were arbitrary enough in dealings with their own subjects (Lach and Flaumenhaft 1965:198).

Rigidities impeding the movement and use of goods and factors of production had to be removed for economies to work efficiently. The lure of profit was sufficient in already commercialised economies to bite into the 'cake of custom' or to get around regulations. Rigidities were less of a bar to development than residual arbitrariness, though the course of market expansion through the maze of inconvenience was not quite as automatic or straightforward as that may suggest. Types of rigidity included gild regulations, monopolies (other than those to encourage the importation of new trades or to shelter infant industries), an excessive schedule of holy days, sumptuary legislation, monasticism (which tied up labour and sometimes forbade the exploitation of mineral rights and woodland), settlement laws, price controls, and taboos and religious sanctions on economic behaviour or even on the study of science and technology. This is a long and bewildering list, but through it we can discern the trend of European history in the stripping-away of the bars and chains handed down from periods of deliberate social control.

If we examine first among the old rigidities the excessive celebration of saints' days we see that the medieval church had handed down or connived at a considerable economic burden. Its frequent, irregular holidays interfered with production schedules and reduced the total year worked. They were pruned and cut back in Protestant countries after the Reformation. Sabbath observance was regularised. There was a similar move in some Roman Catholic countries. Colbert reduced the saints' days celebrated in France to a trifling ninety-two in 1666. In the Rhineland, however, a reduction awaited the acquisition of the area by

Protestant Prussia in 1819. Kamen (1976:13) has put forward the view that given a high level of underemployment the large number of saints' days was not necessarily harmful to production. The evidence for a high average level of underemployment is not however good by late preindustrial times and in any case when producers were busy, the schedule of saints' days would remain rigid. Production schedules, and in agriculture the need to seize spells of good weather, were certain to be harmed by so many interruptions, with a consequent loss of income for all. Any loss of material income was a serious matter where workers were so poor and capital was so easily frightened away from productive activities. Even where workers were delighted to celebrate a release from the confining hours in domestic industry, to frolic and booze, it is not evident that materially or from the point of view of health they were wise to do so. Infant mortality for instance would be sensitive to fluctuations in the real wage. We should perhaps incline to think that Protestant employers, squeezing more regular labour from the workforce in a time of very low material living standards, were actually saving their workers from themselves – though not of course for an altruistic motive.

If we turn to sumptuary legislation, which prescribed the clothing and adornment proper for each social rank, we find the first examples in France in 1294. Laws were enacted in a large number of countries between the fourteenth and seventeenth centuries. Poland revived a dress code in that inauspicious year for economic regulation, 1776. But in England and in some parts of the continent sumptuary laws were decaying long before they were finally laid to rest, even perhaps in Venice, Basel and Zurich, which had special officers and courts to control dress, and in Poland and Spain where legislation persisted into the second half of the eighteenth century. In England such laws were never rigidly enforced, nor did they ever deal with the variety of items proscribed to the lower orders by continental governments or municipalities that wished to regulate consumption. Tudor sumptuary legislation had concerned only apparel and although the statutes were repealed solely for political reasons (when it was understood that this was an area where James I would rule by proclamation if not stopped), the whole apparatus always stood on shifting sands. Its worst enemy was probably economic growth itself, the beneficiaries of which resisted efforts to preserve exact class boundaries, cut spending on luxuries, induce the hoarding of cash which the crown might borrow, and promote the consumption of domestic rather than imported goods. Sumptuary laws could of course be used to bring about change. Peter the Great required the wearing of western dress as part of his modernising programme, and the English tried to impose a dress code on the 'wild Irish' in an effort to civilise them. This shows that it is difficult to be sure *a priori* that any particular sumptuary law was protectionist and hierarchical or intended to encourage economic growth, though the former intent is usually clear on inspection (Baldwin 1926; Harte 1976; Hooper 1915; Plucknett 1936).

As for the gild system, another and more major obstacle to change, we also find a breakdown over time in the enforcement of legislation. When opportunities of vast profit in foreign trade opened up after the Discoveries, merchant gilds moved over to make room for the enterprise of the joint-stock companies. The passing of the influence of the merchant gilds appears in that context understandable and natural, as if restrictions on enterprise are fated to give way before great incentives. That is too bland a view. Craft gilds, certainly, held on longer. They almost seem conspiracies in restraint of trade with their price and quality controls, restrictions on entry through apprenticeship rules, and rights to prosecute unfreemen, i.e. non-members, engaging in a craft. In practice the system was less than adamantine. In some industries it was giving way from the late Middle Ages to freer choice among combinations of factors of production. In textiles, much the largest industrial sector, technological change shook the foundations of the system by provoking intragild competition (Hirshler 1954). The textile gilds and some others were undermined even more forcefully by the dispersal of industry into the countryside, where the putting-out merchant found cheap labour that the town gilds could not control. Members of many gilds removed into the rural areas themselves in order to avoid restrictions on their productive activities, while continuing to sell toll-free in the towns under their gild privileges. Adam Smith noted that customers who wanted work done well hired suburban workmen who did not have exclusive privileges but relied on their reputation. Shopkeepers in London escaped from the sway of the retailing gilds by moving to the suburbs, despite bans on building shops and markets there (Kellett 1958:382). Whether the built-up area of seventeenth-century London really was too big for efficient gild surveillance or whether the greater opportunities opened by London's growth simply eroded the incentive to enforce the restrictions is an open question.

The chief means whereby the expanding market system broke up or bypassed the gild system in Europe as a whole was probably the rise of rural domestic industry. Dispersed producers were difficult to organise. The erosion process was reinforced in England by the growing hostility of the common law to the closed shop principle. The courts elevated the efficiency criterion embodied in individual rights over considerations of equity. The examples are interesting, though it is not certain how far the law was adapting to change or leading the way. A crucial case in 1614 went against an attempt to prevent a man who had been apprenticed to one trade from setting up business in another (Kellett 1958:384). Within two years the gilds had lost other cases at Ipswich and Newbury concerning rights to compel the enrolment of unfreemen engaged in the practice of given trades. These became established precedents. Earlier still, in 1599, the confiscation and forfeiture of goods during searches which gilds were accustomed to make in the course of policing their trades had been declared illegal in a test case involving the Dyers' Company. The ordinances of gilds were granted validity only 'so that they are consonant to law and reason'. In 1699 the Privy Council made the highly significant pronouncement that the statute which had come closest to codifying gild practice, 5 Eliza. c. 4, 'though not Repealed yet has been by most Judges looked upon as inconvenient to Trade, and to the Encrease of Inventions'.

Gild regulation had become like trying to plaster a bad leak with sand. The simplest way of looking on this is to see it as the cumulative spread of the broader interests of the society at the expense of vested interests. Obviously individuals and groups were hurt in this process, and others became very rich. From the *very* long-term point of view we are not called on to make moral judgements about an hypothetical balance of equity; we can see that there were productivity gains ultimately of benefit to all. We may speculate that the overall process, which looks like a series of nasty clashes of interest when examined episode by episode, was an effect of autonomous market growth. Restrictionism began to crumble in sixteenth-century England when some threshold market size was crossed. Four specific forces turned regulation into an increasingly hollow sham and the gilds themselves into friendly societies and dining-clubs, mere shadows of their full intent. Productive tasks became subdivided and every part of a process could no longer be kept under the aegis of one gild. This was the division of labour effect. Gilds that could not from time to time meet some upturn of demand were obliged for fear of community reprisals to grant permission for 'strangers' to sell their goods. Boroughs sold trade privileges to 'strangers' because they wanted more in dues than a local gild could or would raise. The state granted away gild privileges to aliens. With the growth of population and the market, the economy was simply becoming too complicated and changeable for straightforward control, and temptations were being set before backsliders in the gilds themselves. Every law supporting the gild system came to have its exceptions and loopholes (Kramer 1927:187–8, 195–7, 205ff.).

What had happened in Britain was that growth itself stimulated individuals to find ways around customary and legislative barriers to free market activity. Regulation often ceased to be enforced by justices of the peace who had connections with local business (Heaton 1965:228–9). Public authorities were acting in the new spirit when they refused to permit organised labour to impede what was deemed vital economic activity. For instance the Rebuilding Act of 1667 overrode the London craft companies and allowed in artisans from elsewhere to help reconstruction after the Great Fire. Similar derestrictions occurred in the aftermath of other town fires (Jones and Falkus 1979:229). The forces of change rippled out in unexpected ways. If political repression had a demonstration effect, so did revolution: the lord of the manor of Stockport, Cheshire, hastily unloaded the feudal rights attaching to his corn-mill by selling them to a cotton miller in 1791 when reaction to the French Revolution suggested that such rights might anyhow be abolished in England (Unwin 1924:122–3). The Settlement Laws whereby workers were to be shipped back to their parish of birth if they became a charge on the poor rates were allowed to fall into abeyance. The apprenticeship clauses of the Statute of Apprentices had been permitted to become disused before they were finally abolished in 1814, having been whittled away by Judges who 'disapproved of it on principle' (Derry 1931). Of course not all the forms of the past were done away with. European economic institutions have a continuity which is staggering compared with the brief histories of the new lands overseas or those countries where revolution has swept away old trappings. Any European is aware of the hand of the past, not only in the physical landscape but in educational and ecclesiastical institutions and the law. There are some nice examples in business (e.g. the Dutch annuity of 1624 still collecting interest (Homer 1963:128)). It is therefore easy to forget how much change there has been, with the litter of shells of old institutions all around, and because these institutions are animated by age-old ambitions it is easy to forget that they are based now on different groupings of power.

Early in the seventeenth century the English parliament had declared that it was 'to be lawful for every Clothier of what towne or countie soever . . . to make . . . any true woollen cloth . . . albeit the same kind of woollen cloth doe beare specially the name of some other country, city or towne within this realm' (4 Jas. I, c. 2, sect. 12, quoted by Unwin 1963:190). But just at that period France had been setting up privileged industries, and Charles I was soon to extend monopoly privileges in England itself. Charles was summarily dealt with, but change was slower on the continent. Nevertheless the rise of divergent interests and the frequent lack of single sources of authority worked against the ironbound regulation of industry and trade. Industrial development was most vigorous in the freer areas (Barkhausen 1974). Elsewhere noblemen evaded governmental or royal prohibitions on their involvement in business by working through dummies or simply by ignoring the prohibitions with an impunity born of that very status the prohibitions were designed to safeguard (Redlich 1953:83). In time, central authorities turned against restrictions too. The Habsburgs attacked the gilds in Bohemia and Moravia and after 1770 the environment there was definitely more *laissez-faire*, with a large growth in employment and output in the textile industry (Freudenberger 1960:351, 354). Turgot's attempt to abolish the privileges of trading corporations in France in 1776 contributed to his downfall, but they were swept away in 1791, and the Belgian and Dutch gilds were done away with after the French invasions. *La raison à cheval* and the Napoleonic code rid western Europe of much of the archaic lumber of regulation. It is true that gilds survived in Austria and Germany until 1859–60 and in Italy until 1864, but survival is not all. The gilds of the Swiss town still survived in the twentieth century, but without any privileged industrial status (Unwin 1963:1).

In most European countries agriculture dominated the economy and market penetration of that sector was essential for full development. In England organisational changes replaced open-field husbandry by a system of farming free of the hampering vestiges of corporate decision-making. These changes were related to (though, strictly, not indispensable for) the diffusion of more productive methods. Some dismantling of open-field husbandry was a voluntary response to the widening of the market, beginning with bargains over the piecemeal introduction of new crops and ending with enclosures by agreement. Some of the dismantling was forced through by leading members of the rural community in the form of enclosure by private Acts of parliament, and fruitlessly resisted by those whose resultant holdings would be too small without common rights. On the continent, the more to the east we look, so the dissolution of inflexible systems came later and later, and was carried out more and more by the actions of central government. But even in agriculture, by the early nineteenth century, considerable progress had been made towards generalising the freedom from rigidities which the market economy demanded.

Paradoxically, the market economy was a child of the non-market world. Its continuous European life began far back in early medieval history at a period when every return to peace and order prompted an upturn in trade. The dispersed and varied pattern of resources encouraged bulk trade in utilitarian goods among many centres, often far apart. Trade of this kind received the protection of political authorities because, whereas individual consignments were not especially valuable and tempting to seize, a steady flow of them offered revenues from taxes and duties supplementary to revenues from land. The process was cumulative. Growth built growth and business was its own demonstration effect. Arbitrary behaviour such as confiscations could only harm revenues from this source and princes learned the trading benefits of subduing the waywardness of their subjects, and grudgingly of themselves too. In addition the power of the mercantile purse eventually became autonomous enough to abridge royal arbitrariness. Market expansion, which given a favourable political context was a function of rising population, led to specialisation. This helped to undermine the rigidities of custom and law protecting older, less profitable forms of activity. Acts of policy, vested interests, and mercantilist schemers constantly breathed new life into restrictionism; but the momentum of the market was towards *laissez-faire*. That condition, like absolute zero, could never be reached, but as the nineteenth century approached it was ever more nearly touched.

Chapter 6

The states system

That Europe maintained itself in a stable state of division for so many centuries of unexampled progress is historically miraculous

Robert Wesson

EUROPE AS A WHOLE might have adopted one of several political forms. These included theocratic federation, of which the Holy Roman Empire was a waning example; trading networks like the Hanseatic League, or sets of city-states (though these took too little account of power based on land-holding); feudalism, which was however being pressed out into centralised states; and political empire (Wesson 1978:1; Tilly 1975:31). Most of the large populations of the world were organised into empires and the empires had been growing in size for millennia (Taagepera 1978). But Europe's real empires were later creations, the overseas possessions of the individual states. After the fall of Rome no empire was successfully built within Europe, from the time of Charlemagne to the Habsburgs and beyond. The ambitions of Charles V failed in the 1550s, the ambitions of his son Philip II failed, and the Habsburgs failed again in the Thirty Years War, when Gustavus Adolphus, subsidised by Richelieu in one of those cross-alliances that came to typify European rivalries, was able to thwart them.

Europe instead became a single system of states in which change in one cell affected the others. This is as crucial to understanding long-run economic development as it is to explaining the pattern of the industrial world that emerged in the nineteenth century. Certainly Europe neither modernised nor industrialised uniformly. Leadership changed, there were backward regions, even 'protoindustrial' regions that slid into backwardness (Jones 1977a), and the diffusion slope becomes very steep as it traverses from west to east. These are interesting matters – for other purposes. Our perspective agrees with that derived by Lee (1973:582) from studying population history on a European scale, that national or regional differences do not render useless a highly aggregated approach because similar forces were acting over a broad geographic area, and the units in the system were influencing each other.

There appears no *a priori* reason why a states system alone should have introduced the world to sustained economic development. An empire would be expected to generate economies of scale beyond the capabilities of a disarticulated states system. A states system necessitated the maintenance of a balance of power for its very survival, a most difficult tight-rope walk across the centuries. European history has been written before in terms of the system of multiple polities, but we need first to account for the existence of such a system in Europe, and Europe alone. The system endured though the number of constituent states continued to fall over the centuries. It seems to have been based on a characteristic of the environment. This, *fons et origo*, was the scatter of regions of high arable potential set in a continent of wastes and forests. These regions were the 'core-areas' of many states, always excepting those founded by arbitrary dynastic amalgamation (Pounds and Ball 1964; Kiernan 1965:32–4). Since plough husbandry was subject to only the slowest change there was a high degree of continuity in the evaluation of 'good soil' regions, and these 'regions of increment' (Fleure quoted by Pounds and Ball 1964:36) were densely settled by the norms of every period from the Neolithic (e.g. the Paris Basin, central Poland) or early classical times (e.g. Attica, the Roman Campagna). Their progenitors even show up as numerous patches on the map of farming and hunting cultures at 3000 B.C. (Waterbolk 1968:1099). They display evidence of heavy investment in art and architecture from the eighth through the twelfth centuries A.D. Most became the seats of both civil and ecclesiastical administrations and lay at the nodal points of trade.

These core-areas offered the largest tax bases to sustain offence and defence. Given the low agricultural productivity of the past and the need to find tax revenues from the small consumable surplus when seed had been set aside for the next season, 'one can well understand', as Ardant (1975:175) tells us, 'why important state-building efforts succeeded in the relatively wealthy zones, the Parisian basin, the London basin, Flanders, the plain of the Po, and, generally speaking, in the large alluvial plains'. Multiple polities had their nutritional and wealth bases in the core-areas, which were separated by encircling forests, mountains, marshes, or sandy heaths. The extent of wooded land remaining to be cleared as late as the sixteenth century was prodigious. On the modern map the intervening spaces have been cleared, drained, cultivated and filled up with people, but until the end of preindustrial times Europe was a succession of population islands in a sea of forest and heath (Duby 1974:7; Herlihy 1974:14; Kamen 1976: fig. 2; Le Roy Ladurie 1979:179).

Ruling families erected their political fortunes on the scaffolding of these 'islands'. As each island was unified, impulses to expand were liberated (Russell 1972:242), fuelling the outward spread whereby the core-area swelled into a state and then a nation-state, a trend advanced by improvements in communications and military technology which raised the equilibrium size of unit. States began to emerge about A.D. 900; supposedly there were still one thousand polities in the fourteenth century; nation-states began to develop in the fifteenth century; at the beginning of the following century there were 500 more-or-less independent units; by 1900 there were twenty-five (Russell 1972:244, 246; Strayer 1970:61; Tilly 1975:15 cf. 76; Wesson 1978:21). What is noteworthy is that the core-area is clearly traceable in many of the survivors. A large and fertile heart remained an advantage if one were to swallow rather than be swallowed up. Many lesser core-areas had disappeared in the raising of the average size of state.

Belts of difficult terrain lying between the core-areas, and ancient ethnic and linguistic apartheid dating from early folk movements and settlement history, helped to maintain the individuality of political units. Amalgamation went so far but no farther: never to a single empire. Amalgamation costs were high. Major natural barriers protect several parcels of territory the size of modern nation-states and the more durable polities expanded to fit the framework and there stop. Wesson (1978:111) gives as examples mountain chains like the Alps and the Pyrenees and the chain between Norway and Sweden, the riverine marshes protecting the northern Netherlands, and the sea around peninsular Denmark and around Britain and Sweden and Norway. Good natural defences such as Britain, Spain and to a lesser degree France possess have helped to give them greater stability than Germany, Austria and Poland. They cannot stop conflict but they do raise the cost. Ethnic and linguistic diversity also made the cost of assimilating territory high, as the examples of post-Conquest England, medieval and early modern France, and the Prussia of Frederick the Great show (Jones 1976:108; Strayer 1970:51). Perhaps for this reason the expansion of core-areas tended to be along the lines of least resistance, into similar areas with similar languages.

Optimal-size solutions for European states cannot be worked out as simple geometry. The spaces on the board have different values like those in the game of Monopoly and capturing and amalgamating some of them is exceedingly expensive. Where terrain did not provide much protection, units tended to disappear in takeovers by their neighbours. Burgundy seems a case in point. A congeries of smaller regions, some of them individually well demarcated, the fluidity of its outer boundaries and the greater riches of the Ile de France put it at a long-run disadvantage. Burgundy became the region; the Ile de France became the centre of the French nation-state (Commeaux 1977:7 and map 9). Other states that did not conform to the logic of core-areas did sometimes escape absorption. Examples are Switzerland and the United Provinces, countries with inherently poor soils or difficult terrain. Perversely, their initial disadvantage was their strength, in that the great agrarian lords found them too costly to attack, or not worth the candle.

Enough states were constructed each about its core and all of a similar enough strength to resist the logical conclusion of the process of conquest and amalgamation: a single unified European state. This may not have been an absolute bar to the rise of empire, but at least the dice were not loaded at the outset. There remained a large enough number of approximately similar states to preserve the shifting coalitions that successfully opposed control by a single power. History was not determined by this grid of core-areas but was the result of interaction between the environment and a host of other factors, personality, dynastic marriage, chance in battle. The geographers Pounds and Ball (1964:30) admit this when describing the many tiny core-areas supporting primitive or tribal states in the Danube Basin and Balkan peninsula, which meant that 'it thus became the role of historical forces to choose from among the several areas of increment in this area those which were to develop as the foci of their respective states', a point also made by the medievalist, Russell (1972:17–18). What we have, therefore, is a sort of lower-bound theory of European state formation in which other forces decide the precise outcome, but the selection of the nucleus of the rising state will be from among the richer potential cores.

The system was preserved by co-opting counterweights to internal aggressors from outside. A French-based alliance with the Pope even scandalously brought in Islamic forces (the Ottoman Empire) to check the Habsburgs. The Pope called in Protestants against the disillusioned and abdicating Charles V. Campenella in his *Discorsi Politici* of about 1600 referred explicitly to the changing of allegiances in order to trim the balance of Spanish and French power in Italy, and to Habsburg and Ottoman power blocking each other's aspirations to 'universal empire' (Wight 1977:188). The concept of a balance of power, usually dated from the Anglo-Franco-Spanish compromise of the Treaty of Utrecht (1713), was in existence much earlier. It has been dated from Cardinal Wolsey's allying of England with first one, then the other, mainland European monarchy (Holborn 1951:15), but shifting alliances were nothing new, nor does the notion of balancing alliances seem a particularly strange intellectual discovery. What was strange was its prolonged success against a series of powerful contenders for control of Europe.

A long-lasting states system is a miracle. Empires are more understandable since they are formed by straightforward military expansion with obvious rewards for those engaged in it. States systems are fragile and precarious. Any conflict between members is likely to draw others in and threaten the stability and survival of the whole. The checks and balances of decentralised power, and a code of international law such as was developed in Europe, are feeble safeguards against chaos or imperialism. Possibly, despite wars for overseas empires, the availability of extra-European territory provided an essential safety valve.

In longer perspective states systems do have some advantages. Because they spread power around, wrong-headed and incontrovertible systems-wide decisions could not be imposed by some central authority; for all the pretensions of the Papacy or the Holy Roman Empire no commanding focus of authority was universally accepted. Thus no negative centralist decision could thwart change. There was no equivalent of the decision of the Ming court in 1480 not to have Chinese maritime exploration re-opened. The closest parallel was the Pope's division of the globe into Spanish and Portuguese spheres of influence, and of that the king of France smartly said that he was aware of no such clause in Adam's will.

Against the benefits of decentralisation within systems of states, the case in favour of a land empire would presumably rest on economies of scale. There is no *a priori* means of determining the relative merits of the two sorts of advantage. The proof must lie in the historical pudding. In practice centralisation seems to have been at a serious long-term disadvantage. Imperial politics were typically unstable. Unchecked, unresponsive, unrepresentative influence persisted in the hands of those who had the care of the young emperor, often a class of eunuchs. The palace atmosphere was too often a stench of vice, treachery and triviality (Rycaut 1668; Stavrianos 1966:118–19; Wesson 1967). Looking back at the magnificence of empires, the symbolic conspicuous consumption at court, the heavy monuments, it is easy to be impressed. It is easy, too, to impute purpose to what was frequently the sway of spoilt and vicious children imbued with total power. Landes (1969:34) remarks of Muslim history, 'the record of shifting dynasties, palace plots, reigns of terror, and mad rulers reads like an Oriental version of the Merovingian snakepit'. Emperors were surrounded by sycophants. They possessed multiple wives, concubines and harems of young women, a phenomenon that may have been less the perquisite of wealth and power than the assertion of dominance relationships, the propensity to use people as objects. The amassing of households full of slaves for display purposes rather than work may have had a similar ethological significance. Great attention was paid to submission symbols, kneeling, prostration, the kotow, in recognition of the emperor's personal dominance. These forms of behaviour had their counterparts in the history of European royalty, but reading the literature one forms the opinion, which might usefully be quantified, that excessive consumption and debauchery and terror were much more prevalent in the empires of Asia and the Ancient World than in the states of Europe.

To cite a solitary example of conspicuous consumption in Asia, Asaf-ud-daulah, ruler of Oudh, owned in 1782 jewels then valued at £8,000,000. He had 20 palaces, more than 100 private gardens, 4,000 gardeners. His chandeliers cost more than £1,000,000. He owned 1,500 double-barrelled guns, and countless clocks, two of which had cost £30,000. He kept 1,200 elephants, 3,000 saddle horses, and 1,000 hunting dogs. Almost 3,000 servants, including 50 personal barbers, looked after him, and the expenses of his kitchen came to between £200 and £300 per day. His fighting cocks and pigeons were estimated at 300,000 and the deer in his park were too numerous to estimate. He maintained separate establishments for monkeys, snakes, scorpions, and spiders. Oudh was not an oppressed countryside of peasants toiling to support this household, it was 'a chaos of disorder and want' (Young 1959:52).

Many other Asian rulers could match or exceed this catalogue of possessions, but which of the European rulers could compare? The tsars perhaps. The Sun King? Life for the monarch of a country in Europe was spacious, but not on the scale that measures the grandeur of Asian emperors. The habit was simpler in Europe. Monarchs were becoming more purposeful, even if the purpose was military. The organisational tasks attending the wars of the states system were so vast by the late seventeenth century that even kings were obliged to attend to them (Wolf 1962:1–3), becoming in the process more like the heads of corporations than surrogate gods.

These corporations, considered as a group, realised not only the benefits of competitive decision-making but some of the economies of scale expected of an empire. Unity in diversity gave Europe some of the best of both worlds, albeit in a somewhat ragged and untidy way. The senses in which Europe was a unity while remaining decentralised, and the senses in which that mattered for economic development, are what we have to discuss. Viewed under the ordinary arrangement of national

histories Europe is a mosaic of peoples speaking different languages, under rulers often ardently hostile to one another, ardu-
ously hewing their nation-states out of very mixed timber. Tilt
the kaleidoscope and another pattern forms, the pattern of a
common culture. Edmund Burke was typical of the eighteenth
century in proclaiming that 'no European can feel himself a
complete exile in any country of the continent'. This was truer for
the apex of the social pyramid than for the base, but it helps to
justify our looking at a highly aggregated Europe, a system in
which change in one part had an effect on the others. That one
Europe was emerging, or a Europe capable of functioning as one,
is indicated by the increasing uniformity of the calendar. Between
1522, when Venice adopted 1 January as the first day of the year,
and 1752, when a laggard England did so, most European countries including Russia came into line. Between 1582 when Spain,
Portugal, France, and the Italian states adopted the Gregorian
calendar and 1752 when Great Britain came trailing in amid a
clamour of 'give us back our eleven days', that innovation was
also accepted, although Russia held out until 1918. The Balkan
countries and Turkey waited until the Great War or after to chime
in (whereas Japan had adopted the Gregorian scheme in 1872 and
China in 1912). The standardised calendar is as good an indication as most of the bounds of a co-ordinated Europe, which was
in late preindustrial times what we should now call western,
central, northern and southern Europe, with Russia as a slightly
anomalous case, and excluding the Balkans. Co-ordination was
slow and halting, but what is significant is that it was achieved,
and without the strait-jacket of centralism.

True unity based on religion had broken down with the secret
treaty between Venice and the Mongol Empire in 1222, by which
the Venetians were to spy and propagandise for the alien Mongols, who for their part were to destroy all other trading stations
as they advanced, leaving Venice with the monopoly. More generally it broke down with the Great Schism of the fourteenth
century (Chambers 1979:24–5; Dehio 1965:21). Christendom was
more fundamentally fractured by the assault on Venice, despite
the rôle it had assumed as bulwark against the infidel Turks, by
the League of Cambrai, which included the Papacy; and by the
later French alliance with the Ottomans to counterweigh the

Habsburgs. Long before Christ, Herodotus had made a clear enough distinction between European and Asian civilisation, but Christendom had become the preferred label. This reduced 'Europe' to a neutral geographical expression, until in the fifteenth century Europe came again to denote something more. Polish and Habsburg propagandists began to imply that their governments were defending a continental society with a unique value system against the assaults of the Ottomans (Coles 1968:148). Despite the mockeries of its precepts by its wars, Christianity did remain enough of an umbrella, or rather two umbrellas, Roman Catholic and Protestant, to shelter a degree of intercourse among Europeans of diverse language and nationality. In terms of world comparisons it was probably more important for change and innovation that Europeans had, however, escaped the grasp of a single politico-religious order, the equivalent, say, of state Confucianism in China. Limited diversity, for all the blasphemous cruelty and waste of intra-Christian conflict, gave Europeans some togetherness and some freedom of thought. This was a better result than religious totalitarianism or an infinity of splintering.

A similar middle way was taken over the use of language. Two languages were picked out for diplomacy, official business, scholarship and high-society prattle. For diplomatic purposes the usage was Latin until the sixteenth century, thereafter Italian, then increasingly French. Diplomacy was itself a cement. Under the *ancien régime* any one nation's diplomatic advisers were mixed in nationality. Their aim was to preserve the peace, if necessary by bribes. The resultant treaties and conventional usages were not unsuccessful in placing limits on the spread of hostilities: it was for example remarkable that English neutrality and trade were accepted by the belligerents during the Thirty Years War, which might well have become all-consuming (Kepler 1976).

Over and above its diplomatic uses, French became the language of the fashionable set, to the extent that Tsarist nobles preferred it to Russian. By the death of Louis XIV the French language had captured the high society of Europe in a way that French arms had failed to do, and faster even than it was taking over the provinces in France itself, where as late as 1867 ten per cent of the population could still not speak French (Goubert

1974:279; Higonnet 1978:1153). Officialdom tended to use Latin, in some countries into the nineteenth century, despite the rise of literatures in the national languages. Bureaucrats thus had Latin and French in which to converse with foreigners. Students had always been peripatetic, and learning, conveyed in Latin, had been a universal currency under the medieval church, and scholars, still using Latin, continued to admit or suffer no national restrictions on their travel even between countries at war. Their exchange went on as late as the Napoleonic war. As far as they were concerned, there was little of that contradiction in terms, the enforcement of loyalty.

Consider the pan-Europeanism of learning, say, of a science like geology. When early in the nineteenth century Mary Anning's fossil shop at Lyme Regis, Dorset, was visited by the King of Saxony (whose Freiburg had been the world centre for students of geology), she was able to hand back the royal autograph book with a calm, 'I am well known throughout the whole of Europe.' Royal patronage of science was more than mere form, and we find for instance Prince Henry of Prussia travelling to Montbard to call on Buffon, and the Emperor of Austria making flattering remarks about Buffon's own empire. By that period scientific societies had foreign memberships and honoured distinguished non-nationals, and formal western world networks of correspondents and observers were beginning to be set up. The Société Royale de Médecine established a chain of stations in the 1780s to investigate the possible effects of weather conditions on illnesses and epidemics (Gribbin 1979:892). In Germany in 1780 the Elector Karl Theodor of the Rhenish Palatinate founded an observer network under the aegis of the Societas Meteorologica Palatina. This society issued standardised instruments to observers as far apart as Russia, Greenland and North America.

In important respects Europe had become a unified market area, for the factors of production, capital and labour, and increasingly for goods. Obviously it was easiest for commodities of low bulk and high value to surmount the physical and political obstacles to trade, as we may see from the world of fashion. Unification in this field was aided by the Grand Tour and the practice of sending annually round each major city as far afield as St Petersburg, and that western outpost of Europe, Boston,

Massachusetts, a jointed wooden doll dressed in the season's Paris mode (Jones 1973). Dressmakers everywhere copied the style. Generals permitted the 'wooden mademoiselle' to pass through the lines. Fashionable society was animated by periodic crazes for foreign styles, on the continent for things English, in England for things French. Scarcely a corner was remote enough to be exempt: even the National Museum of Iceland contains furniture which represents Danish taste, itself swayed by French, English, German and Dutch influences (cf. Rousell 1957:102, 104). Most striking of all was the dominance of Europe by French *haute couture*, ever since the sixteenth century when France took over the lead from Italy. Many products were therefore interchangeable between countries and faced a market greater than any single land could offer, if they could evade or override the restrictions of mercantilism. Since governments seldom had a large staff of officials they were not well equipped to halt such trade, quite apart from the gaping holes in the net provided by corrupt officials (cf. van Klaveren 1969). At the opposite end of the scale from high fashion, there was a considerable and regular traffic across frontiers in foodstuffs from the lowlands of one country exchanged for the manufactures of cottage industries in the uplands of the next.

The market for news and commercial intelligence was somewhat unified. Marco Polo had been impressed in the thirteenth century by the speed of the mails in the Chinese empire, but in reality a shortage of fodder restricted the Chinese courier service and this was not overcome (Stover and Stover 1976:82). Improved mail services in early modern Europe eclipsed any rivals for volume and perhaps for speed, an advantage being that horses there could usually be foddered. As economies became more complicated there developed, in addition to the flow of legitimate news, a market in industrial intelligence. Espionage and bribery were employed. John Lombe acquired the knowhow of Italian silk manufacturing in this manner in the early eighteenth century and a century later there was an influential underground traffic in machinery blueprints (Jeremy 1977). In the early days of factory industry techniques were spread, lawfully enough, by sales of second-hand machinery down a developmental stairway from more advanced to less advanced European countries. National economic histories cite this as evidence of technological lags, but we should note that by historical standards the very existence of a market for industrial plant is witness to a considerable degree of homogeneity in methods of production and the goods demanded.

The spinning of a political and cultural (and consequently an economic) web had been going on since far back in the Middle Ages, through arranged marriages between ruling houses. These were so important for alliances that they were the normal practice at the level of royalty (Fichtner 1976; Chadwick 1945:103). There was probably a hostage element involved at times. From the present point of view what is important is that royal women who were twice married might carry the lifestyles of a brace of countries to some third court. Other sorts of specialised labour moved too, often on a large scale. To take as an illustration mercenary troops, there was virtually an international officer corps staffing all the national armies (Mockler 1970). Protestant Switzerland exported mercenary regiments even to Papal powers, and the sovereigns of many small states of Germany made a business of hiring out soldiers. As a result Kiernan (1965:31–2) conceives the European states, at any rate in the developing east and north, as a series of joint-stock enterprises attracting the services of the ambitious. We may generalise his observations: in its states system Europe had a portfolio of competing and colluding polities whose spirit of competition was adapted to diffusing best practices.

Skilled civilian labour and entrepreneurs were also willing and often able to migrate, despite a variety of governmental promulgations to the effect that specialist labour should stay put. This has been the subject of wide comment. A literature exists on the history of international labour movement. Medieval cities had their alien communities each with its own church and observing its own saints' days. There were frequent international hirings of labour, initially for the tasks of the state. Thus in the 1470s Ivan III brought Italian engineers and architects to rebuild Moscow and its cathedral, destroyed in a great fire, the connection having come about through Ivan's marriage to Sofia Palaeologia, a Byzantine princess who had been brought up in Rome. The Russians in their relative backwardness were great borrowers. In

1489 Ivan's agents again abroad on marriage business hired gunsmiths, goldsmiths and engineers, two centuries before the mass hiring of Dutch and English artisans on Peter the Great's Grand Embassy (Grey 1967:36–7, 73, 75). Activity of this kind went the rounds, for no one country was permanently in the lead. Thus in the sixteenth century the tin and copper of Cornwall and the Lake District were developed by bringing in miners from the more advanced mining districts of south Germany. The necessity of relying on infrequent forays when some foreign princess was being selected for a dynastic wedding fell away with greater awareness of technological lags and the disadvantages they implied, especially for military standing. Hiring commissions were sent out or government agents were stationed abroad to hire on a regular basis. Private hiring began to supplement royal initiative: one list of skilled men brought into England between the fifteenth and seventeenth centuries includes practitioners of thirteen trades and professions from eight countries (Tilly 1975:529).

Where labour was not officially free to move, it often went anyway. The Murano glassmakers spread their arts across Europe despite severe penalties threatened by the Venetian authorities, who felt more keenly than many governments the loss of an industrial monopoly (Rapp 1975:505–6). Where the user was not able to afford or could not secure all the labour he wanted, he simply set to work anyone who fell into his hands, as when Peter the Great pressed into service the military and technical skills of Swedish prisoners taken at Poltava. Asian empires of course also acquired new skills by bribing foreigners or exploiting prisoners and it is not enough to write this off as labour solely used for developing artillery or squandered on making mechanical playthings. European courts too employed skilled artisans on equally unproductive labours such as turning out mechanical toy bands and roundabouts and ornamental fountains jetted by steam. The difference between Europe and Asia was a statistical one, a 'population difference' in the purposes for which imported labour was employed, rather than a categorical distinction. More of the imported labour in Europe was set productive tasks, and the exchanges of trained labour were far more numerous and systematic.

This picture of a Europe which shared in salient respects a common culture, or series of overlapped lifestyles, and formed something of a single market demonstrates that political decentralisation did not mean a fatal loss of economies of scale in production and distribution. The states system did not thwart the flow of capital and labour to the constituent states offering the highest marginal return. Princes and governments, with the characteristic short-run goals of politicians, often wished to staunch the flow but were largely unable to do so. They even contributed to it, as when they deposited their personal fortunes in foreign money markets, notably Amsterdam and London, or enticed foreign craftsmen to settle in their realms. Conceptions of national loyalty remained vague. The merchants of Holland were ready to supply naval stores to their country's enemies in times of war and hedged their bets by investing in Dunkirk privateers dedicated to preying on the convoys of *fluit* ships making up the Channel to Amsterdam, while Frenchmen were constantly infuriating Colbert by having dealings with the Dutch (Barbour 1963). Lutheran lands invited Calvinist entrepreneurs to set up businesses, as the Dutch Marcellis family did in Denmark and de Geer (from Liège via Amsterdam) in Sweden. So did Roman Catholic countries. Entrepreneurial and managerial skills even more than technical ones were too scarce for scruples. Wallenstein's army was supplied and its pay organised by a Calvinist banker resident in Prague, Hans de Witt, banker to the Viennese Habsburg emperor, banker even to the Jesuits, and controller of the silver and tin reserves of the Holy Roman Empire (Trevor-Roper 1967:7ff.). The Empire was a specially polyglot area. 'Florence, Milan, Trieste, Fiume, Lubljana, Zagreb, Ragusa, Sarajevo, Budapest, Clausenburg, Csernovitz, Lvov, Brno, Prague . . . all of them', writes Leigh Fermor (1977:184n.), 'for varying periods, were part of the Empire. The influx of their citizens to Vienna is the other side of the medal from endemic irredentism and sporadic revolt?

Both buyers and sellers of skilled labour and investment capital were increasingly supplied by the private market. Individuals and whole populations in border areas sometimes shifted their allegiance to that country which was governed best, in Alexander Pope's sense of least taxed (see e.g. Fraser 1971:53). The facility with which the owners of capital might remove to another country is depicted in *The Wealth of Nations* as a restraint on excessive taxation. Montesquieu had previously expressed the view that where citizens held moveable wealth governments would behave more circumspectly than the governments of agrarian states where real estate held the wealth holders tight (Hirschman 1977:94; 1978). The potential 'exit' of propertied men was an implicit rein on arbitrary power even when that power remained harsh enough to render giving 'voice' to political complaints a dangerous luxury. Fundamentally, freedom derived from the states system, from the existence of nearby countries to which one might remove or flee, where one's religion or opinions were not obnoxious and might even be orthodox, and where the way of life was not completely unfamiliar. The device of transportable paper claims to wealth such as bills of exchange greatly increased the chances that the opportunities of flight might be taken. Similar opportunities were not open to subjects sealed, as it were, within vast land empires.

As the European nation-states became more self-conscious they may have begun to raise the costs of exit for both capital and labour by closing borders and pursuing cultural homogeneity as a goal (Friedman 1977:72–6). However according to one authority (Rokkan 1975:589) those absolutist states that did try to block both exit (borders) and voice (political representation) brought political troubles on themselves, probably through forcing heterogeneous peoples too quickly into the one mould of culture and language. But latent competition between states remained a minimal guarantee that the difference between an empire and the European states system would not slide into merely that between one big despotism and a lot of little despotisms.

A large empire which monopolised the means of coercion and was not threatened by more advanced neighbours had little incentive to adopt new methods. The states of Europe on the other hand were surrounded by actual or potential competitors. If the government of one were lax, it impaired its own prestige and military security. If one politically or religiously prejudiced state excluded or expelled disfavoured groups of entrepreneurs or workers, other states of different complexions or greater tolerance might be bidding for services or be open to offers.

The states system was an insurance against economic and technological stagnation. It was as if there were a kind of specie-flow equilibrating mechanism constantly levelling up know-how. Obviously it was imperfect. In the short run it must have seemed to individuals caught in the toils of history quite grotesquely imperfect. The unification of Europe is not yet tidy or complete; *a fortiori* it was not so by the eighteenth century. Possibly the untidiness is a symptom of a deeper and largely positive element of local energy within the system.

A large part of the system's dynamic was an arms race. The goals were dynastic and military rather than developmental. Perhaps first goals always are – 'defence is more important than opulence', as Adam Smith said – and the real difference among states is in their capacity to create economic growth on the side. Yet by functioning as a set of joint-stock corporations with implicit prospectuses listing resources and freedoms, the nation-states insured against the suppression of novelty and unorthodoxy in the system as a whole. Europe offered a series of refuges to the oppressed and its history might be written as a saga of the escape of refugees from its wars, invasions and religious persecutions. There were plenty of oppressions and plenty of conflicts. Few however were tainted by Genghis Khans or 'dawnist' ideologues who in their zeal to make over (and take over) the world afresh were eager to massacre whole populations. Some of this frightfulness had admittedly happened in the religious wars and millenarian uprisings of the sixteenth and seventeenth centuries when individual cities were turned in the space of a fortnight into the autocracy of some demagogic polygamist acting in the name of equality (Cohn 1970). Many Europeans were uprooted from their homes. But by Near Eastern or modern standards few were slaughtered for their beliefs. Refugee movements and the dispersals of war exiles had the incidental effect of transferring skills from one nation-state to the next.

One great wave of Protestants fled from the southern Netherlands as the Duke of Alva was arriving there in 1567. They scattered to England, Holland and Switzerland where they stiffened the workforces of several industries, especially textiles. When Antwerp was sacked in 1585 Flemish artisans fled to England and founded a silk industry. A wave of even greater economic implications was that of the Huguenots leaving France, 200,000 or more of them at and just before the Revocation of the Edict of Nantes by Louis XIV in 1685. They were able to get around various prohibitions on their leaving, though this some-times entailed being smuggled out (Henri de Portal, who founded the firm at Laverstoke, Hampshire, which still prints the paper for Bank of England notes, was shipped from France hid-den in a wine barrel). The Huguenots went to various Protestant countries, including Sweden, Brandenburg and other German states, and Ulster, playing a rôle in metal production as well as paper-making and the establishment of the Ulster linen industry (Scoville 1951; Brierley 1970:152). Scoville (1960) gives extensive details of the industrial effects on England, Ireland, Holland, Germany and Switzerland in a chapter entitled, 'The Revocation and the Diffusion of Technology', for that was what refugee movements amounted to from the point of view of the economic system, a massive process of technological diffusion.

Greek Christians dispersed westwards in response to Turkish wars and conquests between 1460 and 1718. They founded mer-cantile communities in eight countries from England to Russia, as well as in the Balearic islands, Malta, and the Danubian prin-cipalities (Zakythinos 1976:115ff.). There were ample distur-bances to multiply expatriate communities of this type several times over, with the resultant emergence of a sense of European-ness among the bourgeoisie. Contrary to the usual British view of diffusion proceeding from a specially creative Great Britain, commercial and industrial development had roots in these inter-national networks of commercial houses. 'The industrialisation of Britain was a *European* process, in which Germans, Greeks, American Irish, and a smattering of other races (Dutch, French, Italians, and others) contributed their expertise' (Chapman 1977:48).

The European history of the Jews was really the most striking case of all. As early as 1084 northern European princes had licensed Jews as money-lenders, since they were among the few agents available from the advanced lands of the Mediterranean who were willing to participate in the eleventh-century de-velopment of the north. Unfortunately too many loans were taken up for unproductive ventures such as war and cathedral-building. This made lending a burden and made the lenders unpopular in proportion to the inability of the borrowers to pay. In consequence the massacres of Jews associated with the Crusades were apt to start with a burning of deeds of indebtedness. First things first, so to speak. Under this dispiriting régime no Jewish community was able to survive for more than two or three generations, since when kings went broke they were disposed to solve part of their problem and at the same time curry favour with the church by piously expelling their Jews. The first national community to be ousted was from England, where the crown had bled them through a special exchequer until by 1290 they had been bled dry. Edward I prudently made contact with Christian financiers from the continent and then with calculated cruelty expelled the Jews from his dominions. A similar game of cat-and-mouse was played in the other countries of northern Europe. The Christian princes had been in effect using the Jewish money-lenders as fronts for programmes of forced saving, confiscating what wealth remained to them at the point of expulsion (Elman 1936–7; Brierley 1970:150–1; Parkes 1964). Later régimes were more imaginative in their exploitation. Prussia, for instance, repeatedly obliged its Jewries to export the products of its Berlin manufactories to eastern Europe at a considerable cost to them (van Klaveren 1969:268).

The expulsions were not sufficiently synchronised to prevent the Jews, or other refugees, from by and large finding somewhere to go. Braudel (1972 vol. 2:805–17) makes this point about the situation in the politically divided states of Germany and Italy. He stresses how many frontiers there were over which the Jews, and others, might drive their wagons, and the many ports to which they might sail away to safety. The Jews, indeed, homed on the most prosperous countries of the day, bringing skills in languages that necessity had obliged them to acquire, together with the commercial ideas of their own international network and of the lands they had been forced to quit. At the same time a legacy of ideas was often left behind, so that from a long-run and materialistic point of view European society as a whole may have gained from its own failings.

When the Jews were turned out of Spain at the end of the fifteenth century one of the places to which they went was outside the European system: Turkey. The Ottoman empire was then in its short-lived open and receptive phase, and the sultan Bajazet II forecast that the Jews would make him rich at Spain's expense. To the extent that Spain would be unable to replace the lost skills that might have been so, but, in general, expulsions were less damaging than they might have been, and in the Spanish case the Austrian Fuggers and Welsers, and several Genoese families, stepped into the shoes of the departing Sephardic Jews (Koenigsberger 1971:22–3). The Jews followed the Turkish banner to the Near East as the professional classes of the Ottoman empire, replacing the Christian Greeks. The Ottomans went so far as to pull diplomatic strings to have the wealth of the rich Mendes family transferred from Europe in the mid-sixteenth century. They made representations to the Pope against threats to the property of 'their' Jews in Europe (Inalcik 1969:121). Europe, then, was not alone in welcoming minorities. Technological and commercial skills, and investment capital, were scarce enough to make refugees widely welcome, periods of severe ideological stress excepted. The Ottoman empire and the Mughal empire in India were even more cosmopolitan than the most motley court in Europe, which was in Russia. They were 'confluences of fortune-hunters from all over middle and western Asia' (Kiernan 1965:32). Yet those who sought to do business in these régimes did so on sufferance, unprotected by law, and at their daily peril.

Deviant minorities, whom Sir William Petty called 'the Heterodox Party', tended to be influential in the external trade of most economic systems. What distinguished Europe was the extent of its political variety, which offered a compensatory network of refuges to offset the exclusions and rising nationalisms. There was enough competitiveness to permit the recolonisation of expelling states by the expelled or their descendants (see e.g. Trevor-Roper 1967:43), or at the least by their most fruitful ideas. Refugee movements seem perversely to have been energising in the long run. The heterodox parties were successful commercially. They were not files shuffling off the stage of history but were engaged in a game of musical chairs in which with every round, although some poor soul might lose his seat, most, after a flummoxing journey, could find somewhere new to sit down.

European states were alike enough to learn to solve problems precisely because they could see that some neighbouring state had solved them, i.e. by stimulus diffusion. The actual agents who solved technological problems were often refugees. As modern work confirms, technological diffusion is strongly associated at least in its early stages with the physical movement of skilled people.

The economic damage done by expulsions may not have been any greater than that of the confiscations with which they were often linked. The majority of the subjects of a state, or the ruler with their acquiescence, may be able to confiscate the goods of a clearly defined minority without much harm to the economy (Bronfenbrenner 1964), odious as this may be on moral grounds. Growth was not halted by expulsions and confiscations. Where new entrants took over the niche of those who had left, rates of growth may scarcely have fallen. Queen Isabella's coffers were swollen with confiscated Jewish property when she dipped into them to finance Columbus (Birmingham 1972:36). This does not justify expulsions and confiscations, but it does demonstrate the elusiveness of any serious net economic loss. This is admittedly to look on history with a certain Olympian detachment, to see the scrabbling lives of individuals almost as a tired man looks at flies. But there are too many individuals to write sensible history in biographical terms. Even a 'great man' approach prejudges the rôle of individuals in the processes of change, and has to be arbitrarily selective in the figures chosen. The aim of economic history is to see the wood amidst the trees. If we are trying to understand how whole economic systems developed through the *very* long term we have to stand back and take a dispassionate view. A microscope would reveal other patterns, but a telescope is appropriate for our purposes.

All in all, the competitiveness and 'genetic variety' of the states system helped to generalise best practices without, in the event, the penalties that morally may have been right. This was done by voluntary and involuntary movements of capital and labour. Thus the culture, science, technology and commercial practice of the Italian city-states, Antwerp, Amsterdam, and London were passed from each to the next, and were diffused across agrarian and backward economies that showed little sign of attaining the same level on their own. Galileo's trial silenced Italian scientists, but the 'scientific revolution' continued in Protestant lands. Books might be burned and scientists tried by the church, machinery might be smashed by mobs, entrepreneurs banished and investors expropriated by governments, but Europe as a whole did not experience technological regression. The multi-cell system possessed a built-in ability to replace its local losses, a vigorous recombination, regrowth or substitution effect. The system had its own signature and was more than the sum of its parts.

There is a possible alternative hypothesis that development came about not because of the states system but in spite of the associated wars. With or without wars, the states system was not a sufficient cause of economic development, though it was a necessary cause of the form that development took. War is the extension of diplomacy by unacceptable means, but whether or not it was utterly negative in economic effect is a matter of debate. In economies with under-employed resources war and war preparations might drive up production over the short run, but in the longer run war squandered resources and diverted good minds to mindlessness. Associated innovations were a little indirect, like the improvements in crops made by men who had been temporarily exiled during the English Civil Wars, or the sale of heavier war-surplus horses (Jones 1974a; Piggott 1976:115). There was little spin-off from the arsenals of the past in the way of new technology (cf. Kahan 1967:19; and Mokyr 1976:28–9). What for a long time limited the harm done by the wars in the states system was local autarky. Nef (1968:104) points out that the religious wars of sixteenth- and seventeenth-century France came close to bringing about national collapse but this did not happen because areas outside the fighting were accustomed to getting on with the job of producing and consuming more or less in isolation. Wars were in any case less than total, and much business, even international trade, went on as usual.

As time moved on the system developed. The integration of national economies and of the system as a whole went ahead, and the scale of warfare increased. Widescale collapse became a possibility. For reasons which approach the heart of the European miracle – and what shimmers in those depths is the miraculous preservation of the balance of power – the growth of production was enough to weather the storm. Europe was deeply poisoned by dynastic ambition, the endemic *furor teutonicus*, and epidemic religious ideologies – Ortelius's 'Catholic evil, Protestant fever, and the Huguenot dysentery' (Stechow n.d.:22, 25). Its creative act was to ensure the balance of power within this arena of bitterness. Whether there is a theory that can postdict the maintenance of this balance seems doubtful, to say the least, though there was a systematic shift from the days of religious war to a time of dynastic struggle. Since dynastic wars were less bloody than ideological struggle, and were somewhat restricted in scope and duration because they were hard to finance, this may have weighted the scales towards a successful outcome. The balance of power did in practice prevent the rise of monolithic empires and curb some of the waste of the wars among the nation-states. The rules of war were a genuine, if frail, step forward. The pith of the European miracle lies somewhere here, in politics rather than economics.

Eighteenth-century Europeans, as Nef (1968:250) observes, were not entirely absurd in half-hoping, half-believing that their civilisation was merging into a single community with a common culture, expanding trade and industry, and the unfolding of peace. The unification of markets, the rise of international law, and the exchange of ambassadors, all helped to tie Europe together. Modelski (1978:234) suggests that 'oligopolistic' rivalry over power led the existing nation-states to strengthen new allies, and contributed to an all-round, reactive, rise of nationalism. While he is writing of the global influence of the European system, the process began at home, with the support by the leading states of lesser political units geographically so placed as to make them desirable as allies or members of coalitions. In this way the balancing of power had the latent function of strengthening the states system and bringing about an autonomous growth in it. Trade was even more a cement, for it had a habit of crossing coalitions. Trade raised a class with international connections, rising political influence, and probably a greater interest in peaceful intercourse than in the hazardous sweets of trade war. Trade spelled regional specialisation on a basis of comparative advantage. In turn this spelled interdependence. Priestley's (1965:276) optimism, though so soon dashed, was not fatuous when in 1792 he wrote that 'the present commercial treaties between England and France, and between other nations formerly hostile to each other, seem to show that mankind begin to be sensible of the folly of war, and promise a new and important era in the state of the world in general, at least in Europe'. Once the French Revolutionary and Napoleonic wars were over, the anticipated long peace, growing commerce, greater freedom of trade, and the long deflation of the nineteenth century did come about. The self-regulating or homeostatic property of the system was reasserting itself. By the 1840s J. S. Mill (1965 vol. III:706–7, 799–804) had some reason to be both laudatory and optimistic, later strains and the awful collapse of the Great War notwithstanding. The system was fragile, but set on what seemed to him a promising course. He thought that civilised countries would be able to go on extending their command over nature and that other countries would 'successively enter upon the same career', so automatic had the growth process come to seem. He thought that the security of life and property would continue to improve, since the most backward populace in Europe was better protected from crime each succeeding generation, and from predatory acts by the privileged, as well as from 'arbitrary exercise of the power of government'. Mill saw governments everywhere modernising and yet taxing less oppressively. He saw insurance softening the impact of natural disaster. He saw war confined to outlying, savage possessions. If there were not truth in parts of his paean of self-congratulation, Europeans would have been living in the Middle Ages instead of in the age of Victoria.

Chapter 7

Nation-states

Europe, too, was in its own time born, and . . . the circumstances of its
birth were no less extraordinary and perhaps a good deal more paradig-
matic than those of the newer nations

Benjamin Barber

THE NATION-STATE is nowadays the unit of affairs. It is a purely
European form which has been exported to parts of the world
that had hitherto known only tribalism. We may look on national
income accounting as if it deals in categories both natural and
proper, but nation-states are not God-given. They are the creations of post-feudal Europe. By the time the political arithmeti-
cians of the late seventeenth century began to study economic
activity, nation-states had become the dominant vehicles of policy and the most convenient receptacles for quantitative data.
Whereas once states had been federations or amalgams of provinces each of which adapted instructions from the centre to fit an
individual view of its needs, by that time most of Europe had
been organised into centralised states. These states were engaged
in modernising themselves, extending the market system albeit
by political means and for political ends.

The earliest European states had been the products of dynastic
rule by the leaders of warrior bands. These men gathered and
stabilised groups of followers with similar ethnic origins, customs, and languages or dialects. As political expansion drew in
less similar peoples, common organisation was relied on to make
them more alike (Strayer 1966; 1970). But in an agricultural
economy each district tended to be self-sufficient, with weak
economic ties to the centre, and local representatives of the ruler
were constantly tempted to break away. Milton's aphorism that
the history of the Middle Ages was a dreary saga of battles
between kites and crows is explicable in that opportunities were

virtually limited to fighting others for the right to commandeer from the peasantry. The rationale of centralised rule was that in return for a lion's share of the small productive surplus, the ruler supplied justice. By suppressing random violence and obliging the nobles who were his potential competitors to settle their disputes in his courts the king could best secure loyalty and offset centrifugal tendencies. If the courts could prevent undue exploitation of the king's subjects they would be helping to prevent the nobility from amassing the sinews of revolt. Kings therefore tried to monopolise the law and provide enduring legal institutions with a corps of reliable, dependent judges. The best that may be said for this incipient social contract was that the terms were better than the ordinary man received in most of the world. That was not a great deal, but it may have been sufficient to give European life a distinctive cast.

The evolution of the centralised European state appears to have been subject to an almost rhythmic alternation. Tracing a course like a stairway, the state may have been able to extend and consolidate its position when there was population growth and economic expansion but make little headway during phases of contraction. Successful periods seem to have been between the eleventh and thirteenth centuries; again during the late fifteenth and the sixteenth centuries; and once more after the middle of the eighteenth century. Setbacks, rebellions and threats of dissolution were more evident following the Black Death and during the 'General Crisis' of the seventeenth century. By the final phase of consolidation many states were busying themselves with the task of self-modernisation, but before we examine what they were able to achieve in that respect we shall take a closer look at the processes and periodicity of state-building.

When there was economic and population growth there were more buyers and sellers and therefore increasing numbers of transactions. There were more individuals competing for tenancies. This offered the landowning class greater prospects of gain through more market tolls and dues and higher rents. During the High Middle Ages one way in which these opportunities were exploited was by planting new market towns, called Bastides, in the countryside of England, Wales, Gascony, and elsewhere (Beresford 1967). Kings, bishops, and lay lords all carved out town sites on the wastes between existing settlements and let them out in rectangular burgage plots. The grid plans are often still clear on the ground. Some of these new towns failed, but many succeeded and enabled their projectors to tap a share of the contemporary increase in market activity. This and their profitable ownership of land, which was the scarce factor of production, sweetened the temper of the nobility. Kings shared in the prosperity and they could get on with building their states without excessive resistance from the lesser lords.

During phases of contraction there were fewer pickings. There was more discord between and within states. Nobles tended to resist jurisdiction, and both they and the kings made more attempts to lay their hands on what others possessed. Altogether there seem to have been more 'pie-slicing' conflicts over shares of a static or declining total income. Much of the detail of history concerns the frictions as men accustomed to one set of behaviour, and subject to varying degrees of constraint in the shape of tenures and local customs, were obliged to adjust to the big swings in economic activity. We shall leave these short-run incidents aside, but with a finer focus it would be proper to treat particular conflicts (peasant revolts for example) as true signals of what was happening to the economy. Here we are only concerned with broad fluctuations in the ease and acceptance of the building of centralised states. The levels of analysis are merely different and one has no more ultimate legitimacy than the other.

Whereas during the thirteenth century centralism had been in the ascendant, aided by the emergence of a theory of the state, in the less expansive days of the following century it was checked. The consent of powerful lords to adjudication by the royal courts became harder to obtain. Population collapse after the Black Death, a slump in rents and shrinking markets induced the nobility to compete more fiercely for resources. There came the resurgence of baronial power called 'bastard feudalism'. Kings too tried to increase revenues, or deflect internal aggression, by warring with one another for territory. The trend towards larger political units was interrupted. Internally there were however still signs, though fresh ones, of greater centralisation. This does impair the neatness of the fit between growth in population and growth in state-building. What happened was that with the shrinkage of the workforce central authorities began to intervene in the labour market, trying to put a ceiling on wage rates and curb a new mobility of labour. This happened in France and England in the late fourteenth century and in the fifteenth century, for similar reasons, in the Prussian state of the Order of Teutonic Knights (Rosenberg 1958:9). Conceivably what was beginning to happen was that, while the state most easily advanced its frontiers and the degree of central control during economic expansions, some functions of the bureaucracy were actually easier to extend in attempts to cope with the disequilibria of contractions. Perhaps bureaucracy was starting to grow, coral-like, all the time. After all, if there is a natural law of social affairs it is Parkinson's Law.

The existing literature permits no final judgement about the periodicity of state-building and indeed a most active growth phase for the nation-state followed in the fifteenth century. This has been attributed to a shift in military technology which favoured the central authority (Bean 1973), the key episode beginning with the rapid progress of the cannon in the mid-fifteenth century. Renewed demographic and market growth in the late fifteenth century were also favourable, but the main thesis is that changes in military technique raised the optimal size range for states and by about 1500 brought into being the nation-states, which were larger units than existed before. The earliest European reference to the cannon is said to be the report of this armament on board a Genoese ship that accompanied the French fleet on a raid into Southampton Water in 1338, or possibly a reference of 1326. By the time of Crécy (1346) the English bowmen had among them a number of small bombards 'which, with fire, threw little iron balls to frighten the horses' (Green 1888:226; cf. Gimpel 1977:228). A century later the cannon could commit more than the sin of frightening the horses. Its improvement removed the security of fortifications. The lords could no longer defy and dominate the country from their lairs and strongholds. The art of fortification managed to catch up with the severity of bombardment by the 1520s but it necessitated building larger and more expensive castles. This required larger estates to foot the bill, so that the balance of advantage remained with the bigger political units and most of all with the king. As a result the plethora of independent and semi-independent principalities and duchies shrank and the power of central governments grew between 1450 and 1550. Lords tended to give up constructing castles and replaced them with undefended, wide-windowed country houses and châteaux and this meant that capital had been released from the unproductive purposes of fortification.

The concept behind this explanation is the theory of the firm, each state being treated as the equivalent of a firm. Because of indivisibilities and gains to specialisation, large states can attain economies of scale. They provide a larger free-trade area and their *per capita* defence costs are lower since increases in area are not matched by proportionate increases in length of perimeter. However, other costs turn upwards beyond a given size, for instance the costs of administration where conquered minorities have to be assimilated. The long-run average cost-curve of the state was therefore U-shaped. Costs fell over part of the range, where economies of scale accrued, only to rise again as dis-economies made themselves felt. Like firms, states outside the optimal size range tended to be eliminated by competition, the smaller ones being absorbed, the larger ones breaking up. What is envisaged as happening once the cannon and some other military changes came along is that the range shifted outwards and gave birth to the nation-states.

A more benign expansion probably took place during the latter half of the sixteenth century. Population grew quite rapidly and as a consequence of the more frequent encounters in a larger market, transactions costs presumably fell. With the direst strug-gle for revenue abated, it should have become easier to secure consent to the decisions of the royal courts. Bean (1973) indeed agrees that in addition to change in military hardware such fac-tors as transport innovations and the growth of cities were acting to raise the optimal size of state. Subsequently there was another contraction of population and economic activity in the so-called General Crisis of the seventeenth and early eighteenth centuries. This may have at first hit the larger states hardest (Braudel quoted by Wallerstein 1974:32 n. 61). But eventually the centralised state emerged stronger than ever, possibly because of another military development, the great increase in the size of armies by the early eighteenth century. As Louis XIV declared, and confirmed for himself, 'after all it is the last louis d'or which must win' (Green 1888:673).

An interlude in the long, rumbling contest between absolute monarchs and the nobility followed. This was the second stage of a drawn-out transition from the shadows when the kingdom was a proprietorship, through government as a public trust (still under the king and in his name but no longer personal rule), out into the rather dappled sunlight of government by oligarchical bureaucracy. During the eighteenth century this second transition took place in the main continental countries (Rosenberg 1958) and it was, no doubt, a more responsive arrangement than anything that had preceded it. The interest of kings in the tax base induced them to continue to shield the peasantry from depredations by the landowning class. Marc Bloch noted that the French intendants were expected 'to protect rural communities, ripe material for taxation, from intemperate exploitation by their landlords' (quoted by Brenner 1976:71). This was a struggle between taxes and rents.

The uneasy poise of the Absolutist state about this issue was upset by the rapid upturn in population and cereal prices in the middle of the eighteenth century. Landowners were tempted to take a larger share of the land and its revenues. For instance, the east German Junkers began to push their peasants off the land after the Seven Years War. They extended their own holdings and exported the larger harvests to the British market rather than selling to the royal magazines. By 1800 they were sending 150,000 tons of grain per annum to Great Britain. Frederick the Great strove to slow down this entrepreneurial disturbance to the structure of the society as it had been systematised by his father in the 1730s (Tipton 1974:957). Most absolute monarchs tried to protect the peasantry by offering tenurial freedoms which undercut the power of the landlords, and their frequent, though variable, success in so doing was a factor in retarding the rate of productivity growth in agriculture (Jones: forthcoming). The absolutist–monarchist régimes in this respect delayed the all-round growth towards which their policies of modernisation and industrialisation were designed to lead. The monarchist and statist nature of their agrarian policies denied them comprehensive 'growth packages' because they were trying to bring about economic growth while constricting the tenurial framework. We shall see that they made considerable progress in modernisation, but it would be unreasonable to expect fully consistent policies from régimes of their sort.

One absolutist motive was to safeguard the peasantry as the prime source of military recruitment. Bacon had earlier written about England that 'if a state run most to noblemen and gentlemen, and the husbandmen and ploughmen be but as their workfolks and labourers . . . you may have a good cavalry but never good stable bands of foot' (Ashley 1913:177–8). Wrong as this was shown to be by the Englishmen who fought in foam and flames at Trafalgar and on Albuera plains to keep themselves in chains, it was accepted throughout Europe. The policy of Peasant Protection, Bauernschutz, was based on the belief. Nation-states were still in the process of evolving and consolidating and Ardant (1975) has suggested that a factor in this was the healthier tax revenues of the eighteenth-century 'agricultural revolution', deriving from a peasantry whose income was protected by royal curbs on exploitation by the landowners.

Much of the technical improvement made in agriculture – and in the mainland Europe of the eighteenth century this was rather limited – was the result of efforts by landowners. They were the ones who had best access to the international pool of knowledge. The active ones among them founded agricultural societies in their own countries, and diffused English farming methods, inspired by rising cereal prices and potential gains in rental income. Continental nobles had lived in a universe of high risk where a high liquidity preference, and its other face, low productive investment, were understandable. They had lounged and peacocked around the absolutist courts, partly because their royal overlords found it expedient to keep an eye on them, prevent them brooding on their estates, and embroil them in heavy expenses, and partly because sinecures and court offices were the best sources of income (Blum 1978). In slow-growing economies that was where the highest marginal return to their effort was to be had. Rising population and higher cereal prices changed this, altering relative returns in favour of active land management. Better farming methods began to be spread. Power relationships within the absolutist states began to creak and shift.

The problem of discussing development in late preindustrial times is less to explain it within the freer economies of the Netherlands or Britain than to account for the way it was generalised through more Procrustean states. What the absolutist states had done was to start formulating forward-looking policies within one or other philosophical strain of mercantilism. Private citizens took to publishing exhortations to purposeful development, 'growth programmes', virtual national plans. An example was Phillip von Hornick's *Austria Over all, If She Only Will* (1684). Colbert's France was the model of mercantilist centralism and even supposedly localist, *laissez-faire* Britain adopted enough modernising, centralist policies for them to be labelled 'Parliamentary Colbertism'. Britain's trade protection under the Navigation Acts illustrates these policies. Van Klaveren (1968) claims that mercantilism (as distinct from fiscalism) was actually stronger in Britain than anywhere on the continent except France under Colbert. This was because the London merchants who had an interest in seeing policies carried out had political power through Parliament. They were able to press for the formation of courts to try backsliding officials, whereas corruption flourished unchecked on the continent. British policy became decidedly protectionist in the reign of William III, with respect to colonial goods, in effect making linen and silk manufacture protected infant industries (Davis 1965).

Mercantilist policy was an evolving and varied bag of tricks. Not surprisingly, its instruments were at times in conflict with one another. The literature about mercantilism typically concerns itself with inferring intent, but the practice is what is of real interest. The view of several recent authors whose approaches are otherwise diverse is that at the least the spin-off from state policies did have a positive, modernising effect (Anderson 1975; Landes 1969; Rostow 1975; Tilly 1975; the most sceptical observations are by van Klaveren 1969; but cf. also Bronfenbrenner 1964:363; and Tilly 1975:73). Some policies were explicitly designed to lay down an industrial base. 'Reactive nationalism' may be glimpsed among the causes, as when Maria Theresa decided in the 1750s that Bohemia must be made independent of its former market in Silesia, taken by Prussia in 1742. At that period bureaucracies capable of carrying out detailed economic policy were only in the process of formation. Enforcing the regulations was difficult for lack of officials and because corruption was commonplace. Import controls, which were a major policy instrument, were for instance often nullified by smuggling. The strength of the absolutist states lay in their military force. Prussia, indeed, was known as the army with a state rather than a state with an army. Troops were widely used to make good deficiencies of police, customs officers, firemen, and emergency workers. Externally military power was not simply an instrument, it was the goal. At a time when growth was slow, war for territory was logical. Ethical objections aside, what helps to hide this from our post-industrial consciousness and concentrates our attention on the destructive irrationality of war are faster growth rates, higher incomes, greater security, and the more interconnected nature of modern economic systems.

Rulers, whose schemes for glory drove them to prepare for war, began to do so by actively improving the economic base. In addition there were clients for modernisation among the 'middle' and merchant classes. What they prayed for was more public order and fewer obstructions to business, ranging from the abolition of legal and customary restrictions on factor mobility to the removal of nuisances like narrow town gates and constricting walls. They desired the enforcement at law of freely negotiated contracts, the improvement of communications, and all measures to unify the market. The wishes of the ruler and of rising groups in society were thus in many ways confluent. Internal barriers to trade began to be removed, both institutional and physical ones. Native manufactures found protection behind tariffs which encouraged import substitution. Textile works, iron foundries and arsenals were established as government projects. Many of them collapsed through corruption and mismanagement but they served as training schools and had a 'demonstration effect' on the private sector. Such policies were 'pedagogical statism' in Rodinson's (1978:136 and n.54) term. We might today feel a frisson at policies whose tangible legacy was an ant-heap of bureaucrats. Historically they were needed because there was an acute lack of the literate administrators required to carry out minimal social functions.

Mercantilist-absolutist régimes were responsible for introducing new crops, notably the potato. They encouraged the settlement of new land. Measures were taken to codify the law, establish standard weights and measures, and unify the coinage. In 1792 Joseph Priestley (1965:274) could still write that 'the uniformity of weights and measures, as well as of coins, would greatly facilitate general commerce. It seems impossible to effect this throughout Europe; but one would think there could be no very great difficulty to effect it in any particular kingdom.' Tidiness is hard to achieve. Attempts at standardisation in Britain go back to Edgar's unified weights and measures and Athelstan's single coinage (Blair 1959:295–6), and although the Union of England and Scotland took place as long ago as 1707, Scottish banknotes which are not legal tender are still being printed. But despite the inconvenience that a hangover like this can cause, progress was made even in the late preindustrial period.

In this progress lay the nation-state's chance of exiting from medievalism. Cultural homogeneity seemed desirable because it confirmed loyalty to the crown, simplified administration, taxation and trade, and despite some loss of local colour, made everybody better off. Policies successful in one province might more easily be extended to all corners if the state were unified. National centralisers were helped by a nucleus of literate bureaucrats from the church; by the medieval notion that the king's courts were supreme; by the breaking of the trans-ethnic grip of Latin; and by national scripts that tended to lock men more firmly into the culture of wherever they lived (cf. Tilly 1975:597). Their struggle was an uphill one, but these elements of medieval experience could be turned to account in forging more modern states. Localisms and anomalies hanging over from the past had to be smoothed into cultural curiosities. The whole process was slow because Europe was such an ethnic and linguistic motley, set amidst such topographical diversity. Although the upper classes in England had more or less stopped speaking French at the end of the thirteenth century, and English was introduced in schools in 1349 and parliament opened in English in 1362, at the Dissolution, five centuries after the Conquest, the nuns of Lacock Abbey in Wiltshire were still speaking Norman French (Morris 1966:43; Russell 1979:31). Archaisms of this sort (parallels may still be found) were symptomatic of the obstacles. An homogenous culture was not a sufficient cause of modernisation and might even make political autocracy too easy (China for example has had homogenous culture since 200 B.C.), but the extremes of European variety had to be ironed out.

Important elements in the process were internal pacification and colonisation. The suppression of local violence and separatism by central government forces was one more non-market means of extending the market. In addition there were drives in the late sixteenth and late eighteenth centuries to re-open the medieval colonisation of hinterlands. Some of Europe had not then been surveyed; Highland Scots in particular were unaccommodating towards surveyors for ironworks. A motive, therefore, was to secure internal supplies of raw materials. Scientific ventures of the day, such as Linnaeus's Lapland journey, were often just as much resource appraisals as science. Sometimes the motive was to occupy additional land for crops in place of low-intensity grazing. ' '' In this manner'', wrote an observer of the reclamation of the so-called waste in England, ''was more useful territory added to the empire, at the expense of individuals, than has been gained by every war since the Revolution'' ' (quoted by Ashton 1948:7). Europe north of the Alps still possessed a reservoir of land in the shape of the open-field fallows, but better crop rotations brought these into regular use. A further motive, distinct from the aims of earlier periods, was to keep faith with a sense of cultural and political nationalism, and unify and develop the state and the market. The regionalism of old hierarchies, often a disguise for the operation of a spoils system on behalf of local nobles, was struggled against (Rosenberg 1958:55). Yet another motive was to put down the bases of bandits and guerillas, especially where they might be open to use by foreign invaders. Motives and processes were therefore mixed, according to the circumstances, but they all drove towards the settled, occupied and unified nation-state.

Internal frontiers pushed fairly smoothly across low-lying swamps and sandy heaths. Dutch engineers drained marshes from Italy to Britain to Poland. Frederick the Great of Prussia exulted on completing a big drainage project in 1753 that he had 'conquered a province in peacetime'. He 'pursued the policy of internal colonisation on a scale never before attempted', involving planting about 1,200 new agricultural villages and hamlets and settling over 300,000 inhabitants (Henderson 1963:127, 163). The frontier moved with more effort into the forests and up the sides of mountain ranges and with greatest difficulty of all into lands held by self-conscious minorities. Any topographically isolated region tended to cultivate individuality and resist penetration by the larger society. Compounded by the ethnic and linguistic survivals this gave rise to a self-renewing separateness. Consider how strong it remains in the Morvan, a holiday region little over one hundred miles from Paris. The Morvan was to a degree integrated into the national market, its chief speciality being 'l'élevage' or wet-nursing by women who went to Paris or took in infants to suckle. Also, timber was floated out to Paris, cattle were sent to the lowlands for fattening, and the men worked down in the Bazois and Auxois plains. But most of this integration came only in the nineteenth century and even today, as in many Celtic strongholds, a regional personality survives.

A major reason for the survival of underdeveloped upland regions is that they were agriculturally poor. Had their soils been richer they might have been more densely settled in the first place. As it was, while technological change and rising demands could re-evaluate their worth, they were not especially attractive, and economic reasons why the larger society penetrated them are overplayed. The motives for internal colonisation by force were more likely to be strategic. The history of the Scottish Highlands illustrates this. At first sight, the takeover of the Highlands after the Forty-five Rebellion seems neatly timed for the economic interests of an industrialising England and Scottish Lowland. Highlanders tramped south to work in the mills of Lancashire; the moors were left to receive Border sheep moved north to grow mutton and wool for the industrial population. Yet the suppression of the Forty-five was not calculated to these ends. It was a political act by a frustrated Protestant crown, stabbed in the back once too often by the Jacobite sympathies of the clans. Highland resources would not have been sufficient on their own to draw the attention they received and in the early seventeenth century thousands of lowland Scots had actually found emigration to farmland in Poland, Prussia and East Pomerania a better proposition. In short, it was the accident of political intervention and associated government investment that opened the Highlands. After the 1715 rising and the alarm in 1719, and between 1725 and 1737 when General Wade built 250 miles of new road and 40 bridges, the region began to be accessible. Even then the 800 miles of road and 1,000 bridges constructed after the Forty-five were, according to Thomas Telford's report of 1803, so badly aligned and steeply graded as to be of negligible civilian use. The main canal scheme was activated only when military considerations during the Napoleonic wars prompted it, and was afterwards allowed to lapse again (Hamilton 1963:230–2, 242–5). Sheep 'on the hoof' could however come north, and be driven south again to market, and this made it worth annexing Highlands pasturage – and the arable land of the crofters. There was no rush to exploit the general run of resources in the Highlands and what was done was done only as an adjunct to seeming political and military necessity. Without a similar spur, many mountainous regions throughout Europe continued to languish untouched by the internal frontier. They fell below the line of what it was profitable for even such an active continent to embrace. Things might have been different had Europe not acquired its overseas 'ghost acreage'.

The best test of the economic impact of central government policies is where the penalties of failure loomed largest. This was in the realm of disaster management (Cipolla 1976b; Dorwart 1971; Jones 1977b, 1978; McCloy 1946; Meuvret 1965; Rosen 1953; Sølvi 1976; Usher 1973). Perhaps the systematic measures to cope with emergencies that were elaborated by the nation-states are best traced from the efforts of the Italian city-states in the late Middle Ages. Towns elsewhere in Europe began to imitate the procedures, and sometimes to come up with their own, during early modern times. The nation-states took them over and generalised them. As a result the scope of the functions of the state grew and so did the bureaucracy, entwined together in a symbiotic relationship and whipped on by the growth of the expectation that such services would be provided. There was a close association between disaster management and modernisation in general. An example comes from Portugal, where Pombal rose to virtual dictatorship on the powers he was given to cope with the immediate aftermath of the Lisbon earthquake of 1755

(Boxer 1955). 'Bury the dead and relieve the living', Pombal had advised the king, and this was what the king authorised him to do. Success entrenched his position and his subsequent policies went some way towards modernising Portugal – removing the colour bar in her colonies, legislating against anti-semitism, reforming the curriculum of the University of Coimbra and founding a commercial college at Lisbon. The origin of this decisive (and otherwise unpleasant) dictatorship was definitely in the literal and metaphorical shock that the Lisbon earthquake had administered.

A wider type of emergency was epidemic plague. In a burst of creative panic fourteenth-century Italian cities had introduced the quarantine to keep this out, for the shipboard communication of bubonic plague from its endemic foci in the Near East was apparent to quite casual observation in the Mediterranean. An array of regulations to cordon off areas where the plague did get a foothold and to isolate infected households was also drawn up. These practices travelled north and west from the late fifteenth century. Responsibility for control was gradually elevated until it reached the national level. National codes had become quite uniform by the eighteenth century and transgressors were liable to severe punishment. Already in the seventeenth century Brandenburg–Prussia and France had employed emergency quarantining and *cordons sanitaires*, despite their long land frontiers which made cordoning very expensive. The Habsburgs built a cordon 1,000 miles long stretching from the Adriatic to Transylvania along the line of the sixteenth-century Militärgrenze with the aim of shutting out the plague which persisted in the Ottoman empire. After 1770 the Military Border took on the form of a chain of lookouts within musket-shot of one another, with roving patrols under orders to open fire on unauthorised traffic sneaking between them. Passage was only permitted at quarantine stations where goods were disinfected, letters pierced with needles and fumigated, and coins immersed in baths of vinegar. In eastern Europe, Poland was less efficiently organised but the Russian government established a 'southern shield' in the eighteenth century. This consisted of a permanent screening apparatus for people and goods crossing the southern frontier or entering southern seaports. With only twenty-two quarantine offices and checkpoints along a thousand-mile stretch it is not clear that this was an hermetic sealing (Kahan 1979:263–4).

These few examples indicate the wide scope of the administrative effort. How effective was it? We may cite one case of transgression, the kind of case that was not normally put on record (Poynter 1963:70, 75). A Plymouth surgeon, James Yonge, on board the Quaker-captained *Robert Bonadventure* out of Newfoundland via Spain for Genoa in 1664, by his later admission wrote out a false ship's Pratique or health clearance: 'I set my wits and drew up one, as from a Governor of Newfoundland, and signed myself as Secretary. . . . This passed for current.' When the ship reached Messina from Genoa in 1665, 'an old fellow perusing the bill of health we had from Genoa, puts on a great pair of spectacles as big as saucers and, making each man expose his groins and armpits, he looks into them and with a stick thrusts in them, where, finding nothing, we are allowed prattick'. This examination inspired little confidence since one of the men had left Genoa with a bubo, though Yonge claimed to have cured it so that only the 'want of hair' showed.

Was deceit like this common? It would be naive to think that forgery, corruption and evasion did not occur. Yet it is noteworthy that Yonge's trick was perpetrated during one of the last waves of plague in Europe. The failure of the Genoese to detect the fraud is at variance with the record of the public health boards in Italy, which Cipolla (1976b:56) concludes were 'highly reputable and efficient agencies', a judgement borne out by his detailed evidence with its heartwarming testimony that officials did not desert their posts during epidemics. At Marseilles a little later an arriving vessel had to drop anchor at an offshore island and undergo a health scrutiny. The captain was to row across to the office of the health officials at the harbour entrance and from a respectful and sanitary distance announce particulars of his voyage. He was to present his ship's papers and her health clearance, which were picked up in long pincers and dunked in vinegar before being read. The ship and cargo were then quarantined according to the information presented. Now, Marseilles did experience a terrible epidemic of plague in 1720 and this may seem to discredit the quarantine. But it was the last really big outbreak, almost the last of any significance in western Europe.

The cause was discovered to have been the sale of some contraband clothing by sailors. After that, regulations were likely to have been taken more seriously and enforced better. Marseilles administrators and helpers behaved most professionally in the epidemic, after an initial panic, despite horrifying occupational mortality. Their strivings, and the help and direction provided by the French government, make this an episode which demonstrates European determination to cope with disasters.

A sufficient proportion of carriers of the plague were stopped from entering Europe. The degree of organisation, selflessness and voluntary compliance with regulations was worthy of note, comparing very favourably with reports of resistance and evasion going on much later in Asia (Jones 1977b). When workers were so very close to the subsistence line and trade was so vulnerable to stoppages the remedies were severe, but the long-run gains were enormous. There is *prima facie* evidence that the Military Border cordon was effective. As a physician remarked in 1839, 'the simple fact [is] that the plague has never entered Hungary since the border organisation has been completed . . . although it has been as frequent and violent as ever in the neighbouring countries' (Rothenberg 1973:22). Governments were up against a less tractable problem of management once the plague did gain a foothold. Kahan (1968:365–6) cautiously suggests that famines in Russia sometimes caused population movements that ruptured the internal cordons and spread nationwide plagues that might otherwise have been kept to local outbreaks. His evidence suggests a high association of epidemics with the types of calamity that led to famine. But there was not an epidemic every time there was a famine and it may be possible to conclude that quarantining and cordoning had some success in controlling the plague even during some of the stressful famine periods. The Russian government used its army medical corps to isolate plague outbreaks, though relying more and more on a civilian medical service. Altogether, the quarantining and cordoning of settlements, which often amounted to besieging people in their own villages, and which curtailed the movement of persons and rat- or flea-bearing freight, is the best candidate for the honour of eliminating the plague from Europe. This achievement came at the brink of the industrial period, when dense and vulnerable urban populations were about to begin a mushroom growth.

The nation-states also acted purposefully against epizootics. Cattle plagues were a serious economic threat because oxen were the main source of draught power and the harvest was at stake, quite apart from losses of livestock products. Faced with the first of a series of waves of cattle plague in 1709–16, England drew up a policy of slaughter with a government bounty as inducement to comply and as compensation for having done so. By 1714 France had a representative in London reporting on the handling of the outbreak. At first peasant resistance prevented the French from succeeding with a policy of compensated slaughter of their own. The intendants were desperate to replenish devastated regions with enough plough beasts to cultivate the next year's harvest. During the outbreak of the 1740s, France stationed troops along her frontiers to form a bovine *cordon sanitaire*, and used the troops to police the detailed regulations concerning outbreaks. The epizootic of the 1770s was handled with practised sensitivity and thoroughness in the face of a peasantry who remained exasperatingly uncooperative despite compensation at the level of one-third of the value of slaughtered animals and tax reductions for their owners.

Brandenburg–Prussia had established a frontier quarantine of eight days for cattle during the outbreak of 1711. Scientific study of the disease was begun, as it was in other countries – in Italy at the behest of the Pope. Veterinary remedies of the time were admitted failures, but a rigorous policy of compensated slaughter was rightly thought to have some chance of success. The rôle of the nation-states in this respect is highlighted by the inability of the United Provinces of the Netherlands, where central authority was weak, to agree on such a policy until 1799. Between forty per cent and seventy per cent of Dutch cattle died in each of the two worst outbreaks (van der Wee and van Cauwenberghe 1978:174–5), compared with an annual loss in England of only two or three per cent.

Against another form of disaster, settlement fire, Brandenburg–Prussia was the pioneer of state action. Procedures included the inspection of fireplaces and industrial fires and the prescription of tiles for all new roofs. Passive resistance to the roofing edicts unfortunately meant that serious fires continued to break out, especially in rural areas where whole villages were sometimes burned down and not rebuilt for years. As much as anything this was probably a poverty trap, where individuals were unable or unwilling to sacrifice present income despite the prospect of long-term security. At least it was possible to insist on a high ratio of fire pumps to population in the towns. Frederick I set up a state fire insurance monopoly in 1705, but when in 1708 the town of Krossen on the Oder was burned almost to the ground the treasury was found to be empty (because of peculation) and the scheme had to be abandoned. In 1718 property owners in Berlin demanded a mutual fire indemnity scheme and a characteristically compulsory society was formed on their behalf, followed by other successful societies in Stettin, Brandenburg province and the province of East Prussia.

French government experience of coping with fires began in the eighteenth century with a débâcle at Rennes, where soldiers drafted by the intendant to fight a blaze turned to wholesale looting. Despite government aid Rennes was not fully rebuilt more than thirty years later. Subsequent deployment of the army for routine fire-fighting was better managed and the government, through the intendants, channelled immediate relief to fire victims in the shape of food, clothing and tools. Relief in general and the provision of fire-fighting equipment in particular appears to have been administered half on the centralised or compulsory model, à la Brandenburg, and half on the local or voluntary English plan. In England town corporations could on their own initiative seek local acts of parliament banning reroofing in thatch after fires. It is worth adding that the French government also occasionally rebuilt the houses of flood victims (McCloy 1938:528–9).

Thus the nation-states set about codifying and improving earlier local measures to minimise or alleviate disasters. The incentive to do this came from the threat posed to tax revenues and military manpower, and was perhaps the stronger because before 1750 population growth was sluggish and dragged against the ambitions of the state. Inadequacies, peculations and failures in disaster management are easy to catalogue, but they would not give a fair picture of the historical trend. The scope and energy of the response was in reality unprecedented. It was a big step forward from haphazard, local, voluntary or simply non-existent measures. Administrative actions may be seen to have played an independent rôle in the growth of economic efficiency, by reducing losses of food supplies, manpower and capital equipment. Similarities in policy among the countries of Europe are more noticeable than national variations in timing. Governments were responsive to the 'merit good' approach, to tapping the creativity of those middle-ranking men who favoured order and decency (and uninterrupted trade) and possessed a vision of what was best for their fellow men. There was more order and less decency progressing from west to east across the continent, more of the state's untempered martial ambitions. But there was a positive style of government throughout Europe. This was not democracy. It was perhaps only the child of a marriage between dynastic ambition and bourgeois evolutionism; but where the misery caused by inadequate social precautions had been great, mountains could be moved. As Strayer (1970:106) observes, the very looseness of European administration allowed the old bureaucrats to go about routine tasks in routine ways, while policymakers could concentrate on larger schemes: 'more significant than the actual performance of the work was the involvement of larger numbers of men in the political process . . . the old ruling class could not furnish enough men to do all the work'.

The *anciens régimes* have usually been regarded as administratively far too inept to protect the lives and welfare of their subjects, even had they desired so to do. Indeed, they were very much less impressive over what we should describe as social provision than over what we are here calling social precautions. In reality their response to disasters was energetic. Every crisis strained them and found their administrative services barely adequate, but in Strayer's (1970:105) words, 'barely adequate, however, is quite different from failure'. There was nothing with the endurance or cohesion of the European state, he adds, to be found in India, the East Indies, Africa, or the Americas. And even if the Ottoman, Chinese and Japanese states could rival the states of Europe until the eighteenth century, they were beginning to weaken, just at the time when the governments of the West were extending their managerial apparatus.

We have to remember that the resources and scientific knowledge of the time simply could not have solved all the problems of plague and famine. Part of the improvement we observe was certainly due to economic growth reducing the felt impact of disasters. Nevertheless the administrative effort brought real gains. To cite an example, France under Louis XV was to some extent successful in redistributing grain from surplus to deficit regions. No disadvantaged area or town could have the same command over supply that a whole state could have. Systems of internal duties and tolls had restricted the zone from which grain at a price that could be paid might be drawn to any given point. National governments began to dismantle these barriers. Whereas appeals for supplies of grain by individual cities are known to have fallen on deaf ears, the state could exercise some control over its constituent regions and had more bargaining power when facing foreign suppliers. Control over the inter-regional grain trade is said to have begun in the most productive areas of western Europe, such as the Seine Basin (Usher 1973:362), and was extended later to the less fertile deficit areas, until the state had assumed overall direction. A reason for this pattern may have been to ensure food supplies for the capital city, which would usually be situated in the middle of a fertile 'core-area'. European governments were becoming ever more interventionist and mostly continued so until industrialisation was under way and Adam Smith had provided a rationalisation for not intervening. Kahan (1968:363) points out that Russian governments ordered monasteries to despatch and sell their stocks of grain during times of famine from the fifteenth century, as well as engaging in the practices of halting exports, allowing tax relief, and undertaking public works as relief measures. Even Russia, therefore, was behaving in the European manner. In the old dispute as to whether or not Russian society is 'European', part of the argument for excluding her is that culturally she moved apart from the rest of the continent between 1400 and 1700, possibly because of Tartar devastation of her towns (Holborn 1951:9ff.). Clearly borrowings from the West were taking place during that period, even before Peter the Great's Grand Embassy, while managerially we see evidence of a 'European' behaviour pattern in the eighteenth century. As Usher (1973:230, 261) concludes of that European pattern, 'the effort to devise some means to meet the recurring crisis is what transforms medieval into modern society', while 'the recurring famines in the Orient lead to no change. . . . If this attitude had prevailed in Europe none of the modern structure of western civilisation would have come into being.'

State action with respect to disasters achieved economies of scale inaccessible to smaller political units (Jones 1978). This point is now being recognised. It is the thrust of Biraben's major study, *Les Hommes et la Peste*. In a review article, Flinn (1979:142–3) also recognises that when anti-plague measures had been left to local initiative there were bound to remain fatal chinks in the armour. He repeats Biraben's point that the raising of action to national and international levels was the key to eradicating that particular scourge. A scale effect among nations of different sizes in resilience to disaster has been observed at the present day (Lewis 1972:119). What needs to be emphasised is the general point that elevating responsibility to the state and states system (there was a growing exchange of disaster intelligence) enabled Europe to reap economies of scale that its fundamentally decentralised administration might seem to have made inaccessible.

The shift upwards in the level of responsibility for economic crises was part of a wider re-sorting of functions. Productive activities that had been subject to collective controls were becoming individualised. This is a staple of the textbooks. But that Europe moved from the gilds and the common fields towards *laissez-faire* is only half of the story. The missing half is that just when production was becoming fully privatised, services were becoming more of a collective concern, or where they were already communal, now the government was being involved. This does not bear the implication that welfare in the modern sense of social provision and income support was being looked after. The novel functions of late preindustrial times lay more in the background. The nation-states were then becoming service states, supplying a number of social overhead facilities in partial return for taxes. There was a widespread upward shift in responsibility for services, besides that strictly to the level of the national government. In eighteenth-century English towns there was, for example, an improvement in the conditions of safety and trade as municipalities took over from individual householders the tasks of street cleaning, lighting and paving. These were responsibilities that the householder had discharged poorly. Once they were paid for by the rates they were managed more systematically (Jones and Falkus 1979). The rates began to purchase civic fire-engines. Parson Woodforde, at Castle Cary in Somerset, wrote in his diary in 1762: 'Holten preached for Mr. Penny concerning Private Interest giving way to Publick Good in regard to our having an Water Engine to prevent Fire spreading' (Beresford 1978:11).

The direction of change was from individual to civic, from civic to national. Lighthouses, for instance, were moved out of the hands of the private entrepreneur, who had recouped his costs from the right to make a levy on ships using some nearby port, into the hands of a state body and onto the charge of the general revenue (Stevenson 1959; Beaver 1971). Vast private fortunes had been amassed from the old dues but there had been no proper control over the quality of service. The Caistor Light in Norfolk remained unlit in bad weather for over thirty years in the early seventeenth century because the keeper lived some miles away and was reluctant to turn out. A public body like Trinity House was far more reliable. While it might be contended that the state was only moving in to fill a welfare vacuum left by the church (even in the case of lighthouses there were a few St Catherine's Chapels with benefices to light a lamp for seafarers), in practice governments assumed a far bigger rôle. Their administrative, coercive and financial resources were greater and they could provide services that had never been organised before.

Was the all-round transfer of functions the result of some single underlying change? If there was an ultimate force, it may have been located in a complex of persistent technological and organisational change associated with the growth of the market, and then with a hiccough in market growth. Technological progress and reduced costs of freight and information pressed against old institutional forms. We saw how new methods and styles of product raised the cost of enforcing gild regulations and common-field routines. The temptation to sidestep them or let them wither increased. Simultaneously, greater efficiency and growing trade and markets reduced the *per capita* burden of supplying public goods, at a time when political goals were inducing the nation-state to become more interventionist. The slight hesitation introduced into all this by the temporary slowing of population growth in the late seventeenth and early eighteenth centuries, from which period so much government involvement dates, made each citizen implicitly more valuable. The nation-states moved to conserve their subjects, for example by vigorous disaster management. Altogether, Europe switched over to what the conditions of the day made a more efficient mix of production and services. There was no one trigger, no *annus mirabilis*. The general explanation of change lies at the intersection of technological change, increasing market size, and the ambitions of a system of nation-states. To review this from another angle, the European experience is not properly captured by a simple opposition of 'mercantilism' and *laissez-faire*, nor by the phrase 'the rise of capitalism'. This is not just because these terms are vague. It is because the rise of the nation-state and its programme of services was equally vital. Weber's 'rational' western state appeared only at the end of the Middle Ages, when capitalism in the sense of commerce and profit-seeking was already well entrenched, and according to Rodinson (1978:104) this means that the nation-state cannot account for capitalism. What the rise of the nation-state does seem to account for is the establishment of the stable conditions necessary for expanding development and growth, for the diffusion of best practices in technology and commerce, and in several countries for the actual founding of manufactories where there had only been handicrafts. The self-propulsion of market forces explains much, at least in the less authoritarian parts of north-west Europe. A full explanation of the generalisation of novelty must also take the nation-state into account.

The World

Chapter 8

Beyond Europe

Any objective survey of the past 10,000 years of human history would show that during almost all of it, northern Europeans were an inferior barbarian race, living in squalor and ignorance, producing few cultural innovations

Peter Farb

COMPARISONS, or contrasts, with other civilisations are essential for an assessment of Europe's progress. Otherwise conjectures based on a winnowing of the European historical literature are uncontrolled. They may be tested for internal consistency and fit with the evidence, but since there is no generally accepted over-arching theory of *very* long-term economic change there would be no proper check on the chosen explanatory variables. Economic theory is too patently derived from nineteenth- and twentieth-century industrial circumstances to explain the long-run emergence of the developed world. It helps with the sub-processes, but with the *very* long term precisely those elements that theory takes as given, blur and shift and become variables. Where *ceteris paribus* ceases to apply, the comparative method offers the remaining hope for a test of significance.

If we cast around for continents and cultures to set alongside European experience and turn first to Africa, we find that the general level of development and the size and density of population lagged well behind in the historic period. Africa's fascination is *sui generis*. It had no major direct influence on the other continents, except maybe as a source of slaves. Certainly all was not barbarism. There were towns of some size in West Africa and stone building of moderate skill in Zimbabwe and in the chain of fortifications across southern Africa. From time to time large states did emerge, such as the Kongo empire of the fifteenth century A.D. and the empires of Ancient Ghana, Mali, and Songhay that rose and fell in the Niger bend. There was great art at Ife and in the Benin brasses. But no wheel, no plough, and no stable combination of powers that could erect a common front against Arab or European slavers.

In Africa man adapted himself to nature. The hunter felt part of the ecosystem, not outside it looking in with wonder, and definitely not above it and superior. After all, there were large carnivores who sought man as a prey. The most evocative symbol of this ecological oneness may be the honey guides (*Indicator* spp), birds commensal with man. They fly, chattering loudly, ahead of bands of hunters, leading them a quarter of a mile or more to the tree hives of wild bees and feeding on the wax after the men have broken open the hives and taken the honey.

The opinions of the small proportion of Africanists who discuss the matter in the round divide between emphasising the ease of the environment or its difficulty (Davidson *et al.* 1966; Goody 1971; Hopkins 1973; Richards 1973; Turnbull 1976). Perhaps the difference may be reconciled by a division into a wet Africa and a dry Africa, a quick rule of thumb suggested by Michael Havinden. In the wet Africa, notably West Africa, living was easy but infant mortality was horrendously high. In the dry Africa hunting and gathering were not unrewarding, but the agriculture was not productive by world standards. Soils are ancient and poor, having been leached to the poverty line. Rainfall is adequate over vast areas but there is always a dry season. Shifting cultivation over the centuries may have lowered the productivity of forest areas everywhere. Huge tracts of forest are underlain by the charcoal layers and pottery fragments of previous shifting cultivators. Fire and grazing pressure encourage thickets of unpalatable shrubs. Indeed, by the opening of the modern period there were no great virgin tropical forests left in Africa.

African productivity had been raised, it is true, by the arrival of Asian food plants (yams, bananas, rice) as early as 200 B.C. After the fifteenth century A.D. American food crops such as manioc and maize were brought in. But manioc was used to prop up the output of shifting cultivation. This was efficient enough where the population was low, no doubt, but by no means as physically productive as settled farming. At even moderate population densities the land was not given long enough to rest. Output did rise as a result of the new crops, but the availability everywhere of local food substitutes, together with high transport costs, reduced incentives to trade in foodstuffs.

The Negroid peoples, speaking Bantu languages, possessed an Iron Age agricultural technology. They had increased in numbers at the start of the Christian era and were still pushing east and south into the territories of the pygmies and bushmen when the Boers undertook the Great Trek north from the Cape in the 1830s. Population in Africa however remained low by Eurasian standards, held down by disease and the limitations on agriculture. Only forty-six million people occupied the whole immense continent in 1500, only seventy million by 1800. Thus a continent which had held some thirty per cent of the world's population as long before as 10,000 B.C. had not lived up to its promise. In A.D. 500 it was already down to ten per cent of the world's people and a thousand years after that was about the same; by 1800 the proportion had sunk to a mere eight per cent.

Where there were denser populations within Africa they were connected only by long overland routes which made freight charges a large part of the final price of goods. This restricted the market. Land was in general neither a scarce resource nor a particularly rich one. There was scant incentive or pressure for development or invention. Not even the wheel was forthcoming – and to overcome its problem of a small and very widely dispersed market, Africa probably needed not only the wheel but the motor-driven vehicle as well. Any pressure that might have been generated by labour scarcity was apparently offset by the use of slaves instead of the improvement of methods. Such trading profits and agricultural surplus as the tribal chiefs could cream off tended to be invested in slave-owning. Slaves had the advantage that they could be made to transport themselves. Otherwise wealth was spent on luxury items of small bulk and high value, and while this was adapted to the distance and problems of transportation, it did not do what a larger trade might have done to change society. Profitable investment alternatives were lacking. Without a sizeable agricultural surplus there was neither much incentive to develop private property rights in land, nor much room for the emergence of multi-layered social stratification, the accumulation of capital, or specialisation of economic function. At the root of all this seems to have been the infertility of soil; pervasive insecurity as a result of conflict and slave-raiding, even before the advent of the Portuguese (though they may have broken into an agriculture that was stabilising in the Congo Basin as the spread of population was slowing); and a hot environment of such ferocious human and animal diseases that population and market size, and draught power, were held down. This may sound like an argument from environmental imperative. The defects of the environment did indeed strike so close to the heart of economic life that it is not clear what indigenous developments were possible. All told, there was no development of the African economy to set along-side that of Europe in the Middle Ages and after.

Turning to the Americas, we find that they too suffered from low population, as well as isolation from the Eurasian pool of ideas. Agriculture, and the Aztec and Inca states, had emerged and built up populations of some millions only by the time of Columbus. Although the wheel had been invented its use was confined to toys or making pottery. Toy models of wheeled dogs have been found, but not dog carts, which would perhaps have been more viable substitutes for horse transport than is realised (witness their not inconsiderable use in Europe in the nineteenth century). As a result the New World was left far behind in the processes of lifting, carrying, milling and manufacturing for which wheel-based pulleys, cogs and derivative devices are so useful. The poverty of the animal resources available to the New World explains, according to Harris (1978:39), the differential pace of development whereby 'Columbus "discovered" America and Powhatan did not "discover" Europe', and 'Cortes conquered Moctezuma rather than the other way around.' Whatever assessment may be made of this bold interpretation, and the load-pulling potential of the dog throws some doubt on it, the Americas were in practice unable to achieve a European level of development before the arrival of Columbus.

The remaining habitable continent outside Eurasia is Oceania. There were a mere two-and-a-half million people there at the time of Captain Cook. Most of the demographic growth during the historic period had come through Polynesian colonisation of island groups as far spaced as Hawaii and New Zealand. Only one quarter of a million people occupied Australia, described by

McEvedy and Jones (1978:322) as 'an unchanging palaeolithic backwater'. It was in reality not unchanging, though all the changes amounted to were the minute adjustments of aboriginal society to oscillations in environmental circumstances. Australia was admittedly palaeolithic, offering a near-vacuum to European colonists and being the least likely major part of the world to produce spontaneously the economic and technological strength to resist them.

The *very* long-term economic history of the world was thus acted out in Eurasia. Even there, when we come to contrast Europe and Asia, we shall deliberately exclude the tiny and exceptional economy of Japan, despite the immense interest of its later development. Japan provides, intriguingly enough, a comparison rather than a contrast with Europe. Until the equivalent of the Middle Ages, Japanese population was kept low by the vulnerability of an imperfectly insulated offshore archipelago to epidemics from mainland Asia. As a volcanic country Japan was sorely afflicted by geophysical disasters. The country was prone to massive famines in the latter part of the Tokugawa period, though by then there had emerged an economic structure of marked urbanism, monetisation, internal trade (much of it coastal), rising agricultural productivity, and regionally patterned rural industry. This was remarkable for its outline similarity with late preindustrial Britain. Yet there was only the slenderest connection with Europe, through minuscule trade between the Japanese and the Dutch and the semi-secret *rangoku* or Dutch learning. Most foreign contact was flatly forbidden, a prohibition tellingly backed by the weakening of the sterns of all big vessels built. Notwithstanding this, there were excellent coastal fisheries and whale fisheries.

Japan's development in the seventeenth and eighteenth centuries was an unintended result of a kind of absolutist victory over 'feudal' competitors. The Tokugawa shoguns required the samurai to settle in the castle towns and made the lords, the *daimyo*, spend half the year in Edo (Tokyo) under the *sankin kotei* system. This caused 'feudalism' to atrophy. The enforced urban growth caused an expansion of the market. Despite arbitrary acts of government, the private sector fed on the opportunities provided by the pacification. The example of Japan warns against the

wish-fulfilment to which European history lends itself, of equating political liberty and economic progress.

A move from a communal organisation of farming to the nuclear farm family under the early Tokugawa may conceivably have
forged the kind of link between population and environment
which has been postulated for Europe and which was absent in
the major mainland states of Asia. In addition the Japanese
widely practised infanticide. Between 1700 and 1825, zero net
population growth permitted enough capital accumulation for
the country to modernise its structure in many essentials, before
the arrival of Commodore Perry in 1854 initiated the opening of
Japan to the West (McEvedy and Jones 1978:179; Jones 1974a;
Hanley and Yamamura 1972:485–6). We have seen that Europe
undertook a similar modernisation before industrialising.

But Japan was a member of no system of states; interacted very
little with any neighbour; and forbade most foreign trade and
contact. It was symptomatic that the resources of the northern
island, Hokkaido, were surveyed, but then locked away by a
government fearful of change and of conflict with the Ainu
inhabitants. The total market was limited. The smoulderings of
development were damped down. Jacobs (1958:216) nevertheless
claims that capitalism would have emerged spontaneously in
Japan had the experiment not been cut off by Perry's arrival. For
reasons connected with uneven regional development the pro-
gressives among the 'outer daimyo' were already rich and becoming powerful. Perhaps they might have been able to form a
purposeful government, restore the emperor, and usher in
industrialism without the full impact of foreign intervention.
Stray records of technological borrowings before the Meiji Resto-
ration however suggest that they might voluntarily have opened
contacts with the West.

American sociologists in the 1950s used to overturn their students' preconceptions by giving a list of the middle-class characteristics of a lawyer living on a suburban street, until the point at
which the class acknowledged it had got the picture – and then
add, 'oh, by the way, he's black'. One might almost list characteristics of the Tokugawa economy as if speaking of some country
in Europe, and only at the end add, 'by the way, this was Japan'.
In deep-seated economic ratios and social structures Japan was a

surprisingly 'western' country. Jacobs (1958) stresses that Japan and western Europe, without a common cultural heritage, have significant social heritages in common, whereas Japan and China, for all their common cultural heritage, do not. Jacobs' book contains a point-by-point contrast of Japanese and Chinese values and a comparison between the values of Japan and western Europe. Indeed, in certain respects Japan was as 'European' as if it had been towed away and anchored off the Isle of Wight.

We must leave these speculations aside, and in the rest of this book concentrate on the contrasting light thrown on Europe by the economic history of the larger systems of mainland Asia. The proper 'controls' on European experience are China, India and Islam. Two sorts of investigation are possible. Firstly, Europe, China and India were the large and populous cultures of the world, and we may treat Europe as the deviant member. In the fifteenth century China had some 100–130 million inhabitants, India 100–120 million, and Europe 70–75 million. Together they held about eighty per cent of the world's population in 1500 and about eighty-five per cent in 1800. Mackinder (1962:83 and fig. 16) compares the total population of the European and Asian Monsoon Coastlands and recalculating his figures using the modern estimates of McEvedy and Jones (1978; cf. McEvedy 1972:8) we find that the coastlands held seventy-five per cent of the population of the entire world in 1400 and eighty-two per cent in 1800 (and incidentally still sixty-five per cent in 1975). The history of these peoples is the lion's share of world history.

Second, China, India and the Ottoman empire were all imposed, military despotisms and we may look at the ways in which that political fact influenced their developmental prospects. In this case Europe is the deviant member of the quartet of the most powerful systems in the world. Demographically, of course, the Ottoman empire was tiny. The entire Near East held only 20–30 million people in the fifteenth century and ten per cent of these were nomads. There was virtually no growth up to about 1800 – the period that interests us because Europe was then approaching industrialisation. Nevertheless while a large population is *prima facie* important for the production of ideas as well as goods, and does indicate the potential market, it is not the only disposer of change or influence. Culturally Islam was of the first importance; politically the Ottoman empire not only throws light on the impediments to development in a premodern invaders' despotism, but was a direct influence on Europe because it was always in a state of cold or hot war with it. Islam and the Ottomans therefore possess historical significance far beyond their demographic weight, and if the population was small, the Near East was still the fourth most densely settled part of the world. Accordingly we shall look at some general considerations affecting economic change in Asia, and go on to examine in separate chapters the late precolonial Ottoman empire, India, and China.

Several recent authors deride comparisons between European economic history and that of other cultures. They tend to take a very short-run view, and base their objection on compounds of the following three points. Firstly, they urge that economic development leading to industrialisation is inherently so unlikely that it was only arrived at in one civilisation, the European, and then by pure accident. This position is deeply shaken by the reality of the Chinese experience. China came within a hair's breadth of industrialising in the fourteenth century. Second, in a somewhat more general statement of the first position, it is often said that each country's historical sequence is unique. This may well be true as regards the totality of culture or entire complex sequences of events, to the extent that a predictive theory of history may be ruled out, but if the view is carried to the extreme of ignoring all regularities, the very possibility of social science is denied and historians are reduced to the aimlessness of balladeers. Third, some writers claim that non-Europeans were attempting to maximise values other than material ones, the implication being that other values are more worthy. Such a position is racist; or it is simply ignorant of the history of the fight against material poverty – especially in the poorer world beyond Europe. The most plausible assumption is that whatever the details of their cultures, non-Europeans were trying to maximise material gain just as Europeans were, but subject to more stringent constraints.

Nowhere else in the world, not even in mainland Asia, among its old cultures with their physically productive irrigated agricultures, vast and dense populations, marvellous craftsmanship, and stores of treasure, actually released a surge of productivity comparable with that of late preindustrial Europe. As Kiernan (1965:20) has expressed it, 'all men are equal; but only a spurious egalitarianism can reduce the share of all earth's regions in its grand historical advance to one and the same flat level'. The immense relative success of Europe, which is what we wish to understand, implies nothing derogatory about the individual (or 'racial') abilities of non-Europeans. Europe had borrowed from Asia; particular achievements in Asia were spectacular, some of them occurring while Europe was still only a frontier in the forest. The true difference seems to be that non-Europeans laboured under severe handicaps. We shall try to elucidate these in our enquiry into Asian economic history.

The Ottoman empire in the Near East, the Mughal empire in India, and the Manchu empire in China were all military despotisms originating in invasions. Other than politically, however, there was little similarity among Asian cultures. There is no pan-Asian cultural, religious or racial identity. Asia is a collection of subcontinents, themselves divided. Physical and ethnic differences are greater than among Europeans. Religious differences are also wide. There are several types of Buddhist, Hindu, Confucian and Muslim, and only the floundering certainty of the European mind is able to lay Asian poverty at the door of Asian religion (instead of the other way round?). That is as if one could attribute the growth of Europe to the Christian precepts of love, charity and humility which would in truth have censored the actions of the real makers of Europe's destiny. The more sympathetic among observers treat the supposedly fatalist elements in Asian religions as functions of earthly misery too intense to be overcome. In any case, fatalism may not really be a trait. Confucian thought, for instance, attributed natural disasters to maladministration, which is hardly fatalist. The charge that Islam is a predestinarian religion is rejected in that one may always pray to Allah to intercede.

If oriental philosophies do have a common strand it has been said to be the emphasis on emotions, values and cosmologies and the relative absence of the empirical enquiry and criticism of the Graeco-Judaeo-Christian tradition (Fraser 1975:39), though this western tradition is in fact partly of Arab origin. Nakamura (in Iyer 1965), who is a determined opponent of the concept of a single 'Asia' and of common European conceptions of the attitudes of Asians, does admit the characteristic of religious compromise, though it remains unclear whether or not this includes Islam, which shares a certain aggressiveness with Christianity and Judaism. Tolerance of deviation and lack of a crisp tradition of logical debate has been put forward as the kernel of the failure of Chinese and Indian science to develop. In the philosophies of those countries the notion of a consensus in interpreting nature may have seemed absurd (Ziman 1968:22).

There is at any rate no doubt that Asians were responsive to economic opportunity: none more so. We need look no further than Moreland's (1972) conclusions from an extensive scrutiny of the documents, conclusions more firmly based than the speculations of the 'substantivist/formalist' debate among economic anthropologists about motivation. 'A slight experience of the commercial records of the period', Moreland (1972:145) firmly declared, 'will suffice to disillusion any one who may have been tempted to regard the India of the seventeenth century as a country of Arcadian simplicity; buyers and sellers resembled in all essentials the buyers and sellers of the present day, and the commercial aptitudes of Indian merchants were certainly not inferior to those of the foreigners who dealt with them.' Market prices prevailed. Competition was keen. Specialised brokers and a remarkable apparatus of credit, exchange and insurance were in being. Moreland entered only two reservations, neither bearing on motivation but both indicative of the problems of Indian, and Asian, markets. Firstly, transport costs were very high. Markets were kept very local, especially those for food grains. Only along the coast did sea transport succeed in equating prices otherwise subject to the harvest condition of the immediate district. Second, the local governor was all too likely to sweep down at any time and exert *force majeure* to buy up anything, monopolising even the grain for his own or the régime's profit.

Conditions like these, with gluts, scarcities and tyrannical interventions, turned business into speculation. Governments appropriated large shares of the gross product and producers were left little above bare subsistence after allowing for seed. Monsoon agriculture was productive if the rains came, but the rains were not to be relied upon. Terrible famines recurred. Here more than in Europe applies Heckscher's famous remark about nature auditing her accounts with a red pencil. Moreland (1972:233) wrote of India that 'the energies of the unproductive classes were spent in the struggle to secure the largest possible share', and were deflected from the business of production. The incentive system was hostile to it. Confiscatory taxation meant that few could cling onto much of any productive increase they did create. Indians of ability devoted their efforts to the greater prize of distributional shares, embodied in quickly sold produce and items that could be concealed or quickly consumed.

Much the same situation prevailed throughout Asia. Productive effort was very much reduced by the political arrangements. Here is William Dampier on Mindanao in the Philippines in the 1680s: 'These people's laziness seems rather to proceed not so much from their natural inclinations, as from the severity of their prince [an Islamic sultan], of whom they stand in great awe: for he dealing with them very arbitrarily, and taking from them what they get, this damps down their industry, so they never strive to have anything but from hand to mouth' (Purves 1880:205).

Trade was political in complexion, and this impeded the extension of the market. Trade in staples was limited, distant or foreign trade especially. There were a few noteworthy exceptions, such as the trade of fourteenth-century Islamic Malacca, situated at the narrowest neck of the strait between Malaysia and Sumatra where India-bound and China-bound vessels could dock alternately according to the monsoon. Malacca became a big warehousing and entrepôt city which needed to import Java's rice and traded in its spices. This trade was a vehicle whereby Islam spread and it caused the former major east–west mart in the empire of Majahahit to collapse (Pearn 1963:30–5). In addition to this commerce, there was a little short-distance trade in which necessities did predominate. Rice 'fairly regularly' went from South India to Ceylon, from Burma to Bengal, from Vietnam to south China, but the main benefits were indirect, mostly the diffusion of useful plants. China received twenty-nine cultivated plants from the Middle East, but they were economically peripheral vegetables and fruit.

Most of such foreign-going trade as there was involved luxuries, among them the ornamental or reputedly aphrodisiac products of hunting in the jungles. This was sometimes a distant trade. Rome had acquired luxuries from India and competed with China for the spices of Indonesia; the manufactures despatched in return were chiefly ornaments. Later Asian trade was in Indian or Chinese handicrafts, silks, cotton, porcelain and a long catalogue of minor commodities. Simkin (1968:255), who lists them, appends the observation that 'it would thus be wrong to think of Asian trade as involving only luxuries'. He admits that in long-distance traffic luxuries did predominate, supplying the rich with miscellaneous garnerings of the natural world from kingfisher feathers through precious stones to drugs no modern pharmacopoeia would own. He argues however that the needs of ordinary people also generated trade, but his examples are jewellery for Indian women to wear or hoard, aromatics, drugs, and spices to conceal the limitations of diet. Many of these items were little more than biological junk and the growth potential of such a trade was slim. Goods of small bulk required only small ships. With the exception of Chinese tribute rice and some other trades strictly within China, there was little bulk cargo to stimulate ship-building, dock construction and warehousing. Impulses of the kind released in Europe by extensive shipments of wine, salt, wool, codfish, timber, ferrous metals, and grain were missing.

The political nature of commerce was a major limitation. In Malaya for example the royal courts monopolised trading, aided by the ease with which they could block the mouths of the rivers offering the only feasible routes to the interior. Little or no capital was thus formed in the hands of independent traders, and stringent sumptuary laws restricted the size of the market. The lack of an independent legal system to protect the individual merchant was general. In the fourteenth century Pegolotti's commercial handbook had noted that while the Pax Tartarica had made the route from the Crimea right to Peking 'perfectly safe, whether by day or by night', should a merchant have the misfortune to die *en route*, 'everything belonging to him will become the perquisite of the lord of the land in which he dies' (Simkin 1968:135). Traders were permitted to have only a marginal effect on societies commanded by despots who wished to manipulate trade for their personal benefit (and found this quite easy where the trade was small-scale and in fairly valuable goods), or to prevent it from eroding the traditional habits of their peasant tax-payers. Largely agrarian economies were thus watered and fertilised by only a tiny, circumscribed and often inessential trade sector. The degree of responsiveness in the body of the Asian economies was dulled. Where natural and social risks were high, so were liquidity preferences and hoarding. The Asian condition was summed up by Reade (1925:108) as *'property is insecure*. In this one phrase the whole history of Asia is contained.'

There was some urbanisation in traditional Asia but it failed to produce modernisation. For two thousand years before A.D. 1800 one-third or one-half of the four per cent of the world's population living in cities of over 10,000 inhabitants were Chinese. 'The world's premodern urban history has been chiefly a Chinese phenomenon' (Stover and Stover 1976:86). Within Asia it was only in China, on the great navigable rivers, that there were many cities with histories as long as those of Europe, performing comparable port and market functions. Unlike European cities they were permitted no autonomy by the central government (Zinkin 1951:10). Elsewhere capital cities were not independent of the courts and consisted largely of craftsmen and shopkeepers serving the royal entourage. When the ruler decided to remove the court to another location, for whatever reason, the whole population had to uproot itself and move too. Urban improvement was not encouraged. Seventeenth-century Hanoi, for instance, though said to contain a million people on market days remained a city of thatched huts and muddy lanes, ruled by utterly rapacious mandarins.

'Neither the growth of population nor the importation of precious metal', in Weber's (1927:353–4) view, 'called forth western capitalism. The external conditions for the development of capitalism are rather, first, geographical in character.' Recently Wesson (1978:111) has agreed: 'the primary cause seems to be geography'. Was Asia geographically disfavoured? Wesson harks back to Montesquieu's *Esprit des Lois*: 'In Asia they have always had great empires; in Europe these could never subsist. Asia has larger plains; it is cut into much more extensive divisions by mountains and seas . . . in Europe, the natural division forms many nations of a moderate extent, in which the ruling by laws is not incompatible with the maintenance of the state. . . . It is this which has formed a genius for liberty; that renders every part extremely difficult to be subdued and subjected by a foreign power . . . there reigns in Asia a servile spirit.'

Whatever we may think of Montesquieu's theorem of pre-modern geography, there seems a grain of truth in his assertion of a 'servile spirit'. Extremes of wealth and power and a total lack of real legal protection induced such a manner. Clearly there was servility too in eastern Europe, where it was manufactured by serfdom, and in the west of Europe the phenomenon of the 'deference vote' has lingered into the present along with visible and audible class differences. The difference from Asia is one of degree. There was no group in Asia with the self-esteem and independence of the middle-class merchants and professional men of late preindustrial Britain or the Netherlands. As or more important, there was no equivalent of the upper working class of foremen and non-commissioned officers nicely balanced between respecting their superiors and asserting their own authority. The lack of tough, efficient petty officers and sergeants able to handle cannon and conduct war may have been a serious flaw in Asian society (Parkinson 1963).

Montesquieu had China in the front of his mind. In the less stable parts of south-east Asia, struggles between states may have been founded in the environment in that core-areas or 'favourable environmental niches' were large but separated by particularly wide, infertile, lawless tracts. Regions of high yield are numerous and sometimes bigger than the core-areas of Europe. A map of 'favourable environmental niches' by Buchanan (1967) shows over thirty such areas ranging in size up to the entire lower Mekong, half of the island of Luzon in the Philippines, and all of Java. They are mostly lowlands floored by recent alluvium. Soils, rainfall or the possibility of building river-fed irrigation systems have led over the centuries to their selection for agriculture, mainly wet-rice production. The political weakness seems to stem from the fact that they are very widely dispersed, and have lacked adequate cultural exchange, or that they are separated by wide, disputed strips. Often none of the states could acquire a permanent sovereignty over its neighbour, while the territory in between remained a special bone of contention. Indo-China is a prime example. Each of its big river basins or deltas formed the nucleus of an old kingdom, but separating them on the open plateaux from Burma to Laos lay a number of semi-feudal states subject now to Burma, now to the Thai kingdom, now to Annam. In the absence of a natural barrier South Vietnam built two massive defensive walls against the north in the seventeenth century (Spate and Learmonth 1967:177–8; Honey 1968). The concept of a defined frontier is an alien one brought to Asia from the Europe of the nation-states. The indigenous notion was of border zones which were occupied by backward tribal peoples and properly administered by none of the flanking kingdoms or empires. Writing of the Burma–Yunnan region, Fitzgerald (1973) observes that its jungles, mountains, wild rivers, and hot, wet, malarial lowlands were inimical to those who would control or settle them from outside. Even the Mongols retreated from the zone, leaving it to small mingled tribes and principalities. 'Nature has always defined the frontier rather better than the activities of rulers' (Fitzgerald 1973:54–5). Nature really defined insecure borders rather than frontiers.

Endless fighting went on within and among the political units of Asia. But these conflicts over resources – over who was to succeed to the throne or usurp it, over disputed territory, or over who was to grab the other's realm – were not extended outside Asia. There was no addition of overseas 'ghost acreage' to the existing resource base. The marine fisheries within reach, except those off Japan, were inferior to those available to the Europeans of the Discoveries (cf. Dobby 1966). Even the Pacific North-West has no single-species ground as bountiful as the Newfoundland Banks. Away to the African side, the grounds where the Somali current wells up were not discovered until international scientific exploration of the 1960s (sic). The Indian Ocean generally possesses narrow continental shelves and even today accounts for only five per cent of the world's fish catch. Excellent fisheries are scarce. Only where deep water rises all year are there phosphates, rich nutrients, and good fish stocks, and only where the productive layer of the sea touches the land are the fish forced up to where they may be taken. 'In consequence, all the arguments used about the vastness of the ocean cease to apply when one comes to consider the fisheries of historical importance, apart from whaling' (Graham 1956:495). Asians were simply not provided with as good marine fishing-grounds as the North Sea and the far side of the Atlantic offered to Europeans.

Where marine fish are plentiful in Asian waters, as on the Sunda platform between Malaysia and Borneo, they swim in mixed shoals including species unsuitable for food. This increases the necessary catching effort, or it did in the past when there was no means of refrigerating the less palatable species for use as animal feed. Tropical fish are less fleshy and poorer in food value than those of temperate seas. Some tropical species are poisonous. Line fishing is unrewarding because predatory fish are likely to bite off the hooked catch. Fishermen found it difficult to accumulate the capital for deep-sea ships and nets. Distant opportunities were seldom enticing and as a result there could be little of the spin-off in navigation and commercial knowledge that Europeans obtained from deep-sea fishing and sailing. Interestingly, while Europeans balanced their trade with Asia by taking over the carrying trade they did not set up as fishermen for Asian markets. Their techniques were not advanced and there was no mass purchasing power in Asia (though the Chinese found the money to buy opium). When Europeans did begin to supply China with a marine product, in 1778, it was a luxury item, seal fur.

The Chinese were technically quite capable of reaching, say, the Pacific North-West. They chose not to do so. They had made a self-denying ordinance not to re-open their once extensive maritime voyaging in 1480, just when the Portuguese happened to be gearing to round the Cape of Good Hope and spill out European influences into the eastern seas. It was not until 1798 that a British captain, John Meares in the *Felice*, carried the first cargo of logs from north-western America to China.

Asia was locked in, and locked herself in, to her own nutritional base. No power in the monsoon coastlands – 'the Sown' – could make much headway against the warrior nomads of the steppes. For much of Asia limitations of resources may have been a disadvantage, especially as regards supplies of protein. But continental isolation was perhaps less damaging than it might have been to Europe. Pond and paddyfield cultivation of freshwater fish was not difficult. China, though not much else of Asia, possessed internal reserves of land. The human population continued to climb. The lack of maritime exploration was not therefore in itself a decisive check, but it did deny Asia that special European windfall of food, raw materials, colonies and (most important for growth rather than mere expansion) business opportunities. Asia continued to use up her internal resources on a growing population, replicating her existing society and economy.

There seems, indeed, to have been a cycle in which peace and expansion were followed by rapid population growth, diminishing returns in agriculture, an excessive take by rulers or increasingly corrupt administrators, or expensive or unsuccessful wars. Technological change was not sufficient to sustain growth. Political institutions did not evolve and change was limited to a turnover of personnel. Ibn Khaldun in *The Muqaddimah* implies a cyclic history of this type in the Arab world. The heart of the problem lay in pie-slicing politics. Rulers went to war indiscriminately to obtain spoils, with nothing modern man would accept as a *casus belli* (Moreland 1972:2–3). Under strong rulers there were periods of great flowering, but the perpetual conflict over succession, or the unchecked power of the ruler, sooner or later plunged society back into war. Where the personality of the ruler made such a difference, a series ot premature deaths could be demoralising (six Chinese emperors ending with Cheng-te in the sixteenth century died one after another before the age of forty). As Lord Macartney, first British ambassador to China, described it, 'whenever an insufficient man happens to have the command upon deck, adieu to the discipline and safety of the ship' (Dawson 1972:344; see also 275). The Chinese empire was the one that held together through this period, but other Asian systems collapsed in fratricidal war. Havoc was wreaked by the wars, which were fought as *levées en masse*. The dykes of the paddy fields were very vulnerable and although the climate was such that once broken dykes were repaired, production quickly rose again, the intervening famines were appalling. Economic behaviour was distorted by the perpetual sense of insecurity. Thus phases of expansion and order alternated with derelictions on the scale of the collapse of the Sri Lankan irrigated dry-zone farming and the ruin of its capital, Anuradhapura, or the decay of the irrigated agriculture in the Khmer country around Angkor Wat.

Economies with an ever-present threat of confiscation, warfare and natural disaster found it understandably difficult to stimulate enough technological advance even to keep up with the demographic growth released by spells of peace. We have to distinguish three types of historical movement. Firstly, there were the fluctuations just referred to, when the pseudo-stability of strong-man rule alternated with bouts of squandering, oppression and disorder. Second, there was despite these fluctuations and the failure of any real development a marked underlying trend of population growth. This boded ill for some future period when reserves of land and the possibilities of diffusing the better crop strains would give out. Third, there is a body of opinion that Asia was actually entering a synchronised decline somewhat before the arrival of the Europeans. According to Simkin (1968:258–9), Asian trade in general was shrinking. In much of the Islamic world early austerity was turning into a love of luxury, and the merchant class was soon being plundered by the sultans. Islamic countries began to fight one another. China entered its introverted phase and gave up maritime exploration and soon afterwards sea-going trade as a whole. Mughal India, Indonesia and Burma were all in a process of splitting, or were soon to split, into weaker states. The crumbling Khmer Empire was being smashed by the invading Thais. According to Venkatachar (in Iyer 1965:38–9), Hindus as well as Chinese were abandoning the ocean. The lesser Asian societies were withdrawing into parochial shells.

Not all authorities agree on this dismal catalogue, it is true. Van Leur (quoted by Frank 1978:138–9) emphasises how many Asian countries were intact as late as the eighteenth century, and not yet disturbed by European penetration. That does not quite dispose however of the sense of a widespread introversion, or Venkatachar's view of increasingly immobile societies undergoing 'curious experiences'. Horne (1964:115) claims that all that really happened was that the burst of European creative growth temporarily overwhelmed Asia, an opinion approximately in line with Graham's (1973:1) verdict on Chinese science that it merely advanced more slowly than the forced pace of post-Renaissance Europe, and with McEvedy and Jones's (1978:129) view that the Chinese and other Asians did go on improving their technology, though falling behind the Europeans in the area of guns and sails. Yet even that is not quite the picture drawn by Elvin (1973), of an actual retreat by China from her earlier technological heights.

It is in fact pitching the case too high. Technological changes made by the Chinese after the fifteenth century mostly amounted to earlier-ripening varieties of rice and their further diffusion, together with the diffusion of dryland crops brought in by the Portuguese. This in no way compares with Europe's record of technological achievements, which does not need to cite agricultural improvement at all, noteworthy though its advances were in that sector. While there are signs of progress in certain respects, the overall impression of late precolonial Asia is of some societies sliding towards chaos, of others turning inwards, of growing political weakness, of fluctuations without development, and on the horizon a cloud, no bigger than a man's hand as yet, of eventual overpopulation (cf. also Strayer 1970:105). The Asian empires of the period, Ottoman, Mughal and Manchu, were not timeless despotisms. They were régimes of conquest originating from the steppes, unable to survive efficiently without fresh land and spoils, and terrifyingly prone to inhibit development. Adam Smith noted the result: 'In those unfortunate countries, indeed, where men are continually afraid of the violence of their superiors, they frequently bury and conceal a great part of their common stock, a common practice in Turkey, in Indostan, and I believe, in most other governments of Asia' (Smith 1884:115).

Asia

Chapter 9

Islam and the Ottoman Empire

I can say no more, then that the disease yet works internally that must ruyne this empire

Sir Thomas Roe

THE STRONG POINT of the Islamic world of the Near East and North Africa lay in obtaining economies of scale by uniting in one faith, one culture and the one Arabic language, a diversity of peoples from Spain across into Asia. For a time this culture, occupying an area greater than the Roman empire, was most innovative. The 'Arab Agricultural Revolution' which brought crops from India as far west as Spain was based on extensive culture contact and travel (Watson 1974:17–18). Secular gains were made because of the ambition of every man to make a pilgrimage at least once in his lifetime. Ideas were also diffused in books to an extent beyond the dreams of early medieval Christendom. Large, well-lighted cities with universities and great libraries in Muslim Spain stood in contrast to the virtual hutments and spartan monasticism north of the Pyrenees. The generations are said to have passed into the thirteenth century without plague or famine (Goitein 1973:221).

Scientific and technological knowledge was absorbed from India and China and in some respects developed further. Even at late periods Europe had much to learn from Islam. There was in 1550 a lighthouse in the Bosporus much in advance of any in Europe, 120 steps high, with leaded glass windows and a huge glass lantern lighted by twenty wicks floating in a pan of oil (Beaver 1971:15). 'Oriental' bloodstock reached eastern and central Europe only with the Turkish advances of the sixteenth century and only in the second half of the seventeenth century became an ingredient in the larger improved breed of horse essential to the growth of inland transportation as far west as

175

England (Piggott 1976:115). When Thomas Jefferson was considering the grant of a patent for Oliver Evans's automated flour mill, he consulted Shaw's *Travels to Egypt and the Barbary Coast*, for Shaw had noted similar machinery in operation there (Martin 1961:31), in a culture that Christians had come to think of as more advanced in decay than in technology.

Yet a fact and flaw of Near Eastern economic life was that the population remained low compared with China, India or Europe. There were only 28,000,000 people in the Ottoman empire at its peak in 1600. The potential market was limited and spread out over great distances. Political and religious unity did not last as well as did cultural unity. Separate caliphates had begun to break away from Baghdad very quickly after the first triumphant expansion of Islam. Repeated internecine warfare and external attacks culminating in the descent of the Mongol hordes were certainly damaging. The term Islam, too, implies submission and western observers have often seen it as inherently unresistant to autocracy. There does seem to have been a risk that conservative sects, antipathetic to innovation or to borrowings from the infidel, would struggle to impose their own intellectual monopoly, and where they succeeded would roll back the inspirations of other times. It is not however clear what rôle in the disintegration of full unity was played by backward-looking strands in Islamic thought as opposed to the effects of pure power struggles.

The resource portfolio of the Islamic world was seldom a balanced one. This must have hampered development at times – though real complementarities existed which were not properly exploited, for while some areas remained short of raw materials others were exporting them to the richer buyers of Europe. North Africa sent early modern Europe wool and raw silk – 'a clear sign of backwardness' (van Klaveren 1969:50) – as well as metals, wheat and maize, in return for manufactures. There was a great shortage of timber along the Barbary coast and the expedient was adopted by the corsairs of laying Dutch traders under a regular levy of ammunition and ships' timber as a means of obtaining the wherewithal to go on preying on the ships of other European nations. The Algerian corsairs who attacked Baltimore, Co. Cork, Ireland, in 1631 used a Dutch- or Flemish-built vessel (Barnby 1970:27–31).

Voyaging in the Indian Ocean and successful proselytising had given Islam some principalities in Indonesia and trade settlements down the coast of East Africa. These lands were quite different from the scantily peopled and resource-rich spaces seized by Europe in the Americas and had a different economic impact. Their trade was at the luxury end of the spectrum and they did not in general make up for the shortage of real resources, especially timber, in the Near East. For centuries the dhows conveyed mangrove poles from the big Rufiji delta south of Zanzibar for use in the towns of the treeless Arabian shore; but it was a poor haul compared with the large and varied timber imports to north-west Europe. Indeed, Christian powers had early spotted the resource weaknesses in Islam and prohibited exports of iron, timber and sometimes foodstuffs, meaning to keep down the Muslim navy (Strayer 1974:403–4), but no consistent policy was followed and parts of North Africa (where good hard wheat was grown) and even the Ottoman empire eventually became almost resource colonies of the West. Despite clever irrigation practices in some regions, Muslim agriculture and settlement remained oasis-bound over most of its range, and grazing practices, particularly the omnivorous feeding by goats, seem to have extended the margins of the desert in the Near East and North Africa. The Arab peoples seem to have recoiled from land north of the limits of olive cultivation (Glick 1974:77), though this lack of ecological fit did not dissuade them from launching invasions northwards against Europe. In the areas they did permanently occupy livestock production was limited by shortages of fodder. Arabia was so short of forage that vast quantities of tunny were fed to livestock. Sweet are the uses of adversity: because hides were scarce, paper was substituted for parchment, when paper-making had been learned from Chinese prisoners taken in Asia during the eighth century. Paper became an important item in early Muslim trade. In Europe, where hides were more plentiful, the adoption of paper was held up by the availability of parchment (Goitein 1973:20).

The most important segment of the Islamic sphere from the point of view of interaction and comparison with Europe is the Ottoman empire. This was well endowed with resources, for when the Ottoman Turks moved west in the mid-fifteenth

century they captured the Dardanelles and were able to divert the
timber, grain and fish of the Black Sea to their capital at Constantinople. They were able to control trade between the Balkans and
Europe through Ragusa (Dubrovnik), an Italian merchant colony
on the Adriatic, which they surrounded but permitted to buy
immunity. In this beginning, however, may be seen the seeds of
Ottoman weakness, which was never overcome. They were
unable or unwilling to administer all trade themselves and the
Ragusans supplied them with customs officials and tax collectors
(Coles 1968:110–11).

There was at first a heady phase of growth. The Ottomans
imposed a welcome order on Near Eastern affairs. They restored
security to the intercontinental trade routes across the Fertile
Crescent. They ended the phase of their own squabbles with the
Mamelukes by the expedient to taking Egypt from them. The
imperial capital at Constantinople grew from under 100,000 in
1453 to over 500,000, perhaps as high as 800,000, in 1600, at which
date it was larger than contemporary European cities and offered
a big market. The Ottomans came like liberators to the Balkans,
introducing an agreeably decisive form of one-man rule which, in
a manner of speaking, made the trains run on time. Christian
peasants were attracted away from their own oppressive landlords by greater public order and lower taxes. Martin Luther
noted that 'one finds in German lands . . . those who would
rather be under the Turks than under the Emperor and the
Princes', while Barbarossa, who had brought North African
piracy to Ottoman naval service, found revolts raised on his
behalf whenever he invaded the Italian coast (Stavrianos
1966:125; Braudel 1972 vol. 2:663, 778–9).

This empire lay cheek by jowl with Europe, with which it could
trade and from which it initially hired technicians – on such good
terms that many apostasised. The treasury was full in the early
sixteenth century, the capital city was growing fast. Even if the
Ottomans were only frontier Turks culturally below the level of
their Islamic brethren, that heritage was theirs to adopt. As
Europe developed, they could have learned from there too. As it
was they spat on the opportunity, and soon they were held in
terror. The Briefs for alms in the churchwardens' accounts of
English parishes are full of pleas to ransom prisoners from the

Turks. The Ottoman siege of Malta seemed such a hazard to the whole of Christian civilisation, threatening to turn the Mediterranean into a Turkish lake, that the Protestant Bishop of Salisbury went so far as to celebrate the relief of Malta's Roman Catholic defenders, the Knights of St John. But the Ottomans were in the event turned back in the West. Redirected eastwards, they made no great headway there either. As a direct result their economy lost momentum, and the symptoms and causes of that deceleration sufficiently explain why there was no general Ottoman development.

Technological stagnation and intellectual retrogression mark the check to Ottoman ambitions, though whether they were cause or consequence has to be investigated. In their early imperial phase the Ottomans were not cut off and isolated from the adjacent European civilisation, for instance they quickly learned about the Discoveries. A map of 1513 by a Turkish cartographer shows the Atlantic coasts of North and South America, drawn from Portuguese charts and a copy of a chart made by Columbus. But the Ottomans were quite unable to reach out and grasp any share of this prize. Worse, the monopoly of routes to India and the Spice Islands was broken. Sixteenth-century Ottoman rule in Egypt re-opened the overland trade in spices, and the spices travelled better by caravan than tossing around the Cape in little ships, but the tolls soon began to fall off again. When Anthony Wood reported in 1674 that meat was now rarely spiced (Ogg 1934 vol. 1:68–9) he was noticing the effects of the fodder revolution in the most developed parts of Europe. More fresh meat had become available through the year and spices were no longer so essential to mask the taint of over-ripe meat. A nail had been driven into the spice-trade's coffin.

'Sufficient and convincing proof of the necessity of learning this science [cartography] is the fact that the heathen, by their application to and their esteem for those branches of learning, have discovered the New World and have over-run the markets of India' (quoted by Stavrianos 1966:132–3). When the Turkish encyclopaedist Katib Chelebi wrote this in 1656 it was too late. Rycaut (1668:32) remarked that he never saw a good map drawn by a Turk. As to ships and navigation, the Ottomans had too much initial success with borrowed techniques to notice the need to change. Even after the battle of Lepanto in 1571 they rebuilt the same old galleys and took the Spanish fort at Tunis in 1574. They constructed a large navy and won victories in the Black Sea and the eastern Mediterranean, and they captured Egypt. This lulled them into retaining what in ocean-going and sea-battle terms had become an obsolete technology. Their galley fleets out of Aden and Basra were outmanoeuvred and out-gunned by the sailing ships of the Portuguese (Hess 1970; Braudel 1972 vol. 2:1174–5). Europe sailed on to its commercial revolution. The Ottomans were confined to the land.

The Levant fleets of England, Holland and above all France were soon trading with the Ottoman empire under privileges of freedom from taxation and exemption from the jurisdiction of local courts – a valuable privilege in a despotism, and granted to the French as early as 1535. They carried away foodstuffs and raw materials and brought in their own colonial wares and bullion. Thus rice and sugar which had originally been introduced to Europe by the Arab Agricultural Revolution were now brought in from Europe's Atlantic colonies. The bullion did not stick to Ottoman fingers; it drained away eastwards to buy the Ottomans spices for themselves, and precious fabrics. Embargoes on the export of strategic goods to Europe simply were not enforced by a lax officialdom and the Ottoman régime became unable to buy up all the war *matériel* and food needed for its own armies. There were no policies of a mercantilist (rather than a narrowly strategic) kind which might have led them to try to halt, say, penetration by European cloth producers, and had there been, the corruption of officialdom would have nullified them.

There was indeed no political integration capable of matching the organisation of a European nation-state and the loyalties it could command. The empire was a congeries of people with conflicting loyalties. There was open house for renegades but the empire did not harness their energies to full purpose. The system that some early modern Europeans had so much admired could not mobilise its resources a century or so later. Easy circumstances gave way to difficulties. Even had the élite not been disposed to take a giant slice of resources and squander them, the population in general was never rich enough to produce a big margin for investment. Attitudes of resignation came to prevail.

The régime became so oppressive that it depopulated its own countryside. European observers commented on the abandoned holdings and villages of the Balkans. In 1675 one traveller reported that over two-thirds of a region of Thrace was lying uncultivated. Edicts were issued forbidding the peasants to migrate to the cities, and although some movement continued under the stresses of exploitation in the rural areas, after 1600 the urban population began to fall. The internal flaws of the empire eventually became so flagrant that Europe began its colonising assaults on the Near East, beginning with Napoleon's unsuccessful, but ominous, attack on Egypt, which Kiernan (1978:218) describes as 'the soft underbelly of the Ottoman Empire'.

After their tolerant start, typical perhaps of military despotisms in the first flush of confidence, the Ottomans came positively to encourage obscurantist thought. This militated against the borrowing of western techniques and against native inventiveness. Perhaps more serious still, it meant that no precautions were taken against the plague. In Europe, too, a *laissez-faire* attitude to disease as the Will of God was sometimes embraced – but only by backwoods peasants and priests, not by the political or even the Papal authorities. Ottoman obscurantism meant on the contrary that the plague remained endemic, just when it was being eliminated in Europe. The benefits of action across the entire state were therefore lost, for although the Koran enjoins the relief of disaster victims, this could be organised at the local level, and active measures were not sanctioned. The plague flared into an epidemic every few years. Forty thousand people died of it in Constantinople in 1770. Salonika suffered 'repeated and disastrous epidemics' from 1723 to 1741 and lost large sections of its populace between 1741 and 1777. One-third of the populations of Bucharest and Belgrade perished between 1812 and 1814. As late as that, in a bad year, the plague could carry off up to 150,000 people, forcing the closure of trade fairs, leaving the harvest uncut in the fields, and the cattle to starve in their stalls. Some areas were scarcely repopulated (Stavrianos 1966:134–5; McNeill 1976:188–9; Zakythinos 1976:59). Markets and labour supply were thus both depressed and in the prevailing climate of insecurity of investment and hostility to new ways, dearer labour did not lead to labour-saving innovations. Unreason had gained the upper hand. Inalcik (1973), in a chapter entitled 'The Triumph of Fanaticism', cites examples from the late sixteenth century of the reaction against science. The most telling is that, on the pretext that astronomical observations were actually the cause of the plague, the Janissary army in 1580 razed the observatory to the ground.

There was one major exception to passivity in the face of disease. The Turks' Greek subjects did have a treatment for smallpox which was at first unknown in the West. This was inoculation, carried out by old women. The relationship of these folk-doctors to Ottoman orthodoxy is nebulous. Presumably they were left alone to practise their craft, whereas conspicuous health measures taken by more prominent individuals or the government would have attracted the condemnation of religious leaders. It was from Constantinople that Lady Mary Wortley Montagu brought the technique of inoculation to England in the 1720s. After early failures there, inoculation was revived in the mid-eighteenth century and widely adopted in Britain, Europe and the American colonies. Edward Jenner's development of vaccination in 1796 thereafter superseded inoculation and has swept it out of the history books, though her curiosity-value often rates Lady Mary a mention. Conceivably Jenner had himself been inoculated as a boy during an outbreak of smallpox at Wotton-under-Edge.

Thus 'Turkish' inoculation procedures became known in eighteenth-century Europe. They had indeed been described in a book by an Austrian diplomat. One of the intellectuals of the Greek Revival, Iakovros Pylarinos, together with a Chiote physician called Timones, also publicised the treatment. Pylarinos communicated his experiments to the naturalist Sherard, who for a time had lived at Smyrna where Pylarinos was Venetian consul from 1712 to 1718, and Timones communicated his experiments to Woodward at Oxford. Pylarinos further published works on inoculation in Latin at Venice in 1715 and Leiden in 1721 (Zakythinos 1976:109 n.44). The topic was one of enormous significance. Disease control was one part of a mighty triad (with administrative reform and technological invention) that was converging to bring about the development of eighteenth-century Europe. Of course, if a society had to choose between eliminating either smallpox or the plague, the best choice would be to deal with the plague. That administered the greater economic shock, and was what Europe tackled first. The Ottomans did not adopt plague regulations until 1841. But Europe was responsive enough in the eighteenth century to add smallpox inoculation to its measures of disease control, and therefore got the best of both worlds.

Nevertheless, this episode has the salutary function of reminding us of the fragility of generalisations about whole cultures. The Ottomans slipped into an awesome backwardness but even that was not without its very occasional redeeming feature. Generalisation is unavoidable and intentional and proper when we are making *very* long-term or inter-continental comparisons. We can only try to avoid conclusions which are unsupported by the literature. Beneath the cloak of economic systems lie hidden, however, the rich layers of historical individuality, the actors and all the cross-currents. They are not deliberately concealed here, merely set aside because of the larger purpose. None of this is in any way to urge that the mist of obscurantist thought which forbade measures against the plague, and so many other innovations of value, was the root cause of Ottoman decline. There seems nothing inherent in Islam that would forbid economic development; Rodinson (1978) wrote a book to establish just that point. Particular régimes were a different matter, and the Turks' powerful Muslim Institution, whereby the Sheikh of Islam or his mufti could declare any act of the sultan religiously unacceptable (Kiernan 1978:214), worked against novelty and western influence. Economic decline seems however to have set in independently and the sectarian changes may have been a response to it more than they were a cause. Interestingly, theological deviations in Islam were usually 'to the right', towards more conservatism, rigorous observance and spiritual orthodoxy, a point which is also made by Landes (1969:30). In economically developing Christian Europe, breakaway movements tended to deviate 'leftwards' from the established churches towards greater lay participation.

Intellectual backwardness overpowered the Ottoman empire, which was part of that world of Islam which had been the first civilisation to fall heir to all the great cultures of the Old World.

Islamic scientists, wrote Meyerhof (in Arnold 1961:354) in a dazz-
ling metaphor, reflected the Hellenic sun after its day; illumi-
nated the darkest European Middle Ages like a moon; added
some bright stars; but fled at the Renaissance. The untender
ministrations of Selim the Grim and Suleiman the Lawgiver
stamped out originality. The Turks discouraged the use of
Arabic, a language rich in imaginative vocabulary (Kiernan
1978:209). They created in Arab minds 'a psychology of passivity'. The failure of their subject peoples strung out around the
eastern Mediterranean to break away does require some explanation, whether or not this is a sufficient one. The danger to the
Turks themselves of looking only inwards had been forecast by
Chelebi in 1657, but had been disregarded: 'henceforth people
will be looking at the universe with the eyes of oxen' (Stavrianos
1966:133). Policy advice sank to a low level, not that there was in
any case much in the way of purpose other than a perpetual
search for what Gibbon called 'new enemies and new subjects'
(Coles 1968:77, 163). Murad IV (1623–40) did commission a
memorandum on the causes of decline. When it was presented it
proved to be a catalogue of symptoms, and advice to revert to the
purest of traditional practices. Official Ottoman comprehension
of the elementary facts of geography, already poor in the mid-
seventeenth century (Rycaut 1668:32), had quite lost touch with
reality by the close of the eighteenth century and some foreign
governments were sent absurd and bewildering remonstrations
about their supposed geopolitical actions. There was open con-
tempt for infidels and all their works. Ottoman society was illiter-
ate and the introduction of the printing press (after a promising
little start in the sixteenth century) was forbidden for a long time
because it might disseminate ideas dangerous to the state. The
state was governed by the written word, but that written word
turned out to be adamantine precedent.

   From a European standpoint the Ottoman downturn, real
enough, appeared quicker than it was. The Ottomans had shifted
their threatening attentions from Europe. Neither Vienna,
besieged in 1529, nor Malta, in the Great Siege of 1565, had fallen.
The much larger armies fielded by Europe in the late seventeenth
century were hard to match and the Turks were defeated again
outside Vienna in 1683. The unsuccessful Grand Vizier was

strangled on the sultan's orders, but that could not save the Ottoman empire from heavy expenses nor the requirement of the Treaty of Carlowitz (1699) that the trans-Danubian provinces be evacuated. Militarily it had ceased to overawe the Europeans. The Janissaries were jealous of their established military skills and an incapacity to borrow or adapt told against them. A visitor to the Arsenal in Constantinople saw heaps of artillery pieces lying about, all acquired as booty, for the system seemed incapable of manufacturing or even purchasing to a plan (Braudel 1972 vol. 2:802, 1166–7). The system depended on continual victories and its strategy was to make war for no longer than three years, but within that time to make no peace, 'until their Triumphs and Acquisitions would answer the expenses' (Rycaut quoted by Stavrianos 1966:136). Few spoils and high costs spelled, as Sir Thomas Roe put it, 'ruyne'.

The Ottoman state was a plunder machine which needed booty or land to fuel itself, to pay its way, to reward its officer class. Wars to the east (and south along the Red Sea) failed to provide these desirable objects, just as European campaigns had failed. War against the Persians was exhausting. The Turks possessed some slight technological lead against these adversaries but were bogged down by commissariat problems, immense distances, and severe winters. They may have aimed to wrest control of routes to central Asia and to secure the supply of slaves and taxes that might be expected from a conquest of Georgia. But in the event the gains were disappointing. Georgia became a suzerainty but yielded up little in the way of fiefs to distribute among the soldiery (Coles 1968:166, 191).

With military expansion brought to a halt, the state came under severe stress. Revenues sank and the army and navy could not be properly maintained, which in turn reduced the military options. The system turned to prey on itself with a quite indecent haste. Taxes were raised so high as to depopulate. The road to personal wealth for officials and military officers was quickly perceived as the purchase and exploitation of public posts. The rot began to set in as early as the mid-sixteenth century when Suleiman permitted the sale of offices and the accumulation of private fortunes by the Turkish élite within the imperial bureaucracy, the members of the so-called Ruling Institution. This all had to be paid for by the peasant population and their spending power in the market was reduced in consequence. Exemptions from taxes for officers in the Janissaries were the sultans' means of buying off their collective political threat. The unchecked plundering thus allowed was of a different order of magnitude from the peculations and sinecures of *ancien régime* Europe.

To compound the troubles, there followed a deplorable succession of inept sultans. Thanks partly to a change in the laws of succession, the sultans were reared and surrounded by degenerates in the cloying atmosphere of 'boudoir politics' in palace and harem. Coles (1968:162) puts the situation well when he says that the sultans became increasingly impresarios of bizarre troupes of court favourites or prisoners of the harem. The élite Ottoman attitude to females was like that of Kemal Ataturk, who when asked what appealed to him about women is said to have replied, 'availability'. The run of thirteen incompetent sultans who reigned from 1566 to 1703 included lechers like Murad III, who fathered 103 children (though he was outclassed by Moulay Ismail, an eighteenth-century emperor of Morocco who produced 888), drunkards, like Selim the Sot, and mental defectives, like Mustapha, twice deposed for idiocy. Occasionally a sultan would try a vigorous measure or two, but continuity was missing even within the reigns of men like these. It may indeed be that the problem with one-man rule was almost as much the lack of continuity as the despotism (Coles 1968:40; Farb 1978:261; Kiernan 1978:215–16; Stavrianos 1966:117ff.).

Once the flow of fresh resources began to dry up, competition within the system became severe. Christian subjects were now bound to the land by an obligation of perpetual debt, the *chiflik*, which was tolerated by a weakened state (Stavrianos 1966:138–42). Holdings (*timar*) which had formerly been granted to soldiers in return for light payments, and military service in the event of war, were now usurped and became hereditable, again because the government was too weak to stand on the original bargain. The soldiers turned also to exploiting the Christian peasants, especially when more soldiers and officials returned after the loss of the trans-Danubian lands in the late seventeenth century and all of them tried to make a living in the Balkan lands. The average size of holding was pushed down. The once-vigorous Ottoman soldiery sank into the lethargy of unearned landlord incomes. Those who had become artisans were squeezed out of the cities by the shrinkage of urban populations and markets and they, too, set about dispossessing peasants. Ironically, many ousted peasants tried to move to the cities. Others took up large-scale banditry.

The imperial government, concerned about its revenues and political position, had given trade in certain goods into the hands of concessionaries. Far back in Islamic history, the judges of Cordova had protected private property against ministers and the caliph (Wesson 1978:95). There had been little sign of arbitrary seizures of commercial property on the part of medieval Islamic governments (Goitein 1967:268–9). The prominence of Muslim trade in the early Middle Ages had been reinforced by, or maybe even based on, flexible commercial instruments and practices which had sometimes been adopted as early as the eighth century, though they were not taken up in Europe until centuries later (Udovitch 1970:261). The Ottoman empire as heir to all this came instead to operate an economic system that rested on confiscation, despoilment, and a total, calculated, insecurity of life and property. Even of its great men, Rycaut (1668:71) saw in the seventeenth century that 'care is taken to clip their wings'. The Grand Signior, the sultan, seized his inferiors' estates on their deaths, handing back only what he chose to their families. A nobility there was indeed, but an hereditary nobility was contrary to the principles of the state, which, in conformity to terrifying ideals, deliberately set about making and breaking military officers. Ibn Khaldun had long before expressed the view that famines were 'not the result of the land's incapacity to cope with the increasing demand, but of the political chaos and physical oppression which invade the state in its decline' (Cassen 1978:256). The Ottomans fully lived up to this model. Theirs was not however a purely agrarian despotism. It contained, despite everything, an active, profit-maximising trade sector. Rodinson (1978:28) explicitly uses Polanyi's term 'unembedded' of the economy of Mecca where Islam was born. No social relations such as those of the clan interfered with the pursuit of profit in the original Islamic world. Neither did archaic social forms cloud the goals of the traders under the Ottomans, but it would be fair to refer to the economy as politically embedded. No economic decision went undistorted by fear of the polity.

From the time of John Locke, Europeans had scorned the oppressiveness of the Turks. The keys to Turkish poverty lay in confiscatory taxes and the bribes by which justice and administration operated (Fusfeld 1968:21). A Moscow journal, published under the tsars, could claim in 1805 that under the Ottomans, 'the insecurity of life and property take away the stimulus to establish factories. . . . They have no understanding of promissory notes . . . [Borrowers] have to pay 30 to 40 per cent . . .', and more in this deprecating vein (Stavrianos 1966:145). Needless to say, elementary government functions were scarcely carried out. Roads went unrepaired. Brigands abounded, refugees from the *chiflik* system. Officers who had purchased their commissions sent out armies understrength. Great wealth could be made in trade and money-lending but was 'particularly exposed to confiscation by the state' (Inalcik 1969:136). Investment funds were diverted into shops, caravanserais and bath houses, which were hardly worth confiscating, though never quite safe. Much was hoarded. Much went into the madcap 'Tulip Festivals' under Achmed III (1703–30), the 'Tulip Reign', so much indeed that it 'actually began to interfere with State business and to prove a drain on the national resources' (Sitwell 1948:119). Tulip fancying suggests a lack of inviting investment opportunities. The same kind of tulip mania happened in Holland, whence some of the varieties had come among the 1,323 listed by Achmed's Master of the Flowers. But in Holland the scarcity of profitable outlets for funds did not persist as it did in the Ottoman empire. There, at any rate east of the Balkan provinces, investors kept clear of manufacturing with its stocks of goods tempting of confiscation. The nature of the inheritance system and the lack of a means for establishing the legal fiction of a permanent corporation also deflected funds away from the business of production.

The checks to the Ottoman military machine administered by the Europeans and Persians and the Arabs along the Red Sea had been translated into this unedifying scramble for pickings at home. The populace had no legal shield. A policy of despoilment has the merit in the eyes of its initiators of maintaining the existing structure of power. Civilian and military officers of the state were thus bought off, that is as a class, for no individual was ever safe. Despoilment, the Ghazi approach to political economy (the Ghazis were Muslim border raiders) as it has been called, appealed to Ottoman leaders, its philosophy being a nice, direct, 'take the wealth of thy neighbour' (Kortepeter 1973:242). Despoilment was almost automatically resorted to when military stalemate placed its iron grip on the revenues of the state. As a solution it was flawed because the internal struggle it generated caused the management of the state to crumble. There was absolutely no equivalent to the procedure whereby European sovereigns secured their position by offering the service of justice, and very little else in the way of overhead services was offered by the Ottoman state. The decline which overtook that state only widened the technological and military gap between it and Europe. Although Napoleon's incursion into Ottoman lands was a failure, European nations were soon afterwards able to enlarge their trading concessions into outright colonialism.

Out of evil shall come forth good. There was after all one bright spot emerging out of the most unpropitious circumstances in the subject Christian lands of the Ottoman Balkans: an export trade to Europe grew up. This was a trade first of all in maize, which had been adopted as a crop in the sixteenth century, earlier than it was taken up in Italy; and in cotton. European demand for maize and cotton provided an incentive to violate the rights of the Christian peasants, seize control of their land, and oblige them to grow these crops for export. The peasants themselves lived chiefly on sorghum, except in the free mountain villages. To manage the export trade there arose a class of Christian merchants, artisans, mariners and shipowners. This class was the eventual source of opposition to Turkish rule, especially in Greece which was coming to have a degree of *de facto* self-government. Perhaps there are echoes of Britain's American colonies. Native-owned merchant fleets were growing in size, especially as wars between France and Britain ruined western merchants based in Balkan ports. The Greek and Macedonian merchants who controlled much of the trade overland up the valley of the Danube into central Europe, a trade that opened up after the Treaty of Carlowitz, also grew rich. They largely avoided despoilment by the Turks.

These merchants began to make industrial investments, carefully selecting isolated mountain districts where artisans could work with a minimum of Turkish interference. Village artisans in Greece and Bulgaria turned out substantial quantities of textiles. Their regional and occupational specialisation depended on someone else supplying food, that is to say, on a rise in farm output in the lower districts where the demands of the state and the *chiflik* owners were forcing up output. The beginnings of the typical late preindustrial pattern of bifurcation into rural domestic industrial districts and cereal-growing districts (Jones 1974a) can be seen here. The increase in cereal output in the lowland maize districts may indeed have driven upland villages out of the grain market and led them to switch into rural domestic industry. Industrial production did not reach European levels but it did grow sharply during the eighteenth century. Despite the active opposition of western consuls a proportion of the manufactures was exported to Central Europe. By 1800 one of the protoindustrial villages, Ambelakia on the slopes of Ossa in eastern Thessaly, was described as 'rather a borough of Holland than a village of Turkey' (Zakythinos 1976:61). This development included at least one large joint-stock textile and dyeing co-operative noted for the honesty of its management, which had been set up in Ambelakia in 1780. The genesis of so much industry and trade was all the more remarkable in that the country was milked not only by Turkish exactions but by forced levies on the part of 'local notables' employed by the Turkish administration to guard bridges and passes against the outlaws.

The sources of this strong response to western demand are not clear. Zakythinos (1976:111), admitting this, attributes the eighteenth-century cultivation of farmland which had lain abandoned a century before to growth in the subject population and a decline in the local Muslim population. This reflected some weakness in the Ottoman system, which obliged the régime to rely on locally recruited Christian administrators. At any rate the developments in the Balkans left Turkey and the Near East aside. The population of the empire fell from a peak of 28,000,000 in 1600 to 24,000,000 in 1800 as a result of real contraction as well as the breakaway of provinces in the Maghreb and south-eastern Europe. That was a fourteen per cent fall. Greece and Bulgaria on the other hand showed a fifty-five per cent rise over the same period. They were the only expanding pocket within the collapsing dirigible of the Ottoman empire.

Chapter 10

India and the Mughal Empire

I estimate the various administrations strictly from the economist's standpoint, and the conclusions I have reached are sufficiently unfavourable to suggest that the India of the seventeenth century must have been an Inferno for the ordinary man

W. H. Moreland

THE ECONOMY OF INDIA was based on village agriculture. The history of the sub-continent was a fluctuating and unsettled one, yet it has been said (by M. Elphinstone, quoted by Day 1949:120) that 'among all these changes townships remained entire, and are indestructible atoms, from an aggregate of which the most extensive Indian Empires are composed'. In India, according to Cobban (1944:125), 'all that unites China – language, race, common civilisation, tradition of political unity – is absent'. What held this society of atomised townships together was a curiously frozen religious stratification which firmly assigned everyone his place and function. The question that first concerns us here is whether or not the underlying Indian situation prevented development, independently of any particular failings of the Mughal régime which lasted from the sixteenth to the eighteenth century.

Much potential dispute was resolved in India before it could occur, by the prior dispositions of the caste system. Whilst this was more fluid than formal descriptions of it imply, over any single lifetime it cannot have seemed anything but immobile. Caste prescribed occupation and sumptuary rights, the highest castes escaping altogether from involvement with the grime of production. We are not required to enter into an hypothetical discussion about values to see in this the makings of great rigidity in the labour market. Where values clearly had an impact was with Hindu taboos on killing rodents and insects. This must be taken seriously given modern estimates that up to one-third of the crops are lost in store. Hindu distaste for touching refuse or excreta conduced to insanitary conditions and may have helped to maintain the reservoir of bubonic plague. While this may have been functional for the individual in the short run, the taboo was dysfunctional for society.

These arrangements meant, firstly, that the social setting was deleterious, and second that resources were employed in such a way as to produce a lower output than more instrumental combinations of factors might have achieved. Rates of return were kept low and at any given level of savings the incentive to invest, and accordingly the rate of growth, would be driven down (Farb 1978; Morris 1967; Maddison 1971). Consider the individual and social consequences of such prohibitions as that an untouchable might not build himself a brick house. There were endless, rigid restrictions of that sort, applying caste by caste and not simply to the worst-off at the untouchable bottom of the heap. The result of this immensely complicated anthropological pattern was to push the living-standards of the lowest caste to a level that presumably reduced the capacity to work; allocate functions on a basis of heredity, not aptitude; instil ritualistic attitudes to work; restrict the market through caste-defined sumptuary rules; and divide the community and reduce the chances of mutual evasion or resistance to exploitation by affording the Brahmins a privileged position within each village. The caste system might be said to have provided job security and a form of insurance, but the price was high. Tensions in society may be reduced by labelling whole categories of people, in the view of other categories, unpersons. Maybe this is even adaptive in the short run. But accepted for ever, this inserting of an artificial 'individual distance' between persons suppressed social interaction and competition that in the European case, at any rate, has proved energising. And in addition to the developmental liabilities of the caste system, the Indian joint family system was a disincentive to save or limit births because the individual could not be sure of keeping any gains to himself or his nearest kin.

Above the layer of 'indestructible atoms' of village India was a mesh of political units that returned persistently over very long periods. Maps of these 'nuclear areas' appear in Day (1949) and

Spate and Learmonth (1967). Among the political boundaries was a primary division between north and south India, with a belt of uncertain territory between. The art of Indian strategy was to gain control of this middle region and then to unite the Indo-Gangetic Plains with the lowlands of southern India, the Cauvery Plains, and the trading ports of the south. The full game was won only three times in history, with the unifications by Asoka in the third century B.C., Akbar and the Mughals in the sixteenth century A.D., and the British in the eighteenth century. Unity was hard to maintain. Asoka's Buddhist empire split into two on his death, and subdivision quickly followed. 'It may be that a kind of geographical-political "fault" or fracture was already appearing between the Indus system of the north-west and the Gangetic system of the Middle Land' (Tinker 1966:15). The Mughal empire was ruptured by the deep division between north and south India.

Indian history was dominated on one side by vulnerability to invasion through the North-West passes and on the other by the almost impossible task of holding the sub-continent together. Seven cities were built and abandoned in the Doab cockpit between Aryan times and the establishment of British New Delhi. The country seemed to fly asunder at the touch. Contemporary communications and military technology made it difficult to command or retain the loyalty of the nuclear areas. These areas were separated by wide belts of desert, hills or jungle which were militarily difficult to subdue and the interposition of which made it hard to control one nuclear area from the next. Further, the major northern and southern regions formed two poles around one of which a power grouping would tend to form to oppose any grouping around the other.

The matrix of nuclear areas and natural barriers smacks of Europe, especially as the same political divisions recur throughout history. As in Europe, it was clearly costly to try to rule the sub-continent as a single empire. But why, given the makings of a similar set of competing polities, did no states system emerge? The vessels were there but the brew of history was not poured into them. The significance of the framework of nuclear areas is however perhaps reduced by the observation that the Hindu Maratha 'nation' of South India, which was the direct cause of the bankruptcy of the Mughal empire (based in the north), was carved out of the 'badlands' of the Deccan (Wolpert 1965:61–3). The Marathas were not based on a productive nuclear area at all; perhaps we may guess that the zones between the nuclear areas were broad enough to provide better bases for rebels than in Europe. The outcome at any rate was that India remained a congeries of states, sometimes strongly governed, mostly exploitative, and never stable for long enough to encourage purposive government, productive investment, or sustained technological progress.

'India presents a paradox to the student in the sharp contrast between the strength of its social structure, and the fluidity of its political and international systems' (Modelski 1964:559). Modelski's explanation is that the caste system and Brahmin power required and ensured the powerlessness of petty kingdoms. Brahmin priests had the upper hand over princes since it was an immemorially accepted necessity to obtain religious sanction for all acts. But the agency of the Brahmins in this respect was bought at the price of political instability, where princely co-operation was impeded by their various, independent religious advisors. Whether the advice was malicious or random is not clear. A little of both would have a destabilising effect. This explanation is not totally convincing and a similar explanation has been criticised by Rodinson (1978:208) on the grounds that even religiously and politically congruent societies have remained divided for long spells, with presumably the corollary that congruence neither guarantees nor forbids economic development. Nevertheless, while a lack of political and religious congruence may not have been the one fatal flaw, the instability engendered by the lack was probably harmful to investment. The fact remains that an explanation is needed for the failure to build on what Tinker (1966:34) describes as an almost perfect 'natural' set of national and international frontiers.

What distinguished India from early modern Europe and China, in Morris's (1967:594) view, was the degree of political and economic fragmentation and the extraordinarily poor interregional communications. This may reflect the width and difficulty of the terrain between nuclear areas, as well as a paucity of navigable rivers. What needs to be resolved is what we may call

Tinker's paradox: the failure of 'natural' regionalism to house stable states; and what by the same token we may call Thapur's (1966:238) puzzle, which is the failure of Indian rulers to combine for the defence of the North-West passes and to build fortifications across them. Compared with the open frontiers of northern China they were faced with an easy task, for it would not have taken a Great Wall to block the passes. The omission was in the sphere of political creativity. The conclusion seems to be that the structure of Indian society militated against political stability, and the lack of political stability militated against development. In these circumstances the order that the Mughal invaders at first imposed might have been a blessing, but as we shall see the Mughals soon became nearly as oppressive as the Ottomans and their empire quickly broke down.

Mughal India's large scale; the fine workmanship of its handicrafts; its traders exporting luxury goods; its banking system capable of transferring funds across the sub-continent; its glittering, and in the early days brilliant, cosmopolitan and religiously tolerant court; none of these facts can disguise a dismal economic record. Mughal India was run by, and strictly on behalf of, an imposed alien régime and those native princes it was inexpedient to unseat. These men luxuriated in castles and water-gardens, harems, retinues of slaves and servants, Aladdin's caves full of jewels, magnificent wardrobes, vast menageries, warfare as a sport, and absolute uninvolvement with production. An oppressed peasantry did all the work.

The Mughal conquerors left intact cellular village India. They milked this society while remaining a distinct and fundamentally parasitic warlord class throughout their sway from the sixteenth to the eighteenth centuries. A letter to Colbert from a physician, Bernier, who lived in India for twelve years at the court of the emperor Aurangzeb (1659–1707), indicates the extent of the insecurity such a régime could create. Aurangzeb went out of his way to suppress original thought as determinedly as any Ottoman sultan, he razed the temples and sucked the tax system dry. The outcome, according to Bernier, was that the owners of property declined so much as to clean their ditches or repair their houses for fear of confiscation.

Later writers agree on the voluptuous selfishness and conspicuous waste of both Mughals and native princes. 'When the maharajah yawned', it is reported of a Gaekwar of Baroda (Lord 1972:138), 'all present must snap their fingers to discourage flies.' This was one of the milder examples of egoism – absolute power corrupted these men absolutely. The gulf between rich and poor was virtually unbridgeable. Thus Francisco Pelsaert wrote of his seven years in Agra in the 1620s, 'the rich in their great super-fluity and absolute power, and the utter subjection and poverty of the common people' (Maddison 1971:18). Moreland (1972:302–3 n.1) made some calculations of the proportion of the 'take' by the classes he termed 'parasites' and policemen. Given the estimated size of this class, he stated, each producer would have had to have handed over one-sixth of his income for there to have been income equality. Under the revenue system of the emperor Sha-jehan he surrendered in reality one-half. The average income of each parasite or policeman was accordingly five times that of a producer. But since most parasites in fact lived no better than the peasants, a very large proportion of total income was being shared among a tiny élite of non-producers. The assumption seems to be that there were sixteen or seventeen per cent non-producers in the population. At the 1911 census, Moreland thought the proportion was ten per cent.

The peasants were left in destitution by taxes which were collected whatever the state of the harvest. They received no real help in the face of natural disasters, and these were frequent (there was for example a great run of famines between 1540 and 1670 when the empire was at peace). No written legal code existed, no machinery to harmonise orders which might be issued by the ruler one day and countermanded the next. Whether the ruler did effectively rule depended mainly on his character. If he did not, power slid into the hands of officials, and there were no constitutional checks on their rapaciousness. The system was also unstable because there were conflicts over suc-cession, terminally as far as the empire was concerned when Aurangzeb's sons fought at his death in 1707, and again in 1712 on the death of the winner, Bahadur Shah, when his sons too engaged in what *The Oxford History of India* (Smith 1958:433) calls 'the customary war of succession'. When the empire was break-ing apart the capital saw incessant intrigues and treasons which

The Oxford History calls 'unworthy of record or remembrance'. Individually the events may be as unenlightening as they were unedifying. Collectively they denote a total lack of political inspiration, without even stable collusion to plunder the peasantry. Levels of risk were forced up to the skies. Unbridled oppression impoverished the peasants and led to financial ruin for the state. Moreland's (1972) judgement is that according to the evidence of travellers and merchants of many nationalities, the Mughal empire of the seventeenth century was on about the level of Persia or Japan, though well above the appalling straits to which Turkish rule had brought the Ottoman dominions or the situation in some poverty-stricken parts of south-east Asia. Maddison (1971) suggests that at its peak, income *per capita* was equivalent to that in Elizabethan England. By the mid-eighteenth century India's *per capita* income had fallen and may have been only two-thirds that of England. Life expectancy was lower than in Europe and health was poorer, because of a worse diet, debilitating climate, and a disease environment of tropical as well as temperate zone pestilences. Educational provision was not good and the content resembled that of medieval rather than post-Renaissance Europe.

In Maddison's (1971) view the total tax revenue of the state was from fifteen to eighteen per cent of national income, largely collected as a land tax. This is not directly comparable with estimates for Europe as it was used not only for state expenditures, such as they were, but also for consumption by the ruling class, so that it partly represents rental income. Taxation fulfilled nothing like the functions emerging at this period in the service states of Europe. Next to nothing was spent in India on providing an infrastructure. Most taxation was devoted to supporting the élite. The Mughal rulers drew great incomes from state monopolies which extended to grain. Monopolies were also farmed out. Taxation was known as 'eating', as indeed it was in Sri Lanka and Burma. Governors were 'eaters of provinces'. The ruler's contribution to society was thought of as defence and the maintenance of public order, though to put it that way at all invokes an inappropriately Rousseauian notion of a social contract. The maintenance of order was in any case much to the ruler's own advantage. Both parties to any dispute also paid the ruler for adjudicating, the one a penalty, the other a 'present'. The Punjabi proverb was therefore apposite: never stand behind a horse or before an official. Small wonder the peasantry steered as clear of the state as they could, living in an autonomous world regulated by custom and nature, in contact with government only through the taxes they paid. A few public irrigation works were undertaken, but they probably affected at most five per cent of the cultivated area. By the time the British took over, most of the irrigation projects, some of them ancient, had fallen into decay (Davis 1951:40). Apart from the 'Persian wheel' which apparently came in at this period as a means of lifting vessels of water on a chain, using ox or camel power, technology was almost stagnant. Nothing else was copied from abroad.

Agriculture was less productive than in the other great Asian system, China, despite the ability to double-crop if the rains came. The average yield was lower. A much smaller proportion of the land was irrigated. A larger proportion of the total area was however under cultivation (the modern figures are fifty per cent compared with eleven per cent in China) and this meant that in many densely settled regions there was no land to spare for pasture. Draught cattle had to survive by scavenging since cereals could not normally be spared for them (Harris 1978:168–9). Horses were an imported luxury since the scarcity of pasture and the hot climate made breeding and rearing them difficult.

The economy was more varied but no more efficient than this brief résumé may suggest. There was for instance an active class of traders. There was a shipbuilding industry, and exports were carried long distances. Aliens who engaged in trade were however present on sufferance, protected only by custom, not law. The trade was in any case mostly in luxuries, with little traffic in staples like food grains. Poor communications split India into a large number of nearly separate markets and competition between them was prohibited by the high cost of land carriage. The navigable rivers were inadequate and coastal shipping linked only the peripheral regions together, and that only when war and piracy permitted. Trade did not produce great towns, for these were on the whole court and administrative centres, though Agra may have had 500,000–600,000 inhabitants in the seventeenth century and the urban proportion of the population may conceivably have been as high as ten per cent. The towns were 'subsidised' according to Moreland (1972:304), in that peasant farmers were obliged by tax demands to sell much of their crop post-haste after harvest, and had to take low prices from merchants who had coin in hand. If this was so, the size of the urban sector does not reflect its true economic contribution.

Manufacturing in the towns, that is handicraft production, was organised in hereditary gilds. Trading castes stood in the way of artisans who might have wished to move into a merchant rôle. The merchants themselves were equally restricted, for sumptuary rules prevented them from building great town houses or acquiring land, and there was no hope of their acquiring political influence as a class. Banking and money-lending enterprises did exist, with surprising mutual trust across distances and the skilled manipulation of a complicated money market involving many coinages. But this only reveals that financial speculation might prosper. Bankers, like merchants, could not acquire political influence and no systematic pressure could be brought to bear for the improvement of the conditions of distribution and exchange.

The market was depressed because such middle class as there was sought to conceal its wealth from official eyes. Escape from impoverishment 'was barred effectively by the administrative methods . . . which . . . regarded every indication of increased consumption as a signal for fresh extortion' (Moreland 1972:305). Had the Mughal régime persisted, capital formation might actually have become negative. Maddison (1971) concludes that it did fall almost to nothing. A nobility that was not a true landowning class had no incentive not to squeeze the peasantry down to subsistence levels, consume as much as possible, and die in debt. Mughal policy was to prevent the aristocracy from becoming hereditary. Nobles were allocated a collection of villages, called a *jagir*, from which to raise incomes for themselves and revenue for the central treasury or the support of troops. The nobles were posted from one *jagir* to another and their estates were liable to royal forfeit at their death, though when central control was waning towards the end of Mughal times some of them did succeed in bequeathing their land. There were also Hindu notables who retained hereditary control over their villages, and a surprising number of Hindu princes with autonomous states encapsulated within the Mughal empire. Like the *jagirdars* none of them engaged in production. Their comfortable, if subordinate, survival probably reflected a lack of administrative personnel in the régime. The Mughals may have thought the political costs of taking over administration at all levels were beyond them, and assured themselves instead of overall control. The practice of the Hindu princes was to amass their own wealth and leave untouched their predecessor's hoard of precious metals and jewels. In this way they accounted for much of the output of mining and much of the proceeds of the country's export trade. Hoarding was an understandable feature of the economic behaviour of all groups; it was an attribute of risk aversion. We should add that the population did rise over much of the Mughal period, though stagnating or falling in the years of decline. Once again, biomass success was not income success. In Tinker's (1966:46) words, Mughal rule enlarged rather than developed Indian economic life.

An interesting question is whether the system contained similar seeds of disintegration to those in the Ottoman empire. The immediate cause of Mughal breakdown was the excessive cost of futile warfare in Afghanistan and Aurangzeb's twenty-five years of inconclusive effort at quelling Maratha rebellion. War of that scale and duration broke the revenue administration and the Marathas 'pricked the bubble'. There were no stabilising institutions or popular support. A zealotry unlike Asia's usual religious toleration had alienated the Hindus. A régime organised to encourage the producer might just have managed. As it was, 'the student who has acquired even a moderately sound knowledge of the history will be surprised that the empire lasted so long rather than because it collapsed suddenly' (Smith 1958:442). Hindu power waxed after Aurangzeb's death in 1707. The Marathas spilled north; but each of their generals founded a kingdom for himself, true to tradition. Beneath the barrenness of that solution lies the original Indian compromise with social strife, whereby religious acceptance was purchased at the price of a form of mutual apartheid and a fragmentation of political will.

Chapter 11

China and the Ming and Manchu Empires

Europe had some of the most Bureaucratic stations in the world! and imagery

> We have only to compare western/society with China's bureaucratic society to appreciate fully the 'miracle' that occurred in Europe during the sixteenth and seventeenth centuries. The concatenation of circumstances that brought capitalism to birth there and thus set in motion the industrialization of the entire world has all the appearance – when seen in this light – of being a freak of fortune, one of history's privileged occasions, in this case granted solely to that tiny promontory of Asia, Europe
>
> Etienne Balazs

CHINA'S UNIQUENESS lay in retaining an empire and a culture for an immense span of time. The remarkable longevity of the system was symbolised by the presence in Taiwan at least as late as 1970 of the representative of the seventy-seventh generation of the K'ung family, holder of a ducal title conferred on an ancestor by the Sung dynasty emperor Jen Tsung in the fifth century B.C. This is said, credibly enough, to be an unbeatable record for genuine aristocracy anywhere in the world (Stover 1974:229).

Yet an emphasis on the unchanging aspects of the system may unduly stress its monolithic elements. By the fourteenth century A.D. China had indeed achieved such a burst of technological and economic progress as to render suspect the frequently expressed belief that industrialisation was an improbable historical process (cf. Graham 1973; Cipolla 1967:101–2). The developments included a water-powered hemp-spinning machine as advanced as anything in Europe until about 1700. The total Chinese output of iron as far back as the close of the eleventh century A.D. was impressive too, the peak of 150,000 tons being approximately the same as the entire production of Europe in 1700 (Harrison 1972:290). On a *per capita* basis the advantage was six to five in China's favour, leaving aside a five-century advantage in timing. We are so accustomed to thinking that great oaks must from little acorns grow where technology is concerned – European experience demands it – that the occurrence of industrial change on this scale, followed by a retreat, seems a great puzzle (cf. Hartwell 1966; Elvin 1973). The Ming dynasty (1368–1644) was however hostile to mechanical contrivances and actually demolished the astronomical clock that had been built in 1090. The Jesuit Matteo Ricci found little in 1600 to show that there had ever been mechanical clocks in China (Gimpel 1977:152). The Ming shifted Chinese energies back to agrarianism for reasons of state, away from technology and industry, and after initially expanding their navy, they even allowed that to decay, retreated from the sea and became inward-looking (Eberhard 1960:342, note for 250; Filesi 1972:32–3, 69, 71).

We ought not after all to be in the business of accounting for the endurance of a stationary economic system in China, nor for the absence of an 'industrial revolution'. This has often been the aim of historians of China, notably Wittfogel (1957). Certainly some institutional elements were static for long periods; there were big demographic upturns unaccompanied by or not even alternating with detectable movements of *per capita* income; but there was, too, an early development of science and technology, and big improvement in the methods of making iron and textiles, from which however China backed away.

This phenomenon of backing away was even more noticeable in the sphere of maritime exploration. In early historic times Chinese trade with distant East Africa had been quite sizeable; after all, a large empire was better able to mobilise a fleet than, say, little Portugal. But the imports were not of productive significance (they included rhinoceros horn, ivory and pearls), the exports (e.g. porcelain) were insufficient to stimulate the mechanisation of industry, and the Chinese travelled only as navigators and itinerant merchants. Even the great eunuch admiral of the early fifteenth century, Cheng Ho, only 'went a-shopping for the ladies of the Imperial harem' (Duyvendak quoted by Filesi 1972:34). The structure of official China and the luxury nature of its demands muffled the impact that trade might otherwise have made. Nevertheless, seven armadas of junks, as many as sixty-two vessels carrying 37,000 soldiers, sailed as far as Kamchatka and Zanzibar between 1405 and 1430, visiting over twenty countries. Envoys even went to Mecca. Cheng Ho claimed to have brought distant lands under China's sway, receiving tribute on behalf of the emperor and dealing summarily with unwelcoming 'barbarian kings'. The kings of Ceylon and Palembang in southern Sumatra were captured and brought back, and curiosities were collected, including a giraffe from East Africa.

But the ability of China to do these things – what has been called the 'factual history' of her techniques – is beside the point. After 1430 there was an 'inexplicable withdrawal'. The reasons for this may have included a move to prevent the eunuch faction from establishing a power base. The emperor Yung-lo who had launched the great fleets had died. The terms of trade had turned against China. Yung-lo had found the imported goods, the so-called tribute (horses, copper, timber, hides, drugs, spices, gold, silver, even rice), to be well worth acquiring. He had sent in return, besides a certain quantity of silk, ceramics and tea, goods which were of more prestige than intrinsic value, although even so he may have thought the 'tribute' from East Africa unpromising, for that land had been in the grip of a severe drought when it was visited. The Ming government was in any case in financial and military difficulties. China suffered a defeat in 1428 in Annam, the name ironically meaning the Pacified South, and quit in a cloud of platitudes. The resultant fall in her international prestige would have obliged her to supply her missions abroad with goods of real value in return for 'tribute', and on those terms distant voyaging was not worth the candle.

In addition, private trade was growing and this may have persuaded the court to leave the field clear, though before long all maritime trade was declared illegal. There was a strange reason for this. Japan, which was not yet centralised, had sent several missions to China, that is to say, individual *daimyos* (lords) had done so, each believing that he was sending a trade mission. The ideology of the Chinese required them to accept only one such mission as the official one. Thus one was chosen and the others sent back. The disappointed missions promptly turned to smuggling, piracy and the bribery of Chinese merchants, so as not to have to return empty-handed to their masters. It was to quell the resultant disturbances that the Ming banned all trade by

sea. The subsequent reign of the Manchus (1644–1911) adopted a
similar policy of 'coastal defence, but no battles at sea'. In order to
deprive the Formosan pirate, Koxinga, of supplies the Manchu
cleared off the populace and burned the villages of a strip from
eight to thirty miles deep all along the coasts of Kwangtung,
Fukien and Chekiang, a distance of over 700 miles. Merchants no
longer dared to build large vessels for fear of being thought to
engage in distant trade. Mooted conquest and settlement in the
Philippines was abandoned, and as for more distant barbarian
lands, even emperors found that they could at a pinch make do
without ostriches and giraffes (Purcell 1965:24; Fitzgerald
1972:106–12).

The resumption of voyages was proposed in 1480, but was
promptly quashed. This was simply an episode in a perpetual
tussle between the eunuchs and their enemies. The President
and Vice-President of the War Office connived at destroying the
records of previous voyages in order to frustrate the plans of the
eunuch Inspector of the Frontiers, who wished to see them in
connection with a projected expedition to Annam. By 1553 it was
admitted that the art of building large ships had been forgotten.
The arguments advanced by the anti-maritime faction were that
the expeditions were a costly titillation of the desire of court
women for curios and that according to Confucian ideals the very
fact of trade demeaned the emperor. There was some truth in
both of these points. The variant of Confucianism actually
adopted by the Ming did reinforce an empty cultural superiority
(Filesi 1972:69) and seemed to justify the self-engrossment of the
Celestial empire. On the other hand it is certain that the ships
used were not expensive in terms of China's budget, though this
was alleged too.

An important difference from the situation in Europe was that
China was so organised as to permit a dispute which must be
judged trivial in the context of world history to determine the
course of events. Independent bases of power and alternative
states which might have made a different decision did not exist;
yet, as we shall see, this form of centralism does not allow us to
speak of China as a command economy. Another difference was
that China was able to undertake internal colonisation on a scale
not open to Europe. As rice cultivation shifted south to new land,

and when dryland crops from the Americas were introduced by
the Portuguese in the sixteenth century, the Chinese land-base
was revalued upwards and the incentive to seek overseas
territory actually fell.

Collusion rather than dictatorial centralism was the mark of the
Chinese system. The imperial government, like the Ottomans or
the Mughals, left many administrative matters to local gentry
officials. At the detailed level administration was in fact substantially carried out by default. The villages were self-policing, thus
harnessing the energy of peasant envy and suspicion. Feats of
flood control and irrigation were usually government-by-crisis.
The empire was an Asian revenue pump concealed by a mask of
solidarity and any notion of an implicit social contract in which
services of material consequence were supplied by the emperor
in return for his share of the national product is spurious. We
shall have to examine this curious collusive rule and try to find a
reason for its unlikely persistence and success, since the less we
find ourselves dealing with an oriental despotism of the kind
envisaged by Wittfogel (1957), the more baseless the survival of
the empire seems to be.

'The secular officials were hierophants in a political order so
undergoverned by Western standards that it bears closer comparison with the Catholic Church than with the government of
the Roman empire, of which the church was a vestige after the
fall' (Stover and Stover 1976:135, 186). The Stovers add that
'western observers have insisted on seeing in the Chinese imperial polity some version of substantive administration familiar
to them in their own national governments, not believing that
power persons could shape a political realm of continental scope
out of materials as unpromising as religion and high culture'.
Culturalism prescribed codes of behaviour (and correct 'presents')
for all occasions. Protests against imperial authority were unthinkable, yet unlike European (or Japanese) rulers, the emperor
actually possessed few substantive rights to bargain away (Jacobs
1958:104). No private sector could hope to expand as the result of
the tax-bargaining envisaged by North and Thomas (1973) as its
source in Europe, where monarchs distributed rights to trade in
return for guarantees of revenue.

The Chinese system entangled society in a ball of string more than it hammered with a mailed fist. This may not have been how things seemed to individuals entrapped by the emperor's whim, like the poets under the Ming emperor Hung-wu who dared make no reference to natural calamity for fear he would take it as a hint at his tyranny, or his officials who took the precaution each morning before setting out for the court audience of bidding their families a final farewell (Dawson 1972:240). Any individual official or merchant might find himself brought low. Ch'ien Lung's favourite minister, Ho Shen, came to be worth $U.S. 1,500 million (in dollars of the early 1950s), but the next emperor drove him to his death (Murphey 1954:357). On the other hand it was beyond any emperor's power to humble the entire scholar-gentry class. Emperor and élite were bound together by mutual need. Neither was there a totalitarian apparatus capable of controlling the everyday life of the peasants or town dwellers, who were exploited and neglected but not systematically repressed (Moore 1967:173). Quite capable of overawing the populace, putting down local revolts, and torturing, executing or hounding its own officials to their deaths, the system proved weak when faced with a major challenge. 'Dear Mother, don't trouble yourself about me, for I am no more in danger than if I were practising against an old tea-caddy', wrote a British midshipman from China in 1855 (Hibbert 1970:212).

Apart from defence against inner Asia, the emperor kept an army primarily to protect his own interests, such as defending the Grand Canal which was his by monopoly right, the route by which his assigned tribute grain reached the court of Peking. He did not militarily dominate the whole empire. For that reason he may have had less need for a military budget than European monarchs and it has been suggested (Murphey 1954:358) that he did not need the merchant class to finance his ambitions and needed therefore to make no concessions to them. This does definitely offer a contrast with the Europe of North and Thomas (1973). The central government spent a high proportion of its budget on military force, but its total budget was not large. At the end of the nineteenth century it was only one or two per cent of G.N.P. (Perkins 1967:487). Since its expenditures on military, court and civil ends were in the ratios of 25:7:1 (Stover and Stover 1976:113), the trivial volume of investment in an infrastructure is at once apparent, i.e. 0.03 per cent to 0.06 per cent of G.N.P. The imperial purse was not deep enough for the running of a service state, even had such an outlandish notion occurred to the emperor. Nor might he appeal for additional supply. That was not in the nature of the implicit bargain with the élite, that form of social contract for the upper crust. 'The executive government must adapt its wants to the ordinary supplies, instead of calling on the people for extraordinary contributions', noted Barrow in 1805 (quoted by Stover and Stover 1976:90–1).

Remote from the conception of a colossus of hydraulic despotism envisaged by Wittfogel, most of the irrigation schemes were put in on a modest scale under the managerial supervision of local gentry, for peasant clients. Some such work was administered from Peking, to produce further tribute for the Imperial granary, but in the ordinary course of events the bureaucrats had no service function. They were there to supervise the appointment of officials who were to pass up some of the 'take' to the emperor. Officials were not paid, for office was an emolument.

That the central government made little display of force against the Chinese population (as opposed to pre-Chinese tribesmen or foreigners) is partly evidence that the élite found congenial a system that allocated among them rights to make money from the peasants. In Stover's metaphor, they were allocated hunting-licences subject only to a bag limit and a fee. Acquiescence and self-interest were wedded. The aura of legitimation by a state politico-religious authority no doubt seemed to take on a life of its own, but of the basis of the arrangement in a tacit sharing of the agricultural surplus there is little doubt. The system was accepted from early times. There was only token resistance to the destruction by emperors of large Buddhist monasteries, the confiscation of their wealth and freeing of their slaves (to become peasant taxpayers), on several occasions between the fifth and tenth centuries A.D. (Jacobs 1958:187). Secular compliance on these occasions must have been passably like that surrounding the Dissolution of the Monasteries in England.

The system of culturalism therefore replaced the service of adjudication between contesting nobles supplied by the monarchs of Europe. The emperor lacked the footing for such a service. He may have been immensely elevated as a being, but once he had issued a hunting-licence to a provincial governor, and received his 'present', that, for most important purposes, was that. His rôle was liturgical, providing the ceremonial that the élite had been conditioned to expect and which in their eyes legitimated the system. His function was as broker. A rather small percentage of tax revenue (not of course a negligible absolute income) was pumped up through the system to the throne of Heaven. The Ming dynasty certainly failed to penetrate fully into rural areas with their tax administration and under weak emperors the local gentry were able to siphon off funds intended for Peking (Dawson 1972:287). Indeed, a 'squeeze' at every stage of the taxation process was the objective basis of élite support for the imperial system (Moore 1967:172–3). Down to the scholar-gentry came the licences and the obligations of prostrating themselves before Imperial messages (symbolising the dominance relationship and signifying assent to the percentages), of forwarding candidates for examination, and the duty of setting a moral example to the peasants, which last the élite considered to be a valuable contribution on their part.

For the populace the bargain was a poor one. The Chinese paid 24 per cent of G.N.P. to two per cent of their number in return for defence and the co-ordination of irrigation and flood control. No other important services were provided, no civil policing for instance. Villages had to keep their own watch. Where the population was dense there was an exodus of people, including children, from the villages at dusk to guard the crops, just as the workforce had to pour forth again in the morning. Heads of sorghum and millet in particular are all too easily snipped off. Since a holding in the open fields might be in several pieces on different sides of the village, surveillance could only be maintained by forming 'Societies for Watching the Crops'. The cost of guards was rated in proportion to each family's holding. Contiguous villages might meet to make similar arrangements, all this institutional effort having to be provided by the peasants themselves (Sorokin *et al*. 1931:158–9).

Power brought wealth. So it must, urges Stover (1974), because there was no diversity of interests in competition with one another and with the government for the returns that could have come from investing in (and trading between) a diversity of productive landscapes. Wealth of course derived from office and court sinecures in *ancien régime* Europe too, but there were more alternatives. Figures are not available for Europe but the scale of parasitism seems to shift when one comes to Chinese history. More than in India even, divisions within the peasantry sapped the will to resist. A peasant family's every move was apparent to its neighbours. Tiny income differentials denoted status and made the difference between a spartan comfort and sinking into the doomed fringe of the landless. More than in India the villages were the 'indestructible atoms'. The Chinese village landscape was peculiarly hard to modify. Between élite and peasantry lay the social equivalent of a geological unconformity. 'A village located within sight of the municipal walls of Peking is no less remote from the political activity of high culture than one a thousand miles away in a distant province' (Stover 1974:26).

Perkins (1969:174) is definite about the distribution of power: 'pre-modern economic forces favoured regional rather than centralised power in China . . . only conditions outside economics prevented a breakup'. Regional economic power actually grew over time and because it was distributed widely and evenly, the central government was not indispensable to the functioning of the economy. This is Oriental Despotism by default. Western observers saw wealth, ostentatious display, submission symbols like the kotow, big riverine works, hordes of subordinate workers. Who were they to be unimpressed? The scale dwarfed the European. The shrewdest observers, like Lord Macartney at the end of the eighteenth century, were impressed despite themselves; but Macartney could also see the technological backwardness, the gulf between rich and poor, and the precariousness of a system which feeble emperors might not be able to prevent from collapse (Fitzgerald 1972:87).

The spatial distribution of power is of some interest in trying to understand how such a system worked, and survived. Although China is described (Fairbank *et al.* 1973:9) as being broken into a chequerboard of distinct regions by two intersecting sets of parallel mountain chains, two running south-west to north-east and three running west to east, the interstitial units did not form the bases of separatist states. Chi's (1963) work seems to support this by identifying in China not a multiplicity of core-areas but four great 'key economic areas', two of which far outweighed the others. The two largest and most productive of these key areas, lying about the Hwang Ho and the Yangtze respectively, had been linked up by the Grand Canal. Once this link had been made, the joint area might be expected to have dominated the whole country, ensuring the hegemony of empire and closing off the possibility of multiple polities. This would seem the more plausible in that the landscape of irrigated rice is a made landscape. A complex of irrigation canals and ditches, tanks, drainage and flood-control channels, and transport canals had been constructed in chosen regions, 'at the expense of other regions for the purpose of maintaining or building up what may be called a *Key Economic Area*' (Chi 1963:1–2, 11 n.1) or what Wittfogel had earlier labelled 'economic-political kernel districts'. And if they could be built, they could be destroyed, as was shown in the earlier Disunity period of Chinese history. The persistence of the despotism (and geographical locus) of the first overall victor in a struggle seemed assured.

The location of key economic areas was thus more a matter of political choice and less a matter of innate fertility than it was in the case of Europe's core-areas, at least until the agricultural revolution revalued European soils in favour of less fertile, free-draining land. There were anthropogenic aspects of the European distribution – the re-sorting of fertility by grazing and folding so that churches tend to stand in 'made' patches of fertility and the edges of parishes are where names like the Starvealls and Hunger Downs of England are to be found – but these are trivial compared with the man-made aspects of an irrigation landscape in China. The two largest of the 'key economic areas' are far bigger than the core-areas of Europe. They suggest much less decentralisation, much more contrived political domination of the whole by the first few regions to be developed.

Yet, as Perkins (1969:175) observes, only if a region's taxable capacity had determined military strength would the key economic areas have dominated the whole. They did not do so. From the fourteenth century A.D. China was ruled from a capital in one of the poorest regions, Peking in Hopei. Peking was fed from outside, by tribute grain brought along the defended but vulnerable umbilical cord, the Grand Canal. To incorporate this anomaly, the concept of a 'key strategic area' has to be tacked on to Chi's model. Peking was located where it was because of the need for the imperial government to be close enough to direct defence against threats from the steppes and to control enough steppe grazing outside the Great Wall to feed the cavalry horses of its own army. The rice landscape was extremely undifferentiated. A drawback of the concentration on irrigated rice was that a regional division of labour, which in Europe encouraged bulk multi-lateral trade in utilitarian goods, did not blossom. Trade, other than tribute trade in rice, was not stimulated where regional producers were similar rather than complementary. The degree of self-sufficiency and the extent to which nutrition-based power was dispersed in China means that some other explanation than domination by a key region is needed to explain the survival of China as a single empire. We have found this explanation in culturalism. But it is still surprising that such a compact between emperor and élite should have lasted so long, especially since the emperor's power was not founded in a dominant regionalism. What really underlay the persistence of the system?

The population of China has always exceeded that of Europe at the corresponding date. Densities in the settled regions bear no comparison, since ninety-six per cent of the Chinese total is located in less than twenty-five per cent of the area. The difference in densities, like the imposing apparatus of empire, has however a great capacity to mislead. Many of the reports of intense over-crowding in China and the consequent deterioration of the habitat, which draw our attention from equally vital aspects of the system, refer either to the rice region, or to rather recent periods of history, or both. Thus Tawney (1932:27), in the 1920s, seeing grass cut with scissors to burn in the hearths, and never one to pen a dull phrase where an arresting one would do, wrote that 'the provision of warmth is the business, not of the miner, but of the agriculturist'. He drew attention to population so dense and land so scarce that the main source of fodder and hence of fertiliser had in fact to be sent up in smoke. No society, certainly none in preindustrial times, has been able to afford the mass, long-distance distribution of firewood. Relative to its heat efficiency and hence its price, wood is too bulky to carry far from navigable water. Fuel was so scarce that specialists sold hot water in the villages, Chinese houses were so cold that the poor wore heavily padded clothes and the rich fur-lined garments. The shortage of wood was such that the poor, and sometimes the rich, had no furniture. In the old settled areas, fuel wood, construction timber, fodder and fertiliser were alike acutely scarce because the land was settled so densely and had to be given over to rice production.

This would seem to be an incentive to migrate. China had a frontier history. The received version is that the northern border was far more influential on Chinese history than the movement into the south. Wyman and Kroeber (1965:96) argue that the frontier 'was generally fixed . . . it provided no land of opportunity for the masses'. This sole concern with external frontiers is in reality quite misleading. The hidden chapter of Chinese frontier history proves to be about the long movement into the Szechuan Basin and southern forests where, until they were cleared away and the wave rolled on, the Chinese were brought into contact with hostile natives and a strange flora and fauna (the forest is very like that of Georgia, U.S.A.). In what has been called one of mankind's greatest acts of ecological stupidity 670,000,000 acres were felled (Borgstrom 1972a:106). That was twenty-eight per cent of the land surface. Certainly it was an ecological one-way street, and the aftermath of the gains has been soil erosion, gullying, silting and floods. 'The hills and mountains of South China support fewer people in the twentieth century than they did in the first part of the nineteenth' and indeed after 1864 there was a rebound of population from the mountainside frontier into the valleys (Tuan 1970:144, and 168 quoting Ho). Yet for some centuries the movement had pressed on south, without however relieving the densities in the old rice region in any absolute sense. But if as a safety valve the movement seems weak, it is only necessary to contemplate what the densities would have had to become in the old settled areas without an internal frontier.

As Chinese colonists had spilled south, into the lands of the tribal, slash-and-burn agriculturists like the Miao of western Hunan, they had cut over the bottomlands and installed rice paddies, irrigation ditches and terraces. Whenever the Miao overran these areas – against the tide – they found they had regained a different landscape from the one they had lost. 'Like

Humpty-Dumpty the jungle wilderness cannot be put together again. So the Miao lived like Chinese on what they got back from the Chinese' (Stover 1974:74). The Ming dynasty used a system of military colonies called 'ying', state farms worked by soldiers, a device for occupying tribal or uninhabited areas which dated from the second century B.C. Formerly outlying areas of China are dotted with placenames ending in '-ying'. A steady stream of settlers from central China and the coast moved to Kwangtung and Hunan provinces in Ming times, causing innumerable clashes with the indigenous inhabitants but continuing again after each temporary setback. The merchants who carried grain from central China to the border garrisons invested their profits in land on the borders, and attracted farmers from their home areas to be their tenants (Dawson 1972:251; Eberhard 1960:248).

Chinese history is full of figures like the Ch'in governor who irrigated the Chengtu plain and made of it 'a sea on land' (Stover 1974:154). The metaphor catches the sunlight glinting back from the flooded paddies and leads on to the huge fisheries simultaneously formed. During the Tang dynasty (A.D. 618–904) four species of river fish had been added to carp as cultivated species. Fish ate the mosquito larvae and helped therefore to control malaria, not that the connection was understood, and this helped to render habitable large areas of southern China. Fish were applied to the rice as fertiliser and fish supplied the bulk of the non-vegetable protein in the diet (Tuan 1970:129; Eberhard 1960:249). Fish-farming made the limitations of marine fisheries more tolerable and helped in the revaluation of China's interior that irrigated rice farming was bringing about.

The high, forested lands in the south which could not be irrigated were brought into cultivation by American dryland crops introduced by the Portuguese. Wheat, barley and millet from north China also helped. Peanuts were being grown in the Canton district by 1516. Before 1700 they were still only a delicacy but thereafter they colonised light sands unsuited to rice. Sweet potatoes reached Yunnan in the 1560s, came in more widely during the mid-seventeenth century, and became truly widespread during the second half of the next century. The white potato reached Fukien before 1700. Maize arrived overland via India and the Burma–Yunnan route, as well as by sea, but diffused more slowly than the sweet potato and became widespread only after 1700. Then, in the eighteenth century, all these crops spread to sandlands and the formerly forested, thinly peopled highlands of south China (Tuan 1970:140). According to Stover and Stover (1976:115) they came to supply twenty per cent of total food production, though other authorities imply that the proportion was less.

Despite the accounts of overcrowding and the many famines in one province after another, the average food situation in China is reported to have been better than in Europe for the past millennium. Farming methods are regarded as advanced at an early date, an indication being the Chinese use of iron for ploughing while Europe still used wooden ploughs (Dawson 1972:280–1; Ho 1956–7; Tang 1979). There is something in this, though the history of erosion is not accorded its proper place and the real puzzle is why the Chinese went on using iron ploughs while Europe moved to steel. Rice remained the major crop, producing in the seventeenth century seventy per cent of total food output. Early-ripening varieties of rice underwrote the growth of population. Champa rice introduced from Indo-China was hardy and drought-resistant and ripened in three months instead of six or nine. This was improved to a two-month ripening period and in the eighteenth century to forty days. Early-ripening varieties needed less water than older strains and could be extended to higher ground, on terraces. The Persian wheel, brought in during the Ming period well before it was adopted in India, helped with the irrigation problem. In Ming times the early varieties were diffused from the Lower Yangtze area, where the improvements of the Sung period had taken place, throughout the rice region, especially to Hupei and Hunan to which the centre of gravity of rice production was shifting.

The cultivation of wet-rice made China, in Braudel's phrase (quoted by Chaunu 1979:286–8), 'an enormous open space' in terms of carrying capacity and labour requirement. In addition the dryland crops had 'the effect of expanding by millions of acres the Chinese definition of arable soil' (Stover and Stover 1976:114). This is an unexpected slant on the history of such a dense population. Maintaining the agricultural system, in the sense of keeping up *per capita* output, rested on the continual taking-in of fresh land (Perkins 1969:189). Given the growth of population, even maintenance was an achievement. The state encouraged reclamation by permitting the cultivator to become the legal owner once he had paid taxes on the land. After the middle of the eighteenth century, when reserves of suitable land began to run short, merchants were actually being encouraged to import foreign rice and official encouragement was given to the growing of maize and potatoes. By then China had produced in Hung Liang-chi her own Malthus, who believed that population growth must inevitably outstrip production (Elvin 1973:308). Investment however continued to go into extensions of the area under cultivation, by known techniques.

Signs of a grander expansion were by then evident. The Manchu invaded Tibet, Nepal (which had aided Tibetan insurrectionists in the mid- and late eighteenth century), and Burma. They also encouraged Chinese emigration to central Asia. Their control, admittedly sketchy at the edges, was extended from Korea to the Burma border and away again into the interior of Asia. In 1759 they organised conquered territories into the New Dominion, or Sinkiang, though this was sufficiently inhospitable to appear only a Chinese Siberia or New South Wales, fit only for transportees (Jackson 1968:45; Harrison 1972:345–7). Instead, and after centuries of looking inwards, as internal prospects for the Hakka Chinese of the south were dimming, migration began to cross the water. From the last years of the eighteenth century Chinese in some numbers were going by sea to settle in Thailand (Fitzgerald 1973:61).

Several movements had been compounded in the internal colonisation. Massive deforestation in north China during the sixteenth century led the Ming to decree against over-cutting in 1580 and forests grew up once more on the mountain-sides, only for the clearance to be repeated in Manchu times despite a prohibition on logging in 1683. The isolated wet-rice province of Szechuan gained through immigration in Ming times, but the gains were almost wiped out in big peasant uprisings of the second quarter of the seventeenth century and the province became the biggest recipient of immigrants between 1650 and 1850. Under the able emperor Ch'ien Lung (1736–95) emigration was encouraged from 'depressed regions' to areas like Szechuan,

Hopei, and Hunan (Harrison 1972:326, 333). Much of the southern highlands remained heavily wooded until the start of the eighteenth century. A fairly central area like south-western Hupei was still tribal in 1700. Thereafter wet-rice cultivation was introduced to the heavy soils of southern river valleys and lower slopes and Chinese arrived in large numbers. Heavy yields were at first obtained from maize and potatoes planted on the hillsides and by 1800 from white potatoes sown on the steeper mountain slopes. The price, as we have noted, was severe erosion and gullying. This was already evident by the third quarter of the eighteenth century on former forest land in the Yangtze highlands and in the tell-tale silting and flooding of the lower land (Tuan 1970:141–4; Dawson 1972:334).

Population pressure in the old settled areas was not absolutely lessened by the movement to the internal frontier, nor were average incomes raised. There was expansion, not growth. But there *was* expansion, in the sense of the replication of millions of tiny farms and the growth of the élite on the backs of the peasants. The prospects of colonisation were far beyond anything open to either the Ottoman or Mughal empires. The Chinese system survived. The immediate advantage to the élite was perhaps less the bidding up of rents through peasant competition for land than the multiplication of units from which rents might be extracted, and the multiplication of bureaucratic offices in the new provinces (cf. Moore 1967:168, 170). The suggestion has been made that Chinese migration was a push-out phenomenon, not a pull-out like transatlantic migration, and that it was no more than an alternative to the checks of disease and famine (Tang 1979:18–22). Given the physical productivity of Chinese farming and its absorption of new crops, and all the new land that was occupied, we might expect to see a growth of incomes. On the contrary, the growth was all demographic. The advantages of avoiding competition for resources within the élite are apparent, but why was the peasantry's choice what it was? Is it enough to say that the desire to perpetuate the family name overcame the drag on reproduction which phases of rising yield and income must sometimes have exerted (Tang 1979:18), if only in the biggest phases of entry to fresh soil? This standard-of-living effect may have been weak in premodern China, but so it would have

been everywhere before the era of mass consumption made
manufactured goods a real alternative to children. We need to
know why there was not however a preference for a *peasant*
version of stone-age affluence ('bucolic prosperity' (Jones forthcoming)) over maximal reproduction. Perhaps the instabilities of
a disaster-prone environment outweighed the high average level
of production and induced breeding to supply labour as a form of
risk insurance. After all even the labour of very young children
was of value (cf. Farb 1978:143–4).

In contrast with European colonisation, Chinese internal migration added up in the end to no more than static expansion.
Seen in this light it was a miracle of economic history that Europe
was able to undertake so much higher a proportion of its expansion overseas, and secure a massive injection of resources and big
markets without a commensurate growth in her numbers.
Europe and her annexes broke the mould of history, the nexus
between population growth and output gain. Even the prodigal
increase in colonial American families and the forced transfer of
Africans onto Europe's ghost acreage could not drive the
man–land ratio back to the pre-Columbian level. European
farming methods were preternaturally productive in the New
World. Time and time again European travellers complained that
American farmers wasted manure. Their dung heaps rose to
tower over the red Palatine barns of the colonies; why were they
not spread on the land? Such complaints were those of men for
whom fertility conservation was more important than saving
labour. In the overseas annexes of Europe output rose through
natural fertility, the winter blanket of snow, the oppressive heat
and moisture of summer, plus Yankee ingenuity; or through the
sub-tropical conditions of the southern colonies and the West
Indies, plus black sweat; and not through the toil of a fecund
peasantry. The gains were reaped, literally and figuratively, by
fewer men than even Europeans thought possible. Within
Europe disease and restraint reined in the growth of population,
though at minimal standards the ghost acres might have carried
so many more.

But China's colonisation, after an initial surge of yields from
the humus of ancient forests, returned output *per capita* to old
scrimping levels. The energies of the peasantry diverted them-

selves away from higher consumption or even revolt into assarting new land and breeding new people. Peasant payers of rent and taxes were in demand. The land was there for them. 'The principal crop in China, so to speak, is the farm population itself' (Stover 1974:68). Figures of population for all China and for the rice region of the Yangtze and further south show the massive early migration of the Han Chinese. Old and new settled regions outside the rice region cannot be distinguished in the available figures, so that the later Ming and Manchu migrations are blurred. The population share of the rice region can however be seen to have been almost maintained in Ming and Manchu times by the continued increases in wet-rice productivity resulting from earlier-ripening varieties and the wide adoption of double-cropping there during the 'Golden Age' of the eighteenth century.

The systematic reason, as opposed to the incidents of palace

TABLE 11.1 *Distribution and growth of China's population,*
A.D. 2–1770

| Date | Rice Region | | Remainder of China | | Rice Region as a percentage of China total |
	Population in millions	Percentage change	Population in millions	Percentage change	
A.D.2	15	–	43	–	26
700	25	+67	25	−42	50
c. 1300–50[1]	74	+196	16	−36	c. 82
1395–1400[2]	45	−39	25	+36	64
1760–70[3]	170	+278	100	+300	63

Notes [1] Peak before Mongol policy of extermination. 'More than four-fifths' in the rice region is set here as c. 82 per cent and the population is distributed accordingly.
 [2] After the Mongols.
 [3] The expectation of life rose under the early Manchu. In 1726 1.5 million people were reported to be over the age of seventy (Dawson 1972:331).
Sources: Grigg (1974:84–9), following Perkins (1969); McEvedy and Jones (1978). Contrary to my usual reliance on McEvedy and Jones, I have taken the more detailed Perkins–Grigg figures where there are inconsistencies. For maps and discussion of internal migration, see Elvin (1973:204–15).

politics, why the Chinese system could survive intact and at the same time remain inward-looking was therefore that there was an internal frontier. This is not clearly brought out in the literature. The Sung agricultural revolution is allowed pride of place. Elvin (1973:211) indeed argues that after the Middle Ages the impulse given by exploiting the resources of south China ebbed and vanished. By this he appears to mean that productivity gains were unable to do more than keep pace with the growth of population. Certainly land was not spared for growing much cotton at the expense of food crops, and this may have restricted the chances of industrialisation. But the empire survived and its absolute area and absolute population continued to grow. Internal tensions that might have fractured the loosely knit reality of a tightly worded centralism were avoided, until the Taiping rebellion of the mid-nineteenth century (twenty-five million deaths?), which has been called probably the greatest Malthusian crisis in history (Ho 1962:220).

Its inner vacuum was the safety-valve of China. The government ruthlessly put down rebellions by the tribals who were displaced, especially the Miao in the second half of the eighteenth century, and drove paved roads and iron bridges down to the south-west. Territorial expansion provided openings within the existing structure of society for the peasantry, the scholar-gentry and any provincial governor – in earlier times governors had been the rulers of co-opted kingdoms – who might think the unthinkable about breaking away. This was the substance behind the cultural manipulation of empire. It was the key property of a system which actually allowed governors to rule like kings from day to day over provinces the size of European states. That is to say, like kings, subject to a term appointment from the emperor. Like the governors of Mughal India, the governors of Manchu China were rotated to reduce the chances of their establishing bases of power. Where the Indian governors were 'eaters of provinces', the Chinese élite significantly referred to the populace as their 'meat and fish' (Stover 1974:68).

Tactics, organisation, leadership, and discipline, all factors outside economics, says Perkins (1969:176), were what enabled a few million Manchus to dominate what became in the first half of the eighteenth century 400 million Chinese. A regional force could have throttled the Peking government by blockading the Grand Canal. To Murphey (1954:358 n. 14), 'the persistent unity of China despite wide regional diversity is something of a puzzle' and while recent authors do not agree about the diversity, Perkins (1969:180) at any rate does not disagree about the remarkable degree of unity: 'the surprising fact is that China held together at all'. The reasons given by Perkins (cf. Ho 1976) are the consolidating power of Confucian ideology, military skill, the administrative talents of the scholar-gentry, and the ancient certainties of Chinese culture.

We may doubt that by themselves culturalism and administrative flair, factors 'outside economics', would have enabled the Manchu to operate the most successful of the late preindustrial empires. Economic circumstances were uniquely favourable. Theirs was the major civilisation with the biggest and best reservoir of cropland to relieve the pressure of population (Harrison 1972:320) and equally important to unfold opportunity before the Chinese élite whose support the Manchu needed to co-opt. After near-breakdown in the Taiping rebellion of 1850–65, a safety-valve itself in eliminating twenty-five million people, they opened up Manchuria in 1860 to migrants from the overcrowded provinces along the lower Yellow River. Since 1644 the Manchu had been preserving Manchuria for their own people, halting the growth of a Chinese colony in southern Manchuria and 'turning their homeland into a sort of human game reserve' (McEvedy and Jones 1978:168). At length, to preserve for another phase the lateral extension of the Chinese empire, they had to open the flood-gates.

The earlier opportunities of southern forest land had drawn enterprise away from the technological revolution of Sung times, setting Ming and Manchu China on a course of static expansion. But, ultimately, patronising a conservative Confucianism palatable to the literate Chinese blinded the Manchu to the need for systematic change, just as it blinded them to the cost of reclamation in terms of soil erosion. They could not but approve agrarianism. During its long life the system thus always held out to those who had made profits in trade or money-lending the temptation to acquire legitimacy (buy degrees) and 'mainline' on the agricultural rents which were more productive, or at any rate infinitely less risky, than the alternatives. In the eighteenth century there were about one million 'district graduates' licensed to move on to the next, vital stage in the search for office. About one-third of these licences were purchased, mostly by rich commoners protecting themselves from further extortion (Stover 1974:119–20).

Since foreign trade was illegal, except as tribute, no power base could be erected on that which did nevertheless take place. There was none of the political influence and continuity which made trade a powerful engine of growth in Europe. In Europe, according to Harrison (1972:159–60, after J. Levenson), the private trade sector had evolved from the wreckage of central authority during the Dark Ages. The small scale of early government attached itself to trade, as we have seen, for the sake of the revenues that sector could quickly provide. In China, and Asia generally, the private sector emerged only after government, on sufferance. No independent law arose to shield it. Contractual legalism never replaced statist morality. The Chinese system showed signs of development nevertheless, but was turned aside even then by the dead-end opportunity of internal colonisation. The price was structural stagnation, soil erosion, and an eventual Malthusian problem all the same.

Eurasia

Chapter 12

Summary and comparison

Perhaps the absence of fundamental change calls for no special explanation and only the European miracle does.

Ernest Gellner

EUROPE was an innovative, decentralised, yet stable, aberration. Our aim has been to try to understand what there was about it that promoted *very* long-term economic change, as well as what thwarted change in the productive and initially promising lands of Asia. This may seem an abstract, aggregative sort of goal, to which we can only reply, first things first. We tackled the analytical problems by a comparative approach. The colligation problem, that is the problem of when to begin, we resolved by glancing back to the Mesolithic past, but put most weight on the period from about A.D. 1400 to 1800. That was when Europe underwent those political, technological and geographical upheavals which were to make it the birthplace of the industrial world.

The aim has not been to find a specific trigger of industrialisation, which was in any case not a thunderstorm that suddenly arrived overhead but a growth deeply rooted in the past. To deal with the onset of industrialisation we should have needed to write national and regional economic history, and to discuss the rise of domestic industry within the agricultural sector, followed by the rise of factory industry within the domestic industrial sector (Jones 1982). This is not the present purpose, which is to do with context, with the influences of the environment and political action on the genesis and spread of the market system. Industrialisation came earliest in market economies where not only products but factors of production might be freely bought and sold. That world, which was David Ricardo's even more than Adam Smith's, was where modern economic analysis first could and did emerge. There are plenty of opportunities for applying parts of that analysis to earlier times. The most exciting of them lie where the analysis needs to be extended beyond its accepted limitations and applied to decisions about institutions (e.g. open-field farming) hitherto explained *ad hoc* by historians. Whether free market analysis overall is appropriate as its own midwife is another matter. An explanation of the genesis of the modern economy will surely have to incorporate political power into price theory and thus account for that great bulk of human behaviour and choice which otherwise must remain *ceteris paribus*.

An explanation of *very* long-term economic change ought also to take explicitly into account the effects of the different original conditions of production which, as Marx noted, cannot themselves be produced. Europe possessed such special features of site, location and resource endowment that we are bound to try to grasp the nettle of environmental explanation. Fruitful political variety, capital accumulation, and trade all seem partly explicable as adjustments to Europe's particular site and endowments. The very scarcity of large expanses of alluvial delta and river valley, combined with lower temperatures in the growing season, meant that agricultural productivity was lower than in the orient. A less dense population may have helped to avoid the distortions of political centralism. Areas of fertile and level soil were scattered about the map of Europe. These productive areas formed the cores of the most successful political units, the most successful of all becoming the strategic centres of the nation-states. The topographical structure of the continent, its mountain chains, coasts and major marshes, formed boundaries at which states expanding from the core-areas could meet and pause. These natural barriers helped to hold the ring between the varied ethnic and linguistic groups making up the European peoples. They helped to define the nation-states which filled up the matrix so formed and because they were expensive to cross they helped a little in reducing conflict between neighbouring states.

Income *per capita* was higher in Europe than Asia partly because natural disasters were fewer. There was less of the compulsion that Asians felt to breed as many sons as possible in order to ensure family labour for the phases of recovery. Voluntary control of fertility was a safer option, the means being delayed marriage and a lower marital participation rate. The slightly smaller families produced by late marriage made possible a greater investment in the individual: that is in the quality of human capital. The crop of people was not maximised and more land than elsewhere could be devoted to the production of producer goods like livestock and charcoal iron. Further, the accumulation of capital was a little easier than elsewhere because of the shape of the negative economic shocks. The impact of disasters of all kinds, that is including social disasters, was seemingly biassed towards the destruction of human life, the factor of production Labour, away from the destruction of Capital. This effect was reinforced in that early technical changes were capital- rather than labour-saving. Innovations in building-materials and simple improvements such as iron tips for wooden spades made capital goods more efficient.

Europe's very considerable geological, climatic and topographical variety endowed it with a dispersed portfolio of resources. This conduced to long-distance, multi-lateral trade in bulk loads of utilitarian goods. Taxing these was more rewarding than appropriating them. Bulk trade was also favoured by an abnormally high ratio of navigable routeways to surface area, which was a function of a long indented coastline and many navigable rivers. Important political, and therefore eventually market, consequences stemmed from an extensive trade.

Similarly Europe possessed a number of advantages in location. Sheer distance from the Central Asian steppes offered some protection from the worst ravages of their horse nomads, who from time to time devastated or overran the main agricultural civilisations of Asia. Yet the proximity to Europe of one of the eastern cultures, Islam, which was itself a borrower of Indian and Chinese techniques and ideas, was a positive externality. Europe was a peculiarly inventive society, but must have taken much longer to develop without that valuable technology transfer. Subsequently it left its mentors far behind in an array of important fields: according to Reuter, China is publishing in 1980 its first new textbook of forensic medicine since 1247. Finally, Europe's Atlantic seaboard location proved, when activated, to give relatively cheap access to the rich, graspable resources of the Americas and the oceans, and to large external markets. On any historic timescale this expansion of the resource endowment was more rapid and generous than any gains ever made by human populations through migrating to new territories *en bloc*. Earlier maritime migrants, the Vikings in the North Atlantic, the Malays in Madagascar and the Polynesians in the Pacific, had generated too little trade to keep in contact with their homelands or to have a major impact there. In this sense, the novelty of Europe's Discoveries was that it was already complex enough to use the vast resources now within reach, and to develop as a result.

Features of site and location did not determine the course of events. It would be over-simple to treat, say, the invention of labour-saving machinery as an adjustment to the factor proportions of an environment which favoured capital accumulation and where disasters destroyed the marginal unit of labour more freely than the corresponding unit of capital. Leaving aside the difficulties of specifying models of this kind, which is not much of a deterrent to those in the mood, and the problems of estimating *very* long-term parameters, which might well deter the boldest, the state of the inventive art was not so crassly determined. European society always contained a number of individuals whose creative talents were directed to improving the means of production. The supply of their talents was inelastic with respect to material reward: it was their hobby or obsession. This was a deep-seated cultural phenomenon related to that facility of the Germans, *Kraftserwerbsfähigkeit*, of which Werner Sombart spoke, the ability to rebuild from scratch. Political chaos could yet have nullified this drive. That it did not do so is a part of the European miracle.

Social processes had their own logic. The economy of nature, as Marston Bates calls it, does not have to be disregarded on that account. Reality lies where social process and its physical setting interact. The rôle of environmental factors was to sketch out least-cost paths of human action. *Ceteris paribus* we should expect them to have been followed. An environment of relatively cheap capital may well have influenced the rate of innovation. The particular opportunities for minimising cost gave an individual cast to European experience.

Eurasia embraced in the sixteenth, seventeenth and eighteenth centuries four main politico-economic systems. These were the

Ottoman empire in the Near East, the Mughal empire in India, the Ming and Manchu empires in China, and the European states system. The Ottoman, Mughal and Manchu systems were all alien, imposed military despotisms: revenue pumps. They were primarily responsible for the blighted developmental prospects of their subjects: prospects already dimming independently of the colonialism, treaty ports, unequal trade agreements, and indemnities with which Europe was to beset them in the nineteenth century.

The history – and that means the economic history – of Eurasia had been dominated between A.D. 1000 and 1500 by the spillover of Turkish and Mongol peoples from the steppes, infiltrating or conquering the civilisations of the 'coastlands' except the far peripheries of western Europe and Japan. This latest move down the 'steppe gradient' whereby the east–west ethnic and linguistic shading of Eurasia was pencilled in, is said to have been a disturbance comparable only to the conquests of the Bronze Age charioteers between the eighteenth and fifteenth centuries B.C. (Coles 1968:11). Part of it was the Mongol advance of the early thirteenth century whereby China was conquered after a loss of one-third (about thirty-five million) of its population; which reduced the irrigation agriculture of Persia to desert status; and which razed settlements to the ground everywhere it touched. Europe west of Poland and Hungary escaped because of succession disputes among the Mongols, disputes of the kind to which military hordes and despotisms are prone. The later history of the eastern steppes includes the start of the Manchu invasion of China, when the Manchu rolled back Ming Chinese settlement on their grazing lands in what began as the most colossal range war in history and went on to wipe out one-sixth (say twenty-five million) of China's people.

Part of the turmoil of the steppes was absorbed in the Near and Middle East, Islamicised and redirected, and out of this came the Mughal conquest of India, and the Turkish Ottoman empire. Wherever they took over, the steppe nomad warriors made themselves the élite, or the upper élite, of the conquered agrarian civilisations. It is useful to remember their original motives, given here in the words of Genghis Khan: 'The greatest pleasure is to vanquish your enemies and chase them before you, to rob them of their wealth and see those dear to them bathed in tears, to ride their horses and clasp to your bosom their wives and daughters' (Chambers 1979:6). The final sentiment is what is known as a free translation. Did these leopards change their spots? How did military plunder machines of that sort comport themselves as the central organising principle of large-scale peasant economies?

We have discussed how the Ottoman empire ran out of fresh spoils and corrupted itself ever more in the internal struggle for wealth; how the Mughal empire ran aground on the shoals of Maratha resistance; and how only the Manchu empire ran on, despite eventual massive strife, as long as it could cope with population pressure by an internal colonisation that at last drew in even the 'human game reserve' of the Manchu's own homeland. The order at first imposed by a military conqueror may have released initial spurts of productivity in all these systems, but their nature required only a slight check or a weak ruler to bring about intense competition for resources among the élite, enormous oppression, and a corresponding fall in investment. They dare not lose in war, yet could not coexist with peace because it tended to bring such population growth among the subject peoples. Beneath the elaborate ceremonial and display, the worm was already in the apple.

These systems could operate efficiently only within a narrow optimality band. They seemed incapable of bringing about a sustained rise in real incomes or of creating the infrastructure for development. They were prone to harvest the worst of both worlds in the sense that population was outstripping their land resources while at the same time the rate at which it was growing fell behind Europe. Between 1650 and 1850 Europe's population rose 152 per cent, not counting overseas populations of European stock. The population of the Ottoman empire, the least affected by colonialism, fell by 11 per cent. But that of the Indian subcontinent rose 53 per cent and the Chinese demographic monster managed 223 per cent yet ended the period by inflicting the wounds of the Taiping rebellion on itself. The total of the three eastern systems rose by 119 per cent, which was only 78 per cent of the domestic European increase, and without the same gains in income.

The opinion that these precolonial systems were heading for

income and biomass stagnation at the best, or Malthusian crisis at the worst, is hypothetical, counter-factual history. European intrusions destroyed the experiment. Objections on that score seem excessively austere. The driest economic appraisal is bound to contain elements of forecasting. The projection here seems reasonable on the evidence of the late precolonial period and it seems to be consistent with the analysis of the Chinese situation by Moore (1967:169). To talk of homeostatic systems and 'cycles of Cathay' would indeed not be enough. The demographic trend and its reciprocal (cultivable acres per head) must be super-imposed on the cycle. There is a literature from Ibn Khaldun to W. W. Rostow on the failure of the economies of Antiquity and the orient to break out of various types of equilibrium trap, and much of it makes sense. Pie-slicing conflicts always recurred when lack of success in war or over-long periods of peace exposed the developmental barrenness of the past. The underlying trend in late precolonial Asia suggests however that the cycle might soon be taking place about the premodern demographic maximum. The limits of both available land and preindustrial farming techniques were approaching. The post-Columbian exchange of crops had been a once-only boost and the diffusion of best practices was slowing down. Europe had closed out the option of large-scale overseas migration, even had Asia shown much initiative in that direction.

Despite great creative surges in times when Europe had still been primitive, despotic Asian institutions suppressed creativity or diverted it into producing voluptuous luxuries. Palace revolutions were all their internal politics seemed to offer. Maybe there had been 'curious experiences', a turning inwards, just before the arrival of the Europeans, whose real penetration anyhow awaited the nineteenth century (van Leur in Frank 1978:138–9). Systems of despoilment had little to offer when the spoils ran out. All that was promised was a fall in average incomes, the enlargement of the landless class which Stover (1974) labels the 'sink of death', internecine fighting like the Mughal–Maratha struggle, preda-tory behaviour of an Ottoman kind, or upheaval on the wide scale of the Taiping rebellion.

To urge that precolonial Asia was heading into a demographic cul-de-sac is not intended to be, nor could it in fact constitute, a

TABLE 12.1 *Density of population per square kilometre in*
the main Eurasian systems, 1500 and 1800

Date	India	China	Ottoman empire (Anatolia only)	Europe and overseas annexes
1500	23	25	8	8
1800	42	80	12	3

Source: Recalculated from data in Webb (1952) and McEvedy and Jones
(1978).

defence of the colonialism of a later era; any more than urging
that because a premodern states system proved more adaptable
than empires is to say that world government might not be more
effective still in these days of telecommunications; or any more
than pointing out that the nation-state brought Europe benefits
in administration and public health is *ipso facto* a defence of
nationalism. Order and administration could be supplied by
otherwise loathsome régimes, such as Pombal's dictatorship in
Portugal. But whatever the motive and the means, the nation-
states delivered the goods and these goods became part of European expectations. Rosenberg (1958:231) concludes that 'albeit
not free from revolting acts of arbitrariness, reason and order, not
hysteria and violence, were the pillars of the consolidated police
state of the Old Regime'. Comparatively speaking, the world
before the nation-state was indefensible. It is important to clarify
the bird's-eye perspective here, which looks for promising
warmth amidst the welter of events and motives of the past. The
cruelty and waste in the European record is not at issue. Had
Winwood Reade not long ago retired the title, *The Martyrdom of
Man* would serve all too well as a summary. But this is not the
focus of concern in studying broad-front advances, the *very*
long term, or the comparative performance of entire systems. All
histories from Herodotus onwards are crammed with inhuman-
ity. We have to keep a statistical sense. Europe was seldom as
insecure as Moreland's India, 'an Inferno for the ordinary man'.

The historical problem of development is that all economies
were politically embedded. Whatever their cultural virtues, the
Asian empires never overcame for long enough the liabilities of
negative decisions at the top, the lack of incentive for those who

held power to invent or innovate anything productive, and the disincentive for those without power to risk setting up productive plant. Where life expectancies were low, planning horizons were in any case short. Since technological and organisational problems do not yield instantaneous solutions, a long gestation period was vital for development in any civilisation. For political reasons long, easy spells were rare in Asia.

Europe, however, had avoided the plunder machine. The invasions of the tenth century had been repulsed, the thirteenth-century Mongol plans to invade had been abandoned, and resistance to the Turks had succeeded in the sixteenth and seventeenth centuries. Asia may begin at the Landstrasse, but Vienna's walls, built with the ransom paid for Richard the Lionheart, fended off the last Turkish siege in 1683. After a prudent interval, in the 1860s the walls were pulled down. Strauss wrote the Demolition Polka to celebrate the fact that the eastern threat to Europe was over.

European political forms reflected a victory for certain elements within a feudal system and not the imposition of despotism by invaders. But how did Europeans escape crippling exploitation by their own rulers? How was risk reduced and the depressants on investment lifted? The answer is a compound of processes, but what stands out is that the rulers of the relatively small European states learned that by supplying the services of order and adjudication they could attract and retain the most and best-paying constituents – for their subjects must be thought of as constituents in some degree. Within each state there was a clash between kingly interest in taxes and noble preoccupation with rents, an unsettled competition in which the royal concern offered the peasantry some faint protection and some provision of justice. Competition among states led later to programmes of services. Once more there was an environmental component, since, had the core-areas of their states been larger and richer, kings might have felt less inspired to offer as much as they did in return for taxes (it was little, but in the *very* long term it was enough to make European history special).

European kings were never as absolute as they wished. The power dispersed among the great proprietors was a check on them, as was the rising power of the market which, for the sake of regular taxation, they had themselves encouraged. This abridged the worst arbitrariness of kings, and it was in their interest to check it among their nobles. Dishoarding and productive investment became less penalised than they had been. The market expanded under the impetus of its own regional specialisation. Opportunities for profit ate into Walter Bagehot's 'cake of custom' and into new restrictions on factor mobility which arose as side-effects of acts of government prompted by special interests. Development was cumulative. Long-run development must indeed seem to a European to have been the normal condition of history. There is of course a danger in assuming that it must have been inevitable. The dismal record of the remainder of the premodern world shows that purposive government, regular technological change, and a population response reined back from swamping any gains in income were far from inescapable attributes of human society, but were specific processes each requiring explanation. Against this, it is worth reiterating that European optimism about progress was not self-evidently absurd, either towards the end of the eighteenth century or in the Victorian age. Life had become more secure and technologically and organisationally more competent in more and more of the continent. After Waterloo, war had been thrust away to the colonial corners of the globe. The expectation of continued development was not simply an English, whiggish interpretation of history and certainly predated the influence of the theory of evolution as put forward by Charles Darwin in his *Origin of Species* of 1859. Mill had deeply sensed the momentum of change in the 1840s; so had Priestley in the early 1790s. Their projections were wrong in important respects, especially as regards the power of commerce to keep the peace among nations. But they were not foolish. A deteriorationist position would have been hard to hold in the face of Mill's view of cumulative improvement in the underlying economic structure – of efficiency gains, certainly, more than equity gains, but of betterment nevertheless. The observables of history lent support to the beliefs of the progressive school of thought.

An underlying thrust of our argument has been that *very* long-term growth was less the result of a conjunction of growth-promoting forces than of the removal of impediments. As usual the literature contains an apposite remark. Adam Smith said in a lecture of 1755 that 'little else is requisite to carry a state to the highest degree of opulence from the lowest barbarism, but peace, easy taxes, and tolerable administration of justice; all the rest being brought about by the natural course of things'. On such a view secondary institutions like banks, which depended on there being a demand for their services, although they arose very early, are no more powerful in explaining growth than the old *dei ex machina* of steam-engines, coke-smelted iron and turnips. What was important instead was the slow planing away of roughness and risk, so that entrepreneurs might not merely maximise profits but retain them too. And as interest rates were brought down so choices among investments became technical exercises in deciding what the market demanded, rather than matters of guessing merely where it was least risky to hazard resources. The economy became regulated by economic rather than political decisions. This emphasis on the withering away of arbitrariness, violence, custom, and old social controls, seems to leave little scope for direct assaults on the old order. That seems to be about right. The bourgeoisie pressed its interest, but in a peasant- and craftsman-dominated continent, the working class did not have much chance to make a mark. In any case, where insecurity was so rife the working class was understandably too fearful of losing what it had to push for the development of risk capitalism.

As far back as the tenth century Europe had rebounded fast from its catastrophes. This betokens considerable economic resilience. Speedy recovery after disasters was not unique to Europe. It was a feature of the aftermath of plagues and famines in India (Davis 1951:41), though apparently not of floods in China. Europe however made special efforts to limit the damage done by wars. Three hundred conventions for the humane treatment of the sick and wounded were signed in the centuries after the first such convention at Tournai in 1581, including treaties of broad scope between France and Spain in 1683 and between England and France in 1743 (Magill 1926:10). Even more noteworthy was the extent of rebuilding and new development given momentum by the ending of each war.

To resilience and progress may be added the similarity of developmental forms throughout much of Europe. In the literature so much is made of a supposed 'take-off' into sustained growth, and the switches that took place in international economic leadership, that they tend to mask how coherent and widespread progress already was in late preindustrial Europe. In its trade expansions, handtool revolutions (distaff to spinning-wheel, sickle to scythe), and the regional specialisations of rural domestic industry, development had become the normal condition (Jones 1974a; 1977a). The rapid spread of factory-and-steam industrialisation from Britain to many regions on the continent suggests that their economic matrices were remarkably alike or capable of remarkably efficient substitutions. In retrospect some of the preparatory processes can be detected at very early periods, cumulative technological advance and changes in political forms for instance, but it would have been difficult to guess which way these would evolve and that they might fuse into the productive and modernising shapes of industry and the nation-state. Synergy is as difficult to predict as mutation.

Commercial and manufacturing advances were first conspicuous in the trading cities of Italy, in the Netherlands, Britain, 'Belgium', Bohemia, and a few other patches (Barkhausen 1974). They were creations of the market. What Europe had hit on in addition in the states system and the nation-state was a framework in which decentralisation could offset malfunction in any one part and yet where unity was provided by competitive exchanges of know-how and factors of production. It was a bit rough and ready, for instance much diffusion of ideas took place by the backdoor of refugee movements which otherwise traumatised so many European families, Marx's and Weber's among them (Adam Smith was merely stolen by gipsies). Admittedly, within the nation-states, many government industrial enterprises actually collapsed. The state as a benign manager may seem an English rather than a European conception, but probably it is not. Central European governments supervised the details of life more fruitfully than anywhere.

There were unintended consequences since bureaucracies took on a life of their own. When bureaucrats deal with drains, so to speak, they are useful; when they extend themselves to organising the supply of potable water, that is a bonus. In the period with which we have been dealing there were plenty of these humdrum tasks needing attention. It was not yet a reasonable fear that bureaucracies might become Parkinsonian. It is almost unnecessary to add that national purpose in the *anciens régimes* was largely a cloak for ruling interests; that the effects of forward-looking policies are hard to separate from the independent effects of growth itself; that measures to reduce risk were still feeble by modern standards; that any cherishing of human capital often thought of people as no more than tax-payers and cannon-fodder; and that the distribution of wealth, and social relations, remained preposterously unequal. For all these reservations, the modernising effect of state action is clear. The results were out of all proportion to the motives. The latent function was to extend the market farther and faster than its evident attractions could do unaided.

The scissors movement whereby production became individualised while services were somewhat collectivised conferred both efficiency and stability gains. Security of life, property and investment were not security of employment, income and health. They remained nevertheless essentials for development, parts of its definition. Individualism, Cunningham (1896:167) claimed, 'won its way, step by step and bit by bit, in commerce, and industry, and agriculture'. An Englishman of his day might tend to take public services for granted, but they too had won their way by stages, until Europe as a whole possessed a far more efficient mix of functional agencies than ever before, or than anywhere else possessed. The attainment of minimum stability conditions for economic growth lies so far back in the history of the developed world that we all now take it for granted. Arguably, there is more relevance for the less-developed world in the history of this kind of provision than in those staples of Industrial Revolution history, canals and cotton mills. European, and Western, man came to expect security, order and services undreamed of by his medieval forebears or the rest of mankind. The search for further growth or greater social justice, or some mix of the two, could now begin from a basis of virtually guaranteed security and social precaution. The export of these products of the administrative revolution is witnessed by the faster population growth in the colonial empires once internecine wars, arbitrariness, disease and the worst disaster shocks were on the way to being suppressed. The service state may not be a sufficient condition for rapid income growth, as colonial and post-colonial experience unfortunately seems to show, but it may well be a necessary condition.

In the present state of knowledge we must resist the notion that any simple model will account for the whole developmental process. We cannot model it, say, as a production function which makes modernisation, eighteenth-century industrialisation, or the sustained rise of real incomes, the output of a handful of stylised inputs, while hoping to retain any sense of the historical complexity involved. Too many parameters shift and dissolve; *very* long-term economic change was much more than the usual conception of an economic process. The model implied by the results of this enquiry resembles a giant combination lock. There is no one key. The parts fit together well enough to work, but perhaps not even in a unique combination: it is difficult to gauge retrospectively what the tolerances of the system may have been. The problem is that economic history has been searching too much in the foreground, in the late eighteenth and nineteenth centuries and among too limited a range of variables, to find all the clues to the process of development. There are many ways of studying the totality, since it is 'not possible to maximise simultaneously generality, realism and precision' (Levins 1968:7). For the moment one pays one's money and takes one's choice. Europe's *very* long-term development appears miraculous. Comparable development in Asia would have been super-miraculous.

An annotated bibliographical guide to Eurasian economic history in the very long term

Miscellaneous reading turns up all sorts of stray ideas for such broad themes as have appeared in this book and the complete list of 400 references, many cited in the book only once, is not as helpful a guide as it might be. What is included here is therefore only what I relied on most. There is an element of the misleading about even the present guide, since only the dullest mind would find its inspiration entirely within the field's own subject matter. One individual's catalysts are not however likely to be as helpful to anyone else with different preparations and anticipations. I find a more enticing literature in natural history, ecology and biology, and the history of science than in plain history or economic history. But I have confined myself here to indicating references from the (fairly) standard historical literature where they contain leading ideas, together with a minimum number of descriptive books and articles.

The works cited are in English. The opportunity costs of learning another language, which would have had to be an Asian tongue, were too high. Even in English there is no hope of completeness, scarcely a definition of it. I took comfort from a comment Stan Engerman made to me about a batch of the learned tomes that had come out on 'big picture' history, that each was a *tour de force* for its author without really succeeding in explaining economic change over the *very* long term or at a continental or global level. This accorded with my own reading and led to the conclusion that while more knowledge obviously helps, diminishing returns soon set in as regards its helpfulness in explanation. The operational conclusion was that one should compile one's material, collect one's ideas, have one's say, and then let someone else have a go.

As I found when progressing from writing a review article on North and Thomas, *The Rise of the Western World* ('Institutional determinism and the rise of the western world', *Economic Inquiry* 12 (1974), pp. 114–24) to writing an essay of my own ('A new essay on western civilization in its economic aspects' *Australian Economic History Review* 16 (1976), pp. 95–109), this is a field where the usually wide gap between precept or critique on one side and practice on the other becomes a chasm, and

239

where one's own ideas freeze fast and are not thawed by descriptive histories read thereafter.

Chapter 1. Environmental and social conjectures

Very long-term economic history has never been fashionable, though it has been receiving more notice lately. The general references with which I began are listed under Chapter 12. The question of Europe's population : resource balance in the *very* long term is almost nowhere directly tackled, but a background of similar considerations is provided by Marvin Harris, *Cannibals and Kings: the origins of cultures* (London: Collins/ Fontana, 1978). Colin McEvedy's three atlases set the demographic scene well: *Penguin Atlas of Ancient History, Penguin Atlas of Medieval History* and *Penguin Atlas of Modern History to 1815* (Harmondsworth, Middlesex: Penguin Books, n.d.), as does his indispensable compilation (with Richard Jones), *Atlas of World Population History* (Harmondsworth, Middlesex: Penguin Books, 1978). An older paper by A. P. Usher, 'The history of population and settlement in Eurasia', *Geographical Review* 20 (1930), pp. 110–32, also describes the pattern of Europe's late demographic growth. See also W. M. S. Russell, 'To seek a fortune', *The Listener* 80 No. 2060 19 September 1968, pp. 365–7, and S. C. Gilfillan, 'The coldward course of progress' *Political Science Quarterly* 35 (1920), pp. 393–410.

Adjustment mechanisms in European demography are discussed by five writers: J. Hajnal, 'European marriage patterns in perspective', in David Glass and D. E. C. Eversley (eds), *Population in History* (London: Edward Arnold, 1965), pp. 101–43, a classic paper; John T. Krause, 'Some implications of recent work in historical demography', in Michael Drake (ed), *Applied Historical Studies* (London: Methuen, 1973, pp. 155–83); Alan Macfarlane, 'Modes of reproduction' in Geoffrey Hawthorn (ed), *Population and Development* (London: Frank Cass, 1978); R. S. Schofield, 'The relationship between demographic structure and the environment in pre-industrial western Europe', in *Sozialgeschichte der Familie in der Neuzeit Europas: Neue Forschungen Herausgegeben von Werner Conze* (Stuttgart: Klett, 1976, pp. 147–60); and E. A. Wrigley, 'Family limitation in pre-industrial England', *Economic History Review* 2 Ser. 19 (1966), pp. 82–109.

The early setting of the structure of European society is described in Grahame Clark and Stuart Piggott, *Prehistoric Societies* (London: Hutchinson, 1965). David Kaplan, 'Man, monuments and political systems', *South-western Journal of Anthropology* 19 (1963), pp. 397–410, casts doubt on the adamantine despotism usually associated with monument building in the ancient empires. On resources and environmental processes,

W. L. Thomas (ed), *Man's Rôle in Changing the Face of the Earth* (Chicago: University of Chicago Press, 1956, two volumes), has worn well, and R. E. Baldwin, 'Patterns of development in newly-settled regions', from *Manchester School of Economic and Social Studies*, 1956, reprinted in Carl Eicher and Lawrence Witt (eds), *Agriculture in Economic Development* (New York: McGraw-Hill, 1964), pp. 238–51, is suggestive about production possibilities and economic systems in different natural settings.

Chapter 2. Disasters and capital accumulation

There is a considerable literature on categories of natural and other disasters and compilations exist such as C. Walford, 'Famines of the world: past and present', *Journal of the Statistical Society* 41 (1878), pp. 433–535, 42 (1879), pp. 79–275, and A. Keys *et al.*, *The Biology of Human Starvation* (Minneapolis: University of Minnesota Press, 1950, vol. 2, pp. 1247–52, 'Some notable famines in history'). One of the most comprehensive is J. H. Latter, 'Natural disasters', *The Advancement of Science* 25 (1968–9), pp. 362–80. Recent examples of this literature include Editors of *Encyclopaedia Britannica*, *Disasters! When Nature Strikes Back* (New York: Bantam Books, 1978), and James Cornell, *The Great International Disaster Book* (New York: Pocket Books, 1979), which is the most useful of all. No good generalising commentary on the economics of disaster in history seems to exist, nor on the economics of recent disaster. Big shocks are treated as little shocks writ large, which may capture the essence of the disturbances they set up as far as neo-classical theory goes, but smooths out a past made up of frequent deviations from a highly abstract norm. It is a pity that this is allowed to blinker perceptions of the past; deviations from theoretical expectations are precisely what should be most interesting, not least to economic theorists.

In the historical literature disasters as an influential category of processes faded in and promptly out again with Henry T. Buckle, *History of Civilization in England* (London: O.U.P. 1903. First published 1857–61. vol. 1, chapter 2). An attempt to determine the global distribution of disasters of many kinds was Raoul Montandon, 'A propos du projet Ciraolo: Une carte mondiale de distribution géographique des calamités', *Revue Internationale de la Croix-Rouge*, 5 (1923), pp. 271–344. The growing modern literature on disasters is too static and cross-sectional in approach to be as stimulating as the subject warrants, though this will probably change.

There is a recent study of the overall historical importance of epidemics, W. H. McNeill, *Plagues and Peoples* (Garden City, N.Y.: Anchor Press/Doubleday, 1976), and one hopes that this swallow does portend a summer. An ingenious reconstruction of epidemic losses century by century for Italy is L. Del Panta and M. Livi Bacci, 'Chronologie intensité et diffusion des crises de mortalité en Italie, 1600–1850', *Population*, Numéro Spécial, 32ᵉ année (1979), pp. 401–46. I mentioned the possibility of a different shape to the shocks affecting Europe and Asia in my chapter, E. L. Jones, 'The environment and the economy' in Peter Burke (ed), *The New Cambridge Modern History, XIII Companion Volume* (Cambridge: Cambridge University Press, 1979), pp. 15–42, and develop the idea here.

Chapter 3. Technological drift

The share of their attention historians and economists have given to disasters, say, or *very* long-term change has been astonishingly slight. Technology is another orphan. Few good general treatments are available. Economists have too often abstracted technological change away (but see for an honourable exception the works of Nathan Rosenberg, notably *Perspectives on Technology* C.U.P. 1976). R. J. Forbes, *The Conquest of Nature. Technology and its Consequences* (New York: Praeger, 1968), and Lynn White's chapter 'The expansion of technology 500–1500' in Carlo M. Cipolla (ed), *The Fontana Economic History of Europe: The Middle Ages* (London: Collins/Fontana, 1972), are good starting-points. Lynn White's *Medieval Technology and Social Change* (Oxford: Clarendon Press, 1962), was savaged by R. H. Hilton and P. H. Sawyer, 'Technical determinism: the stirrup and the plough', *Past and Present* 24 (1963), pp. 90–100, but it is interesting to see that a professional ecologist, R. S. Loomis, takes White's ideas seriously ('Ecological dimensions of medieval agrarian systems: An ecologist responds', *Agricultural History* 52 (1978), pp. 478–83).

J. P. M. Pannell, *An Illustrated History of Civil Engineering* (London: Thames and Hudson, 1964) is fascinating.

On environmental control S. F. Markham, *Climate and the Energy of Nations* (London: O.U.P. 1947) is unconvincing but suggestive.

On the history of science, as regards comparisons of China and Europe, Joseph Needham has made all the running. See especially his 'The roles of Europe and China in the evolution of oecumenical science', *The Advancement of Science* 24 (1967), 83–98. W. P. D. Wightman is a terse, sometimes cryptic, but stimulating introduction from the European side, *Science in a Renaissance Society* (London: Hutchinson University Library, 1972). I also enjoyed Kurt Mendelssohn, *Science and Western Domination* (London: Thames and Hudson, 1976), especially on the Discoveries, and of course Jacob Bronowski, *The Ascent of Man* (London: B.B.C. Publications, 1975).

Chapter 4. The Discoveries and ghost acreage

Much the most comprehensive book on the origins of the Discoveries is Pierre Chaunu, *European Expansion in the Later Middle Ages* (translated by Kate Bertram) (Amsterdam: North-Holland Publishing Company, 1979).

Exceptionally interesting material also occurs in Carl O. Sauer, *Northern Mists* (San Francisco: Turtle Island Foundation, 1973); R. L. Reynolds, 'The Mediterranean frontier, 1000–1400', in W. D. Wyman and C. B. Kroeber (eds), *The Frontier in Perspective* (Madison: Wisconsin University Press, 1965); and Carlo Cipolla, *Guns and Sails in the Early Phase of European Expansion 1400–1700* (London: Collins, 1965). I enjoyed Christopher Bell, *Portugal and the Quest for the Indies* (London: Constable, 1974) and thought K. G. Macintyre, *The Secret Discovery of Australia: Portuguese Ventures 200 Years Before Captain Cook* (Mendindie, S.A: Souvenir Press, 1977) a superbly constructed thriller.

The 'ghost acreage' concept appears in works by Georg Borgstrom, e.g. *The Hungry Planet* (New York: Collier Books, 2nd rev. ed, 1972). For the neglected aspect of maritime exploitation, see C. L. Cutting, 'Historical aspects of fish' in G. Borgstrom (ed), *Fish as Food* (New York: Academic Press, 1961–5); Michael Graham, 'Harvest of the seas' in W. L. Thomas (ed), *Man's Role in Changing the Face of the Earth* (Chicago: University of Chicago Press, 1956, vol. 2); and Gordon Jackson, *The British Whaling Trade* (London: Adam and Charles Black, 1978).

On the impact of the Discoveries on Europe, the *locus classicus* is W. P. Webb, *The Great Frontier* (Boston, Mass.: Houghton Mifflin, 1952); for a recent work of similar originality see Alfred Crosby, *The Columbian Exchange* (Westport, Conn.: Greenwood, 1972).

The beginnings of a typology of areas settled or traded with appears in D. W. Meinig, 'A macrogeography of western imperialism: Some morphologies of moving frontiers of political control' in Fay Gayle and G. H. Lawton (eds), *Settlement and Encounter* (Melbourne: O.U.P. 1969).

Chapter 5. The market economy

To my surprise I found little directly on the rise of the market in all except the oldest literature (but see the books by Sir John Hicks and D. C. North and R. P. Thomas listed under Chapter 12). Important side-lights are to be found in Norman Cohn, *The Pursuit of the Millennium* (London: Paladin, 1970), on areas of social disturbance and by inference growth outside the agrarian social structure; and in Jan de Vries, 'On the modernity of the Dutch Republic', *Journal of Economic History* 33 (1973), pp. 191–202, on the development of the non-feudal Netherlands. Karl Polanyi's work is having a vogue. Douglass North gives him his due in 'Markets and other allocative systems in history: The challenge of Karl Polanyi', *Journal of European Economic History* 6 (1977), pp. 703–16. The decline of arbitrariness is best approached through a thoughtful and pleasing essay by Albert O. Hirschman, *The Passions and the Interests: Political Arguments for Capitalism before its Triumph* (Princeton, N. J.: Princeton University Press, 1977). The erosion of rigidities such as gilds and sumptuary law has been quite out of fashion in economic history but a recent return to part of the field has been made by N. B. Harte, 'State control of dress and social change in pre-industrial England', in D. C. Coleman and A. H. John (eds), *Trade, Government and Economy in Pre-industrial England* (London: Weidenfeld and Nicolson, 1976).

The 'core area' pattern of the European landscape with its implications for trade has been most recently discussed by N. J. G. Pounds and S. S. Ball, 'Core-areas and the development of the European states-system', *Annals, Association of American Geographers* 54 (1964), pp. 24–40.

Chapter 6. The states system

Robert Wesson is the modern champion of states systems and documenter of the characteristics and failings of the imperial alternative. See his *The Imperial Order* (Berkeley: University of California Press, 1967) and *States-Systems* (New York: The Free Press, 1978). The Pounds and Ball paper listed under Chapter 5 above may suggest an environmental basis for multiple polities in Europe (contrast with India and China where political units did not conform to seemingly 'natural' units). Hints as to the precarious nature of the European system are found in Ludwig Dehio, *The Precarious Balance: Four Centuries of the European Power Struggle* (New York: Vintage Books, 1965); Hajo Holborn, *The Political Collapse of Europe* (New York: Knopf, 1951); and recently in T. K. Rabb, *The Struggle for Stability in Early Modern Europe* (New York: O.U.P. 1975).

The view that the failure to return to empire in the sixteenth century was critical for European development, and that the development was determined by a transnational economic system, is the theme of Immanuel Wallerstein, *The Modern World System: Capitalist Agriculture and the Origins of the European World-Economy in the Sixteenth Century* (New York: Academic Press, 1974). The essence of Wallerstein's argument is also contained in his 'Three paths of national development in the sixteenth century', *Studies in Comparative International Development* 7 (1972), pp. 95–101. Much the most effective criticism of this influential work is by Robert A. Dodgshon, 'The modern world system: A spatial perspective', *Peasant Studies* 6 (1977), pp. 8–19.

Suggestive material on the economic rôle of refugees occurs in studies of two groups who certainly needed a refuge, James Parkes, *A History of the Jewish People* (Harmondsworth, Middlesex: Penguin Books, 1964) and W. C. Scoville, 'The Huguenots and the diffusion of technology', *Journal of Political Economy*, 60 (1952), pp. 392–411.

Chapter 7. Nation-states

The birth of the nation-state is explained, differently, by R. T. Bean, 'War and the birth of the nation state', *Journal of Economic History* 33 (1973), pp. 203–21, and Joseph R. Strayer, *On the Medieval Origins of the Modern State* (Princeton, N.J.: Princeton University Press, 1970), as well as in Strayer's 'The historical experience of nation building in Europe' in Karl W. Deutsch and W. J. Foltz (eds), *Nation Building* (New York: Atherton, 1966). A more general account is J. H. Shennan, *Origins of the Modern European State 1450–1725* (London: Hutchinson, 1974), and a major collection of essays, better drawn together by an editorial hand than most collections, is Charles Tilly (ed), *The Formation of National States in Western Europe* (Princeton, N.J.: Princeton University Press, 1975).

An interesting treatment is David R. Friedman, 'A theory of the size and shape of nations', *Journal of Political Economy* 85 (1977), pp. 59–77. The internal workings of the nation-states are discussed in studies dealing with Absolutism, such as the book by Wallerstein, noted under Chapter 6 above, and the second volume by Perry Anderson, noted under Chapter 12 below. A review article on Wallerstein and Anderson by Keith Thomas, 'Jumbo history', *The New York Review of Books*, 17 April 1975, pp. 26–8, is perceptive. I found the strains of the system and the influences on continental-landowner behaviour pointed up in J. Blum, *The End of the Old Order in Rural Europe* (Princeton, N.J.: Princeton University Press, 1978), supplemented with remarks about liquidity preferences in Nathan Rosenberg, 'Capital formation in under-developed countries', *American Economic Review* 50 (1960), pp. 706–15. On the service state, see especially R. A. Dorwart, *The Prussian Welfare State before 1740* (Cambridge, Mass.: Harvard University Press, 1971), and on disaster management, Carlo Cipolla, *Public Health and the Medical Profession in the Renaissance* (Cambridge: Cambridge University Press, 1976), and Shelby T. McCloy, *Government Assistance in Eighteenth-Century France* (Durham, N.C.: Duke University Press, 1946), as well as two papers of my own, the latter of which is an expanded version of the former, with references: E. L. Jones, 'Disaster management and resource saving in Europe, 1400–1800' in Michael Flinn (ed), *Proceedings* of the Seventh International Economic History Congress (Edinburgh: Edinburgh University Press, 1978), vol. 1, and in Antoni Maczak and William N. Parker (eds), *Natural Resources in European History* (Washington, D.C.: Resources for the Future, 1978). On economic policy in general, Eli Heckscher's book on mercantilism is the standard source and there is the usual long library list. Jacob van Klaveren, *General Economic History, 100–1760* (München: Gërhard Kieckens, 1969) is more interesting than most, and plausibly iconoclastic. I could find no general work on internal colonisation as either process or policy, but enjoyed W. C. MacLeod, 'Celt and Indian: Britain's old world frontier in relation to the new' in Paul Bohannon and Fred Plog (eds), *Beyond the Frontier* (Garden City, N.Y.: The Natural History Press, 1967).

Chapter 8. Beyond Europe

Surprisingly little work comparing European and Asian development seems to be available. In commenting not long ago on a batch of papers on the economic history of the Third World, Henry Rosovsky observed of Europe's mysterious technological overtaking, 'the big question is: What happened? Why did most of the Third World fall behind? And the interesting thing is that the authors of these papers don't care' (*Journal of Economic History*, 31 (1971), p. 255).

There are honourable exceptions, to be noted in their places. At a very general level Halford Mackinder is one: *Democratic Ideals and Reality* (New York: Norton and Co., 1962, first published 1942). C. N. Parkinson, *East and West* (London: John Murray, 1963) is a good beginning, and Ragha-van Iyer (ed), *The Glass Curtain between Asia and Europe* (London: O.U.P. 1965), raises questions about comparisons from an Asian viewpoint. Max Weber, *General Economic History* (translated by Frank H. Knight) (New York: The Free Press, 1927), of course examined the matter, but one would not expect to have to go back so far in one's reading, given the general explosion of historical literature. 82 per cent of all the books I used turned out to have been published since 1958 and the journal article literature would be more modern still, yet this outpouring does not gush over some of the most important topics.

J. R. Levenson (ed), *European Expansion and the Counter-Example of Asia 1300–1600* (Englewood Cliffs, N.J.: Prentice-Hall, 1967) is an astute comparative writer; Maurice Zinkin, *Asia and the West* (London: Chatto and Windus, 1951) is another. I found Karl Bekker, 'Historical patterns of culture contact in southern Asia', in Bohannon and Plog (eds), as cited under Chapter 7 above; B. R. Pearn, *An Introduction to the History of South-East Asia* (Kuala Lumpur: Longmans of Malaysia, 1963); and C. G. F. Simkin, *The Traditional Trade of Asia* (London: O.U.P. 1968), all helpful.

Chapter 9. Islam and the Ottoman Empire

In view of Islamic and Ottoman significance for European development their study plays an astonishingly small part in English-language economic history. This makes Paul Coles, *The Ottoman Impact on Europe* (London: Thames and Hudson, 1968) an eye-opening survey. Coles himself has a scholarly bibliography which is not short; the fact remains that the topic has vanished from the mainstream in favour of studying Europe overseas. No doubt it will reappear with O.P.E.C.'s demonstration of the fascination of things Arab. Although it would be unrealistic not to expect some change in emphasis according to contemporary geopolitics, this is not the proper way to determine historical significance. The investigation of Islam should have been in curricula all along, and we should look to see what else of historical moment is neglected, regardless of whether or not it is also geopolitically fashionable.

Pertinent works on Islam and the Ottomans include the recent facsimile reproduction (1972) by Gregg International Publishers of Paul Rycaut, *The Present State of the Ottoman Empire* (1668); L. S. Stavrianos, *The Balkans since 1453* (New York: Holt, Rinehart and Winston, 1966); Halil Inalcik, 'Capital formation in the Ottoman Empire', *Journal of Economic History* 29 (1969), pp. 97–140, and *The Ottoman Empire: The Classical Age 1300–1600* (translated by Norman Itzkowitz and Colin Imber) (London: Weidenfeld and Nicolson, 1973), and Maxime Rodinson, *Islam and Capitalism* (Austin, Texas: University of Texas Press, 1978), which is a more subtle book than my occasional critical comment may imply. A. M. Watson, 'The Arab agricultural revolution and its diffusion, 700–1100', *Journal of Economic History* 34 (1974), pp. 8–35, is useful (compare Reynolds 'The Mediterranean frontier, 1000–1400' cited under Chapter 4 above). D. A. Zakythinos, *The Making of Modern Greece* (Oxford: Basil Blackwell, 1976), contains some observations on the development of the Greek economy under (and despite) Ottoman rule. Mostly, however, one has to rely on snippets.

Chapter 10. India and the Mughal Empire

Once again generalising work is scanty. Indian specialists may know better, but they have definitely not catered for the non-specialist anything like as well as China specialists. Angus Maddison, *Class Structure and Economic Growth: India and Pakistan since the Moghuls* (New York: Norton, 1971), is at an appropriate conceptual level. Maddison's book is a rare example of development questions systematically asked of an historical literature. Hugh Tinker, *South Asia: A Short History* (London: Pall Mall Press, 1966) is also helpful, but more conventional, as is Stanley Wolpert, *India* (Englewood Cliffs, N.J.: Prentice-Hall, 1965). Of the older works, W. H. Moreland, *From Akbar to Aurangzeb* (New Delhi: Oriental Books Reprint Co., 1972, first published 1923) is pithy and refreshing.

The core (or nuclear) area problem may be approached through O. H. K. Spate and A. T. A. Learmonth, *India and Pakistan* (London: Methuen, 3rd ed, 1967) and W. M. Day, 'Relative permanence of former boundaries in India', *Scottish Geographical Magazine* 65 (1949), pp. 113–22. George Modelski, 'Kautilya: Foreign policy and international system in the ancient Hindu world', *American Political Science Review* 58 (1964), pp. 549–60, grapples with the remote source of *very* long-term governmental instability in India.

Chapter 11. China and the Ming and Manchu Empires

China is much better served. Its overall experience became accessible in the early 1970s with the publication of two books, Mark Elvin, *The Pattern of the Chinese Past* (London: Eyre Methuen, 1973), and Leon E. Stover, *The Cultural Ecology of Chinese Civilization* (New York: Mentor Books, 1974).

Stover keeps up a steady use of veil-piercing concepts and language. See also Leon E. Stover and Takeko Kawai Stover, *China: An Anthropological Perspective* (Pacific Palisades, Calif.: Goodyear Publishing Co. Inc., 1976), and Dwight Perkins, *Agricultural Development in China 1368–1968* (Edinburgh: Edinburgh University Press, 1969). Before this breakthrough the field was dominated by Karl Wittfogel, *Oriental Despotism* (New Haven, Conn.: Yale University Press, 1957). Wittfogel's views are also sketched in 'Chinese society: An historical survey', *Journal of Asian Studies* 16 (1957), pp. 343–64.

General histories include John A. Harrison, *The Chinese Empire* (New York: Harcourt-Brace Jovanovich Inc., 1972) and Raymond Dawson, *Imperial China* (Harmondsworth, Middlesex: Penguin Books, 1972), both good, the latter a narrative antidote to the virtual personification of whole systems to which social scientists lean (*mea culpa*). One must not pass over the many publications of Ping-ti Ho, see especially 'Early ripening rice in Chinese history', *Economic History Review* 2 Ser. 9 (1956–7), pp. 200–18 and 'The Chinese civilization: A search for the roots of its longevity', *Journal of Asian Studies* 35 (1976), pp. 547–54, nor Robert Hartwell, 'Markets, technology, and the structure of enterprise in the development of the eleventh-century Chinese iron and steel industry', *Journal of Economic History* 26 (1966), pp. 29–58. Norman Jacobs, *The Origin of Modern Capitalism and Eastern Asia* (Hong Kong: Hong Kong University Press, 1958), is an important and rare comparative work. See also Rhoads Murphey, 'The city as a center of change: western Europe and China', *Annals, Association of American Geographers* 44 (1954), pp. 349–62, and for some incisive scepticism about the comparative exercise, A. C. Graham, 'China, Europe, and the origins of modern science: Needham's *The Grand Titration*', in Shigeru Nakayama and Nathan Sivin (eds), *Chinese Science: Explorations of an Ancient Tradition* (Cambridge, Mass.: The M.I.T. Press, 1973).

The landscape and colonisation are the subject of Yi-Fu Tuan, *The World's Landscapes: China* (London: Longman, 1970), and the core-area problem ('Key Economic Areas') is the subject of Ch'ao-ting Chi, *Key Economic Areas in Chinese Economic History* (New York: Paragon Book Reprint Corp., 1963, first published 1936), a matter also discussed, with a map, in Stover's book listed above. After reading the first volume of Han Suyin's autobiography, *The Crippled Tree* (London: Jonathan Cape, 1965), I could almost believe Bertrand Russell's comment that he learned more from it than from living a year in China. A survey and penetrating critique of answers to the 'why not China?' question – the 'Needham question' writ large – came out right at the end of my sabbatical: Anthony M. Tang, 'China's agricultural legacy', *Economic Development and Cultural Change* 28 (1979), pp. 1–22. After that I had to call a halt to compiling sources – in January 1980.

Chapter 12. Summary and comparison

I list here those works on global history or *very* long-term economic change, or major aspects thereof, which have been central to the whole exercise. They codify what one would never find or assemble for oneself in a month of Sundays:

Perry Anderson, *Passages from Antiquity to Feudalism*, and *Lineages of the Absolutist State* (London: New Left Books, 1975);

Clarence Ayres, *The Theory of Economic Progress* (New York: Schocken Books, 1962, first published 1944);

Fernand Braudel, *Capitalism and Material Life 1400–1800* (London: Collins/ Fontana, 1974);

Robert Brenner, 'Agrarian class structure and economic development in pre-industrial Europe', *Past and Present* 70 (1976), pp. 30–75;

C. M. Cipolla, *An Economic History of World Population* (Harmondsworth, Middlesex: Penguin Books, 1974 6th edn), and *Before the Industrial Revolution: European Society and Economy, 1000–1700* (London: Methuen, 1976);

Ralph Davis, *The Rise of the Atlantic Economies* (London: Weidenfeld and Nicolson, 1973);

Jan de Vries, *The Economy of Europe in an Age of Crisis, 1600–1750* (Cambridge: C.U.P., 1976);

Maurice Dobb, *Studies in the Development of Capitalism* (London: Routledge, 1963, first published 1946);

W. T. Easterbrook, 'Long-period comparative study: Some historical cases', *Journal of Economic History* 17 (1957), pp. 571–95;

Peter Farb, *Humankind: A History of the Development of Man* (London: Jonathan Cape, 1978);

J. D. Gould, *Economic Growth in History* (London: Methuen, 1972);

Marvin Harris, *Cannibals and Kings: The Origins of Cultures* (London: Collins/Fontana, 1978);

Sir John Hicks, *A Theory of Economic History* (Oxford: O.U.P., 1969);

V. G. Kiernan, 'State and nation in western Europe', *Past and Present* 31 (1965), pp. 20–38;

David Landes, *The Unbound Prometheus* (Cambridge: C.U.P., 1969);

Colin McEvedy, the four works mentioned under Chapter 1 above;

W. H. McNeill, *The Rise of the West* (New York: Mentor, 1965), and *The Shape of European History* (New York: O.U.P., 1974);

George Modelski, 'The long cycle of global politics and the nation-state', *Comparative Studies in Society and History* 20 (1978), pp. 214–35;

W. Barrington Moore Jr, *Social Origins of Dictatorship and Democracy* (London: Allen Lane, the Penguin Press, 1967);

John U. Nef, *Cultural Foundations of Industrial Civilization* (New York: Harper Torchbooks, 1960), and *The Conquest of the Material World* (Chicago: University of Chicago Press, 1964);

D. C. North and R. P. Thomas, *The Rise of the Western World: A New Economic History* (Cambridge: C.U.P., 1973);

Goran Ohlin, 'Remarks on the relevance of western experience in economic growth to former colonial areas', *Journal of World History* 9 (1965), pp. 30–8;

W. W. Rostow, *How It All Began: Origins of the Modern Economy* (New York: McGraw-Hill, 1975);

W. M. S. Russell, *Man, Nature and History* (London: Aldus Books, 1967);

L. S. Stavrianos, *The World Since 1500: A Global History* (Englewood Cliffs, N.J.: Prentice-Hall, 1966);

Charles Tilly (ed), *The Formation of the National State in Western Europe* (Princeton, N.J.: Princeton University Press, 1975, for chapters by Ardant, Finer, Rokkan and Tilly);

Immanuel Wallerstein, *The Modern World System* (New York: Academic Press, 1974);

Robert Wesson, the two works cited under Chapter 6 above;

Richard G. Wilkinson, *Poverty and Progress: An Ecological Model of Economic Development* (London: Methuen, 1973); and

A. J. Youngson (ed), *Economic Development in the Long Run* (London: Allen and Unwin, 1972).

Among these it would be invidious to offer prizes, but for the sake of knowing where to start, the best value per page on 'why Europe first?' is in my view David Landes, *The Unbound Prometheus*, pp. 12–40, which does identify contrasts with Asia and the Middle East. I have had economics students who disagree; it should however be the rôle of the economic historian to persuade them that creative ideas are to be preferred to mere formalism. The truly distinguished economists who have contributed to this literature obviously do agree with a 'no-holds-barred' position. The best short essay from that side of the fence is Goran Ohlin, 'Remarks on the Relevance of Western Experience' (cited above). Finally, water of a sufficiently icy temperature to be taken serious notice of is poured on the notion of stable theories of economic history by P. T. Bauer, 'Economic history as theory', *Economica* N.S. 38 (1971), pp. 163–79. That helped to dissuade me from looking for a monocausal, determinist explanation of *very* long-term change; that and the record itself.

Bibliography

Allmand, C. T. 1973. *Society at War: The Experience of England and France during the Hundred Years' War*. Edinburgh: Oliver and Boyd.

Ambraseys, N. 1971. Value of historical records of earthquakes. *Nature* 232, 375–9.

Ambraseys, N. 1979. A test case of historical seismicity: Isfahan and Chahar Mahal, Iran. *Geographical Journal* 145, 56–71.

Anderson, Perry. 1975. *Lineages of the Absolutist State*. London: New Left Books.

Anon. 1645. *The Desires, and Resolutions of the Club-men of the Counties of Dorset and Wilts*. London. In Wiltshire Tracts, 40. Wiltshire Archaeological Society Library, Devizes.

Ardant, Gabriel. 1975. Financial policy and economic infrastructure of modern states and nations. In *The Formation of National States in Western Europe*, ed. Charles Tilly, 164–242. Princeton: Princeton University Press.

Arnold, T. W. 1961. *The Legacy of Islam*. Oxford: Oxford University Press.

Arrow, Kenneth J. 1969. Classificatory notes on the production and transmission of technological knowledge. *American Economic Review, Papers and Proceedings* 59, 29–35.

Ashley, W. J. 1913. Comparative economic history and the English landlord. *Economic Journal* 23, 165–81.

Ashton, T. S. 1948. *The Industrial Revolution, 1760–1830*. London: Oxford University Press.

B., S. ('S.B.'). 1979. The black rat in Britain. *Nature* 281, 101.

Baldwin, F.E. 1926. *Sumptuary Legislation and Personal Regulation in England*. Baltimore, Md.: The Johns Hopkins Press.

Baldwin, Robert E. 1964. Patterns of development in newly settled regions. In *Agriculture in Economic Development*, ed. Carl Eicher and Lawrence Witt, 238–51. New York: McGraw-Hill.

Barback, R. H. 1967. The political economy of fisheries: from nationalism to internationalism. *Yorkshire Bulletin of Economic and Social Research* 19, 71–84.

Barbour, Violet. 1963. *Capitalism in Amsterdam in the Seventeenth Century*. Ann Arbor: University of Michigan Press. (First published 1950.)

Barkhausen, Max. 1974. Government control and free enterprise in western Germany and the Low Countries in the eighteenth century.

In *Essays in European Economic History 1500–1800*, ed. Peter Earle, 212–73. Oxford: Clarendon Press.

Barnby, Henry. 1970. The Algerian attack on Baltimore 1631. *The Mariner's Mirror* 56, 27–31.

Barraclough, Geoffrey. 1976. *The Crucible of Europe: The Ninth and Tenth Centuries in European History*. London: Thames and Hudson.

Barton, Robert. 1974. *Atlas of the Sea*. London: Heinemann.

Båth, M. 1967. Earthquakes, large, destructive. In *Dictionary of Geophysics*, ed. S. K. Runcorn, vol. 1, 417–24. Oxford: Pergamon Press.

Bauer, P. T. 1971. Economic history as theory. *Economica* n.s. 38, 163–79.

Bean, Richard. 1973. War and the birth of the nation state. *Journal of Economic History* 33, 203–21.

Beaver, Patrick. 1971. *A History of Lighthouses*. London: Peter Davies.

Bell, Christopher. 1974. *Portugal and the Quest for the Indies*. London: Constable.

Beresford, John (ed.). 1978. *James Woodforde: The Diary of a Country Parson 1758–1802*. London: Oxford University Press.

Beresford, M. W. 1967. *New Towns of the Middle Ages*. London: Lutterworth Press.

Berg, Alan. 1973. *The Nutrition Factor: Its Role in National Development*. Washington, D.C.: The Brookings Institute.

Bernard, Jacques. 1972. Trade and finance in the Middle Ages 900–1500. In *The Fontana Economic History of Europe: The Middle Ages*, ed. C. M. Cipolla. London: Collins/Fontana.

Biraben, J. N. and Le Goff, J. 1969. La peste du haut moyen âge. *Annales E.S.C.* 24, 1484–1510.

Birmingham, Stephen. 1972. *The Grandees: America's Sephardic Elite*. New York: Dell Publishing Co.

Blair, P. H. 1959. *An Introduction to Anglo-Saxon England*. Cambridge: Cambridge University Press.

Bland, A. E., Brown, P. A., and Tawney, R. H. (eds.) 1914. *English Economic History: Select Documents*. London: Bell.

Blum, J. 1978. *The End of the Old Order in Rural Europe*. Princeton: Princeton University Press.

Borgstrom, Georg. 1972a. *The Hungry Planet*. 2nd rev. edn. New York: Collier Books.

Borgstrom, Georg. 1972b. Ecological aspects of protein feeding – the case of Peru. In *The Careless Technology: Ecology and International Development*, ed. M. T. Farrar and J. P. Milton. Garden City, New York: The Natural History Press.

Boserup, Ester. 1965. *The Conditions of Agricultural Growth*. London: Allen and Unwin.

Boxer, C. R. 1955. Pombal's dictatorship and the great Lisbon earthquake, 1755. *History Today* November, 729–36.

Braudel, Fernand. 1972. *The Mediterranean and the Mediterranean World in the Age of Philip II*. New York: Harper and Row.

Braudel, Fernand. 1974. *Capitalism and Material Life 1400–1800*. London: Collins/Fontana.

Brenner, Robert. 1976. Agrarian class structure and economic development in pre-industrial Europe. *Past and Present* 70, 30–75.

Bridbury, A. R. 1969. The dark ages. *Economic History Review* 2 ser. 22, 526–37.

Bridbury, A. R. 1973. The black death. *Economic History Review* 2 ser. 26, 577–92.

Brierley, John. 1970. *A Natural History of Man*. London: Heinemann.

Bronfenbrenner, M. 1964. The appeal of confiscation in economic development. In *Two Worlds of Change*, ed. Otto Feinstein. Garden City, New York: Anchor Books.

Buchanan, Keith. 1967. *The Southeast Asian World*. London: G. Bell and Sons.

Buck, J. L. 1937. *Land Utilization in China*. Chicago: University of Chicago Press.

Carefoot, G. L. and Sprott, E. R. 1969. *Famine on the Wind: Plant Diseases and Human History*. London: Angus and Robertson.

Cassen, Robert H. 1978. *India: Population, Society, Economy*. London: Macmillan.

Chadwick, H. Munro. 1945. *The Nationalities of Europe and the Growth of National Ideologies*. Cambridge: Cambridge University Press.

Chambers, James. 1979. *The Devil's Horsemen: The Mongol Invasion of Europe*. London: Weidenfeld and Nicolson.

Chapin, Henry and Walton Smith, F. G. 1953. *The Ocean River*. London: Victor Gollancz.

Chapman, S. D. 1977. The international houses: the continental contribution to British commerce, 1800–1860. *Journal of European Economic History* 6, 5–48.

Chaunu, Pierre. 1979. *European Expansion in the Later Middle Ages*. Amsterdam: North-Holland Publishing Co.

Chi, Ch'ao-ting. 1963. *Key Economic Areas in Chinese History*. New York: Paragon Book Reprint Corp.

Cipolla, C. M. 1967. *Clocks and Culture 1300–1700*. London: Collins.

Cipolla, C. M. 1976a. *Before the Industrial Revolution*. London: Methuen.

Cipolla, C. M. 1976b. *Public Health and the Medical Profession in the Renaissance*. Cambridge: Cambridge University Press.

Clark, Grahame and Piggott, Stuart. 1965. *Prehistoric Societies*. London: Hutchinson.

Cobban, Alfred. 1944. *The Nation State and National Self-Determination*. London: Oxford University Press.

Cohn, Norman. 1970. *The Pursuit of the Millennium*. London: Paladin.

Coles, Paul. 1968. *The Ottoman Impact on Europe*. London: Thames and Hudson.

Commeaux, Charles. 1977. *Histoire des Bourguignons: Des origines à la fin du règne des ducs*. Paris: Fernand Nathan.

Cornell, James. 1979. *The Great International Disaster Book*. New York: Pocket Books.

Crafts, N. F. R. and Ireland, N. J. 1976. A simulation of the impact of changes in age at marriage before and during the advent of industrialization in England. *Population Studies* 30, 495–510.

Crosby, Alfred. 1972. *The Columbian Exchange*. Westport, Conn.: Greenwood.

Cunningham, W. 1896. *Modern Civilisation in some of its Economic Aspects*. London: Methuen.

Darby, H. C. 1961. The face of Europe on the eve of the great discoveries. In *The New Cambridge Modern History*, ed. G. R. Potter, vol. 1, 20–49. Cambridge: Cambridge University Press.

Davidson, Basil *et al.* 1966. *A History of West Africa to the Nineteenth Century*. Garden City, New York: Anchor Books.

Davis, Kingsley. 1951. *The Population of India and Pakistan*. Princeton: Princeton University Press.

Davis, Ralph. 1965. The rise of protection in England, 1689–1786. *Economic History Review* 2 ser. 19, 306–17.

Davis, Ralph. 1973. *The Rise of the Atlantic Economies*. London: Weidenfeld and Nicolson.

Davison, C. 1936. *Great Earthquakes*. London: Thomas Murby and Co.

Dawson, Raymond. 1972. *Imperial China*. Harmondsworth, Middlesex: Penguin Books.

Day, Winifred M. 1949. Relative permanence of former boundaries in India. *Scottish Geographical Magazine* 65, 113–22.

Deane, Phyllis. 1960–1. Capital formation in Britain before the railway age. *Economic Development and Cultural Change* 9, 352–68.

Dehio, Ludwig. 1965. *The Precarious Balance: Four Centuries of the European Power Struggle*. New York: Vintage Books.

Derry, T. K. 1931. The repeal of the apprenticeship clauses of the statute of apprentices. *Economic History Review* 3, 67–87.

Dobby, E. H. G. 1966. *Monsoon Asia*. London: University of London Press.

Dodgshon, Robert A. 1977. The modern world-system: a spatial perspective. *Peasant Studies* 6, 8–19.

Dorwart, R. A. 1971. *The Prussian Welfare State before 1740*. Cambridge, Mass.: Harvard University Press.

Duby, George. 1974. *The Early Growth of the European Economy*. London: Weidenfeld and Nicolson.

Dunstan, Helen. 1975. The late Ming epidemics: a preliminary survey. *Ch'ing-Shih wen-t'i* 3, 1–59.

Duyvendak, J. J. L. 1938. The true dates of the Chinese maritime expeditions in the early fifteenth century. *T'Oung Pao* 34, 341–412.

Eberhard, Wolfram. 1960. *A History of China*. London: Routledge and Kegan Paul.

Editors of *Encyclopaedia Britannica*. 1978. *Disaster! When Nature Strikes Back*. New York: Bantam Books.

Eisenstein, Elizabeth L. 1970. The impact of printing on European education. In *Sociology, History and Education*, ed. P. W. Musgrave, 87–95. London: Methuen.

Elman, P. 1936–7. The economic consequences of the expulsion of the Jews in 1290. *Economic History Review* 7, 145–54.

Elvin, Mark. 1973. *The Pattern of the Chinese Past*. London: Eyre Methuen.

Fairbank, John K., Reischauer, Edwin O., and Craig, Albert M. 1973. *East Asia: Tradition and Transformation*. London: Allen and Unwin.

Farb, Peter. 1978. *Humankind: A History of the Development of Man*. London: Jonathan Cape.

Febvre, Lucien. 1932. *A Geographical Introduction to History*. London: Kegan Paul, Trench, Trubner and Co.

Febvre, Lucien. 1976. *The Coming of the Book: The Impact of Printing 1450–1600*. London: New Left Books.

Fermor, Patrick Leigh. 1977. *A Time of Gifts: On foot to Constantinople*. London: John Murray.

Fichtner, Paula S. 1976. Dynastic marriage in sixteenth century Habsburg diplomacy and statecraft: an interdisciplinary approach. *American Historical Review* 81, 243–65.

Filesi, T. 1972. *China and Africa in the Middle Ages*. London: Frank Cass.

Fitzgerald, C. P. 1972. *The Southern Expansion of the Chinese People*. London: Barrie and Jenkins.

Fitzgerald, C. P. 1973. *China and Southeast Asia since 1945*. London: Longman.

Flinn, M. W. 1979. Plague in Europe and the Mediterranean countries. *Journal of European Economic History* 8, 131–48.

Frank, Andre Gunder. 1978. *World Accumulation, 1492–1789*. London: Macmillan.

Fraser, George Macdonald. 1971. *The Steel Bonnets: The Story of the Anglo-Scottish Border Reivers*. London: Pan Books.

Fraser, J. T. 1975. *Of Time, Passion, and Knowledge*. New York: Braziller.

Freudenberger, Herman. 1960. Industrialization in Bohemia and Moravia in the eighteenth century. *Journal of Central European Affairs* 19, 347–56.

Friedman, David R. 1977. A theory of the size and shape of nations. *Journal of Political Economy* 85, 59–77.

Fusfeld, Daniel R. 1968. *The Age of the Economist*. New York: Morrow and Co.

Gatty, Harold. 1958. *Nature is your Guide*. London: Collins.

Genicot, Léopold. 1966. Crisis: from the Middle Ages to modern times. In *Cambridge Economic History of Europe*, ed. M. M. Postan, vol. 1, Cambridge: Cambridge University Press.

Gilfillan, S. C. 1920. The coldward course of progress. *Political Science Quarterly* 35, 393–410.

Gilfillan, S. C. 1935. *Inventing the Ship*. Chicago: Follett.

Gimpel, Jean. 1977. *The Medieval Machine*. London: Gollancz.

Glamann, Kristof. 1974. European trade 1500–1750. In *The Fontana Economic History of Europe: The Sixteenth and Seventeenth Centuries*, ed. C. M. Cipolla. London: Collins/Fontana.

Glick, Thomas F. 1974. Discussion of Watson: *The Arab agricultural revolution*. *Journal of Economic History* 34, 74–8.

Goitein, S. D. 1967. *Mediterranean Society: Volume I: Economic Foundations*. Berkeley: University of California Press.

Goitein, S. D. 1973. *Letters of Medieval Jewish Traders*. Princeton: Princeton University Press.

Goody, Jack. 1971. *Technology, Tradition, and the State in Africa*. London: Oxford University Press.

Goody, Jack. 1976. *Production and Reproduction*. Cambridge: Cambridge University Press.

Goubert, Pierre. 1974. *The Ancien Régime: French Society 1600–1750*. New York: Harper Torchbooks.

Gould, J. D. 1972. *Economic Growth in History*. London: Methuen.

Graham, A. C. 1973. China, Europe, and the origins of modern science: Needham's *The Grand Titration*. In *Chinese Science: Explorations of an Ancient Tradition*, ed. S. Nakayama and N. Sivin, 45–69. Cambridge, Mass.: The M.I.T. Press.

Graham, Michael. 1956. Harvests of the Seas. In *Man's Role in Changing the Face of the Earth*, ed. William L. Thomas, vol. 2, 487–503. Chicago: University of Chicago Press.

Grant, Bruce. 1967. *Indonesia*. Harmondsworth, Middlesex: Penguin Books.

Green, J. R. 1888. *A Short History of the English People*. London: Macmillan.

Grey, Ian. 1967. *Ivan III and the Unification of Russia*. New York: Collier Books.

Gribbin, John. 1979. Eighteenth century patterns may indicate future patterns. *New Scientist* 83, 891–3.

Grierson, Philip. 1975. *Numismatics*. London: Oxford University Press.

Grigg, David. 1974. *Agricultural Systems of the World*. Cambridge: Cambridge University Press.

Hajnal, J. 1965. European marriage patterns in perspective. In *Population in History*, ed. David Glass and D. E. C. Eversley, 101–43. London: Edward Arnold.

Hamilton, Henry. 1963. *An Economic History of Scotland in the Eighteenth Century*. Oxford: Clarendon Press.

Hamilton, Sir William. 1783. Of the earthquakes which happened in Italy, from February to May, 1783. *Philosophical Transactions* 73, 373–83.

Hanley, Susan B. and Yamamura, Kozo. 1972. Population trends and economic growth in pre-industrial Japan. In *Population and Social Change*, ed. David Glass and Roger Revelle, 451–99. London: Edward Arnold.

Harris, Marvin. 1978. *Cannibals and Kings: The Origins of Cultures*. London: Collins/Fontana.

Harrison, John A. 1972. *The Chinese Empire: A Short History of China from Neolithic times to the end of the Eighteenth Century*. New York: Harcourt Brace Jovanovich.

Harrison, Paul. 1979. The curse of the tropics. *New Scientist* 84, 602–4.

Harte, N. B. 1976. State control of dress and social change in pre-industrial England. In *Trade, Government and Economy in Pre-Industrial England*, ed. D. C. Coleman and A. H. John, 132–65. London: Weidenfeld and Nicolson.

Hartwell, Robert. 1966. Markets, technology, and the structure of enterprise in the development of the eleventh century Chinese iron and steel industry. *Journal of Economic History* 26, 29–58.

Hartwell, Ronald Max. 1969. Economic growth in England before the industrial revolution: some methodological issues. *Journal of Economic History* 29, 13–31.

Hawthorn, Geoffrey (ed.) 1978. *Population and Development: High and Low Fertility in Poor Countries*. London: Cass.

Heaton, Herbert, 1965. *The Yorkshire Woollen and Worsted Industries*. Oxford: Clarendon Press.

Heers, Jacques. 1974. The 'feudal' economy and capitalism: words, ideas and reality. *Journal of European Economic History* 3, 609–53.

Henderson, W. O. 1963. *Studies in the Economic Policy of Frederick the Great*. London: Cass.

Herlihy, David. 1957. Treasure hoards in the Italian economy, 960–1139. *Economic History Review* 2 ser. 10, 1–14.

Herlihy, David. 1971. The economy of traditional Europe. *Journal of Economic History* 31, 153–64.

Herlihy, David. 1974. Ecological conditions and demographic change. In *One Thousand Years: Western Europe in the Middle Ages*, ed. Richard L. De Molen, 3–43. Boston: Houghton Mifflin.

Herodotus. 1954. *The Histories*. Harmondsworth, Middlesex: Penguin Books.

Hess, Andrew C. 1970. The evolution of the Ottoman seaborne empire in the age of the oceanic discoveries, 1453–1525. *American Historical Review* 75, 1892–1919.

Hewitt, H. J. 1966. *The Organisation of War under Edward III 1338–62*. Manchester: Manchester University Press.

Hibbert, Christopher. 1970. *The Dragon Wakes: China and the West, 1793–1911*. London: Longman.

Hicks, Sir John. 1969. *A Theory of Economic History*. London: Oxford University Press.

Higonnet, Patrice. 1978. Reading, writing and revolution. *The Times Literary Supplement* 13 October, 1153–54.

Hillaby, John. 1972. *Journey through Europe*. London: Constable.

Hilton, R. H. and Sawyer, P. H. 1963. Technical determinism: the stirrup and the plough. *Past and Present* 24, 90–100.

Hirschman, Albert O. 1977. *The Passions and the Interests: Political Arguments for Capitalism before its Triumph*. Princeton: Princeton University Press.

Hirschman, Albert O. 1978. Exit, voice, and the state. *World Politics* 31, 90–107.

Hirshler, E. E. 1954. Medieval economic competition. *Journal of Economic History* 14, 52–8.

Ho, Peng-Yoke. 1964. Natural phenomena recorded in the Dai-Viet Su'-Ky Toan-Thu', an early Annamese historical source. *Journal of the American Oriental Society* 84, 127–49.

Ho, Ping-ti. 1956–7. Early ripening rice in Chinese history. *Economic History Review* 2 ser. 9, 200–18.

Ho, Ping-ti. 1962. *The Ladder of Success in Imperial China, Aspects of Social Mobility, 1368–1911*. New York: Columbia University Press.

Ho, Ping-ti. 1976. The Chinese civilization: a search for the roots of its longevity. *Journal of Asian Studies* 35, 547–54.

Holborn, Hajo. 1951. *The Political Collapse of Europe*. New York: Knopf.

Hollingsworth, Thomas H. n. d. Population Crises in the Past? University of Glasgow, typescript.

Homer, Sidney. 1963. *A History of Interest Rates*. New Brunswick, N.J.: Rutgers University Press.

Honey, P. J. 1968. *Genesis of a Tragedy: The Historical Background to the Vietnam War*. London: Benn.

Hooper, W. 1915. Tudor sumptuary laws. *English Historical Review* 30, 433–49.

Hopkins, A. G. 1973. *An Economic History of West Africa*. London: Longman.

Horne, Donald. 1964. *The Lucky Country*. Harmondsworth, Middlesex: Penguin Books.

Hoskins, W. G. 1950. *The Heritage of Leicestershire*. Leicester: City of Leicester.

Hudd, A. E. 1957. Richard Ameryk and the name America. In *Gloucestershire Studies*, ed. H. P. R. Finberg, 123–9. Leicester: The University Press.

Hutchinson, Sir Joseph. 1966. Land and human populations. *The Advancement of Science* 23, 507–28.

Inalcik, Halil. 1969. Capital formation in the Ottoman empire. *Journal of Economic History* 29, 97–140.

Inalcik, Halil. 1973. *The Ottoman Empire: The Classical Age 1300–1600*. London: Weidenfeld and Nicolson.

Innis, Harold A. (revised by Mary Q. Innis). 1972. *Empire and Communications*. Toronto: University of Toronto Press.

Iyer, Raghavan (ed.). 1965. *The Glass Curtain between Asia and Europe*. London: Oxford University Press.

Jackson, W. A. Douglas. 1968. *The Russo-Chinese borderlands*. Princeton, N.J.: D. Van Nostrand Co.

Jacobs, Norman. 1958. *The Origin of Modern Capitalism and Eastern Asia*. Hong Kong: Hong Kong University Press.

Jankovitch, Miklos. 1971. *They Rode into Europe: The Fruitful Exchange in the Arts of Horsemanship between East and West*. New York: Scribner's.

Jeremy, David J. 1977. Damming the flood: British government efforts to check the outflow of technicians and machinery, 1780–1843. *Business History Review* 51, 1–34.

Johnson, H. T. 1967. Cathedral building and the medieval economy. *Explorations in Economic History* N.S. 4, 191–210.

Jones, E. L. 1968. The reduction of fire damage in southern England, 1650–1850. *Post-Medieval Archaeology* 2, 140–9.

Jones, E. L. 1970. English and European agricultural development 1650–1750. In *The Industrial Revolution*, ed. R. M. Hartwell. Oxford: Basil Blackwell.

Jones, E. L. 1973. The fashion manipulators: consumer tastes and British industries, 1660–1800. In *Business Enterprise and Economic Change*, ed. L. P. Cain and P. J. Uselding, 198–226. Kent, Ohio: Kent State University Press.

Jones, E. L. 1974a. *Agriculture and the Industrial Revolution*. Oxford: Basil Blackwell.

Jones, E. L. 1974b. Institutional determinism and the rise of the western world. *Economic Inquiry* 12, 114–24.

Jones, E. L. 1976. A new essay on western civilization in its economic aspects. *Australian Economic History Review* 16, 95–109.

Jones, E. L. 1977a. Environment, agriculture, and industrialization in Europe. *Agricultural History* 51, 491–502.

Jones, E. L. 1977b. Societal adaptations to disaster. *Biology and Human Affairs* 42, 145–9.

Jones, E. L. 1978. Disaster management and resource saving in Europe, 1400–1800. In *Natural Resources in European History*, ed. Antoni Maczak and William N. Parker. Washington, D.C.: Resources for the Future. Shorter, undocumented version in *Proceedings*, Seventh International Economic History Congress, ed. Michael Flinn, vol. 1, Edinburgh: Edinburgh University Press.

Jones, E. L. 1979. The environment and the economy. In *The New Cambridge Modern History* 13. *Companion Volume*, ed. Peter Burke, 15–42. Cambridge: Cambridge University Press.

Jones, E. L. 1982. *Agricoltura e Rivoluzione Industriale*, Roma: Editori Riuniti.

Jones, E. L. and Falkus, M. E. 1979. Urban improvement and the English economy in the seventeenth and eighteenth centuries. *Research in Economic History* 4, 193–233.

Kahan, Arcadius. 1967. Nineteenth-century European experience with policies of economic nationalism. In *Economic Nationalism in Old and New States*, ed. Harry G. Johnson. Chicago: University of Chicago Press.

Kahan, Arcadius. 1968. National calamities and their effect upon the food supply in Russia. *Jahrbücher für Geschichte Osteuropas* 16, 353–77.

Kahan, Arcadius. 1979. Social aspects of the plague epidemics in eighteenth-century Russia. *Economic Development and Cultural Change* 27, 255–66.

Kamen, Henry. 1976. *The Iron Century: Social Change in Europe 1500–1660*. London: Cardinal.

Kaplan, David. 1963. Man, monuments and political systems. *Southwestern Journal of Anthropology* 19, 397–410.

Kellenbenz, Hermann. 1974. Technology in the age of the scientific revolution, 1500–1700. In *The Fontana Economic History of Europe: The Sixteenth and Seventeenth Centuries*, ed. C. M. Cipolla. London: Fontana/Collins.

Kellett, J. R. 1958. The breakdown of gild and corporation control over handicraft and retail trade in London. *Economic History Review* 2 ser. 10, 381–94.

Kepler, J. S. 1976. *The Exchange of Christendom: The International Entrepot at Dover 1622–1651*. Leicester: Leicester University Press.

Keys, A. *et al*. 1950. *The Biology of Human Starvation*. 2 vols. Minneapolis: University of Minnesota Press.

Kiernan, Thomas. 1978. *The Arabs: Their History, Aims and Challenge to the Industrialized World*. London: Abacus.

Kiernan, V. G. 1965. State and nation in western Europe. *Past and Present* 31, 20–38.

Kisch, Herbert. 1964. Growth deterrents of a medieval heritage: the Aachen-area woolen trades before 1790. *Journal of Economic History* 24, 517–37.

Knoop, D. and Jones, G. P. 1967. *The Medieval Mason*. Manchester: Manchester University Press.

Koenigsberger, H. G. 1971. *The Habsburgs and Europe 1516–1660*. Ithaca, New York: Cornell University Press.

Kortepeter, C. M. 1973. *Ottoman Imperialism During the Reformation: Europe and the Caucasus*. London: University of London Press.

Kramer, Stella. 1927. *The English Craft Gilds: Studies in their Progress and Decline*. New York: Columbia University Press.

Krause, John T. 1973. Some implications of recent work in historical demography. In *Applied Historical Studies*, ed. Michael Drake, 155–83. London: Methuen.

Kuznets, Simon. 1965. Capital formation in modern economic growth (and some implications for the past). *Contributions to the Third International Conference of Economic History, Munich*, vol. 3, 15–33. Paris: Mouton.

Lach, Donald. 1965, 1970. *Asia in the Making of Europe*. 2 vols. Chicago: University of Chicago Press.

Lach, D. F. and Flaumenhaft, Carol (eds.). 1965. *Asia on the Eve of Europe's Expansion*. Englewood Cliffs, N.J.: Prentice-Hall.

Lamb, H. H. 1977. *Climate Present, Past and Future*, vol. 2. London: Methuen.

Lambert, L. Don. 1971. The role of climate in the economic development of nations. *Land Economics* 47, 339–44.

Landes, David. 1966. *The Rise of Capitalism*. New York: Macmillan.

Landes, David. 1969. *The Unbound Prometheus*. Cambridge: Cambridge University Press.

Lane, Frank W. 1965. *The Elements Rage*. Philadelphia: Chilton Books.

Langer, W. L. 1972. Checks on population growth: 1750–1850. *Scientific American* 226, 92–9.

Large, E. C. 1940. *The Advance of the Fungi*. New York: Holt.

Latter, J. H. 1968–9. Natural disasters. *The Advancement of Science* 25, 362–80.

Lauwerys, J. A. 1969. *Man's Impact on Nature*. London: Aldus Books.

Le Roy Ladurie, E. 1979. *The Territory of the Historian*. Hassocks, Sussex: The Harvester Press.

Leary, Lewis (ed.). 1962. *The Autobiography of Benjamin Franklin*. New York: Collier Books.

Lee, Ronald. 1973. Population in preindustrial England: an econometric analysis. *Quarterly Journal of Economics* 87, 581–607.

Leibenstein, H. 1957. *Economic Backwardness and Economic Growth*. New York: Wiley.

Levins, Richard. 1968. *Evolution in Changing Environments*. Princeton: Princeton University Press.

Lewis, A. R. 1958. *The Northern Seas: shipping and commerce in Northern Europe, A.D. 300–1100*. Princeton: Princeton University Press.

Lewis, James. 1979. The vulnerable state: an alternative view. In *Disaster Assistance: Appraisal, Reform and New Approaches*, ed. Lynn H. Stephens and Steven J. Green, 104–29. New York: New York University Press.

Lewis, P. S. 1972. *The Recovery of France in the Fifteenth Century*. New York: Harper and Row.

Loomis, R. S. 1978. Ecological dimensions of medieval agrarian systems: an ecologist responds. *Agricultural History* 52, 478–83.

Lord, John. 1972. *The Maharajahs*. London: Hutchinson.

Loture, Robert de. 1949. *Histoire de la grande pêche de Terre-Neuve*. Paris: Edition Gallimard.

McCloy, Shelby T. 1938. Some eighteenth century housing projects in France. *Social Forces* May, 528–9.

McCloy, Shelby T. 1946. *Government Assistance in Eighteenth Century France*. Durham, North Carolina: Duke University Press.

McEvedy, Colin. 1972. *The Penguin Atlas of Modern History (to 1815)*. Harmondsworth, Middlesex: Penguin Books.

McEvedy, Colin and Jones, Richard. 1978. *Atlas of World Population History*. Harmondsworth, Middlesex: Penguin Books.

Macfarlane, Alan. 1978. Modes of reproduction. In *Population and Development: High and Low Fertility in Poor Countries*, ed. Geoffrey Hawthorn, 100–20. London: Frank Cass.

Macfarlane, K. B. 1972. *Wycliffe and English Non-Conformity*. Harmondsworth, Middlesex: Penguin Books.

McIntyre, K. G. 1977. *The Secret Discovery of Australia: Portuguese Ventures 200 years before Captain Cook*. Mendindie, South Australia: Souvenir Press.

Mackinder, Halford J. 1962. *Democratic Ideals and Reality: with Additional Papers*. New York: Norton and Co. (First published 1942.)

MacLeod, W. C. 1967. Celt and Indian: Britain's old world frontier in relation to the new. In *Beyond the Frontier*, ed. Paul Bohannan and Fred Plog. Garden City, New York: The Natural History Press.

McNeill, W. H. 1964. *Past and Future*. Chicago: University of Chicago Press.

McNeill, W. H. 1965. *The Rise of the West*. New York: Mentor.

McNeill, W. H. 1976. *Plagues and Peoples*. Garden City, New York: Anchor Press/Doubleday.

Maddison, Angus. 1971. *Class Structure and Economic Growth: India and Pakistan since the Moghuls*. New York: Norton.

Magill, Col. Sir James. 1926. *The Red Cross: The Idea and its Development*. London: Cassell.

Mallory, Walter H. 1926. *China: Land of Famine*. New York: American Geographical Society.

Markham, S. F. 1947. *Climate and the Energy of Nations*. London: Oxford University Press.

Martin, E. T. 1961. *Thomas Jefferson: Scientist*. New York: Collier.

Mason, Peter. 1978. *Genesis to Jupiter*. Sydney: Australian Broadcasting Commission.

May, Jacques M. 1961. *The Ecology of Malnutrition in the Far and Near East*. New York: Haffner Publishing Co.

Meinig, D. W. 1969. A macrogeography of western imperialism: some morphologies of moving frontiers of political control. In *Settlement and Encounter*, ed. Fay Gale and G. H. Lawton, 213–40. Melbourne: Oxford University Press.

Metcalf, D. M. 1967. The prosperity of north-western Europe in the eighth and ninth centuries. *Economic History Review* 2 ser. 20, 344–57.

Meuvret, J. 1965. Demographic crisis in France from the sixteenth to the eighteenth century. In *Population in History*, ed. David Glass and D. E. C. Eversley. London: Edward Arnold.

Mill, John Stuart. 1965. *Principles of Political Economy*. Toronto: University of Toronto Press.

Milne, J. 1911. *A Catalogue of Destructive Earthquakes A.D. 7–1899*. London: British Association for the Advancement of Science.

Mockler, Anthony. 1970. *Mercenaries*. London: Macdonald.

Modelski, G. 1964. Kautilya: foreign policy and international system in the ancient Hindu world. *American Political Science Review* 58, 549–60.

Modelski, G. 1978. The long cycle of global politics and the nation-state. *Comparative Studies in Society and History* 20, 214–35.

Mokyr, Joel. 1976. Government, finance, taxation, and economic policy in old regime Europe. *Journal of Economic History* 36, 28–9.

Montandon, Raoul. 1923. A propos du projet Ciraolo: une carte mondiale de distribution géographique des calamités. *Revue Internationale de la Croix-Rouge* 5, 271–344.

Moore, Barrington, Jr. 1967. *Social Origins of Dictatorship and Democracy*.

London: Allen Lane

Moreland, W. H. 1972. *From Akbar to Aurangzeb*. New Delhi: Oriental Books Reprint Co. (First published 1923.)

Morris, A. E. J. 1972. *History of Urban Form: Prehistory to the Renaissance*. London: George Godwin.

Morris, Christopher. 1966. *The Tudors*. London: Collins/Fontana.

Morris, M. D. 1967. Values as an obstacle to economic growth in south Asia: an historical survey. *Journal of Economic History* 27, 588–607.

Murphey, Rhoads. 1954. The city as a center of change: western Europe and China. *Annals of the Association of American Geographers* 44, 349–62.

Musgrave, P. W. (ed.). 1970. *Sociology, History and Education*. London: Methuen.

Narain, Brij. 1929. *Indian Economic Life*. Lahore: Uttar Chand Kapur and Sons.

Nath, Pran. 1929. *A Study in the Economic Condition of Ancient India*. No place or publisher stated.

Nef, J. U. 1960. *Cultural Foundations of Industrial Civilization*. New York: Harper Torchbooks.

Nef, J. U. 1968. *War and Human Progress*. New York: Norton.

North, Douglass C. 1968. Sources of productivity change in ocean shipping, 1600–1850. *Journal of Political Economy* 76, 953–70.

North, Douglass C. 1977. Markets and other allocative systems in history: the challenge of Karl Polanyi. *Journal of European Economic History* 6, 703–16.

North, Douglass C. and Thomas, Robert Paul. 1973. *The Rise of the Western World: A New Economic History*. Cambridge: Cambridge University Press.

Ogg, David. 1934. *England in the Reign of Charles II*, vol. 2, Oxford: Clarendon Press.

Pannell, J. P. M. 1964. *An Illustrated History of Civil Engineering*. London: Thames and Hudson.

Paré, Ambroise. n.d. Journeys in diverse places. In *The Harvard Classics*, vol. 38, *Scientific Papers*. New York: Collier.

Parkes, James. 1964. *A History of the Jewish People*. Harmondsworth, Middlesex: Penguin Books.

Parkinson, C. N. 1963. *East and West*. London: John Murray.

Parris, G. K. 1968. *A Chronicle of Plant Pathology*. Starkville, Missouri: Johnson and Sons.

Parry, J. H. 1964. *The Age of Reconnaissance*. New York: Mentor.

Pearn, B. R. 1963. *An Introduction to the History of South East Asia*. Kuala Lumpur: Longman of Malaysia.

Pearson, Harry W. 1977. *The Livelihood of Man: Karl Polanyi*. New York: Academic Press.

Perjés, G. 1970. Army provisioning: logistics and strategy in the second half of the seventeenth century. *Acta Historica Academiae Scientarium Hungaricae* 16, 1–51.

Perkins, Dwight. 1967. Government as an obstacle to industrialization: the case of nineteenth-century China. *Journal of Economic History* 27, 478–92.

Perkins, Dwight. 1969. *Agricultural Development in China 1368–1968*. Edinburgh: Edinburgh University Press.

Piggott, Stuart. 1976. *Ruins in a Landscape*. Edinburgh: Edinburgh University Press.

Pike, Ruth. 1962. The Genoese in Seville and the opening of the new world. *Journal of Economic History* 22, 348–78.

Pipes, Richard. 1974. *Russia under the Old Regime*. New York: Scribners.

Pipes, Richard and Fine, J. V. A. Jr (eds.). 1966. *Of the Russe Commonwealth by Giles Fletcher 1591*. Cambridge, Mass.: Harvard University Press.

Pirenne, Henri. 1913–14. The stages in the social history of capitalism. *American Historical Review* 19, 494–515.

Plucknett, T. F. 1936. Some proposed legislation of Henry VIII. *Transactions of the Royal Historical Society* 4 ser. 19, 119–44.

Polunin, Ivan. 1976. Disease, morbidity, and mortality in China, India, and the Arab world. In *Asian Medical Systems*, ed. Charles Leslie. Berkeley, Calif.: University of California Press.

Pounds, N. J. G. and Ball, S. S. 1964. Core-areas and the development of the European states system. *Annals of the Association of American Geographers* 54, 24–40.

Poynter, F. N. L. 1963. *The Journal of James Yonge, Plymouth Surgeon*. London: Longman, Green and Co.

Priestley, Joseph. 1965. *Priestley's Writings on Philosophy, Science and Politics*. New York: Collier Books.

Purcell, Victor. 1965. *The Chinese in Southeast Asia*. London: Oxford University Press.

Purves, D. Laing (ed.). 1880. *A Voyage round the World by Sir Francis Drake and William Dampier*. Edinburgh: William P. Nimmo and Co.

Rapp, R. T. 1975. The unmaking of the Mediterranean trade hegemony. *Journal of Economic History* 35, 499–525.

Reade, Winwood. 1925. *The Martyrdom of Man*. London: Watts.

Redlich, Fritz. 1953. European aristocracy and economic development. *Explorations in Entrepreneurial History* 6, 78–91.

Reynolds, R. L. 1965. The Mediterranean frontiers, 1000–1400. In *The*

Frontier in Perspective, ed. W. D. Wyman and C. B. Kroeber. Madison, Wis.: Wisconsin University Press.

Rich, E. E. and Wilson, C. H. (eds.). 1977. *The Cambridge Economic History of Europe* 5 *The Economic Organization of Early Modern Europe*. Cambridge: Cambridge University Press.

Richards, Paul W. 1973. Africa, the 'odd man out'. In *Tropical Forest Ecosystems in Africa and South America*, ed. Betty J. Meggars *et al.* Washington, D.C.: Smithsonian Institution Press.

Rodinson, Maxime. 1978. *Islam and Capitalism*. Austin, Tex.: University of Texas Press.

Rokkan, Stein. 1975. Dimensions of state formation and nation-building. In *The Formation of National States in Western Europe*, ed. Charles Tilly, 562–600. Princeton: Princeton University Press.

Rosen, George. 1953. Cameralism and the concept of medical police. *Bulletin of the History of Medicine* 25, 21–42.

Rosenberg, Hans. 1958. *Bureaucracy, Aristocracy, and Autocracy: The Prussian Experience, 1660–1815*. Cambridge, Mass.: Harvard University Press.

Rostow, W. W. 1975. *How it all Began: Origins of the Modern Economy*. New York: McGraw-Hill.

Rothenberg, G. E. 1973. The Austrian sanitary cordon and the control of the bubonic plague, 1710–1871. *Journal of the History of Medicine and Allied Sciences* 28, 15–23.

Rousell, Aage. 1957. *The National Museum of Denmark*. Copenhagen: The National Museum.

Russell, J. C. 1972. *Medieval Regions and their Cities*. Newton Abbot: David and Charles.

Russell, W. M. S. 1967. *Man, Nature and History*. London: Aldus Books.

Russell, W. M. S. 1979. The palaeodemographic view. Lecture to the Royal Society of Medicine and the Academy of Medicine, Toronto, International Meeting on Disease in Ancient Man, London, March. Typescript.

Rycaut, Paul. 1668. *The Present State of the Ottoman Empire*. Farnborough, Hants: Facsimile reproduction by Gregg International, 1972.

'S. B.' (*See* B., S.)

Samhaber, Ernst. 1963. *Merchants Make History*. London: Harrap.

Sauer, Carl O. 1973. *Northern Mists*. San Francisco: Turtle Island Foundation.

Schofield, R. S. 1976. The relationship between demographic structure and the environment in pre-industrial western Europe. In *Sozialgeschichte der Familie in der Neuzeit Europas: Neue Forschungen Herausgegeben von Werner Conze*, 147–60. Stuttgart: Klett.

Scoville, W. C. 1951. Minority migrations and the diffusion of technology. *Journal of Economic History* 11, 347–60.

Scoville, W. C. 1960. *The Persecution of Huguenots and French Economic Development 1680–1720*. Berkeley, Calif.: University of California Press.

Shepard, Francis P. 1977. *Geological Oceanography*. St Lucia, Queensland: University of Queensland Press.

Shepherd, James F. and Walton, Gary M. 1972. *Shipping, Maritime Trade, and the Economic Development of Colonial North America*. New York: Cambridge University Press.

Simkin, C. G. F. 1968. *The Traditional Trade of Asia*. London: Oxford University Press.

Sitwell, Sacheverell. 1948. *The Hunters and the Hunted*. New York: Macmillan.

Slicher van Bath, B. H. 1963. *The Agrarian History of Western Europe A.D. 500–1850*. London: Edward Arnold.

Smith, Adam. 1884 and 1937. *An Inquiry into the Nature and Causes of The Wealth of Nations*. London: T. Nelson and Sons; New York: Modern Library.

Smith, Vincent A. 1958. *The Oxford History of India*. Oxford: Clarendon Press.

Sølvi, Sognar. 1976. A demographic crisis averted? *Scandinavian Economic History Review* 24, 114–28.

Sorokin, P. A. *et al*. 1931. *A Systematic Source Book in Rural Sociology*, vol. 2. Minneapolis: University of Minnesota Press.

Spate, O. H. K. and A. T. A. Learmonth. 1967. *India and Pakistan*. London: Methuen.

Speaight, Robert. 1975. *Burgundy*. London: Collins.

Sprague de Camp, L. 1974. *The Ancient Engineers*. New York: Ballantine Books.

Stavrianos, L. S. 1966. *The Balkans Since 1453*. New York: Holt, Rinehart and Winston.

Stechow, Wolfgang. n.d. *Pieter Bruegel the Elder*. New York: Harry N. Abrams.

Steinberg, S. M. 1961. *Four Hundred Years of Printing*. Harmondsworth, Middlesex: Penguin Books.

Stevenson, D. A. 1959. *The World's Lighthouses before 1820*. London: Oxford University Press.

Stover, Leon E. 1974. *The Cultural Ecology of Chinese Civilization*. New York: Mentor.

Stover, Leon E. and Stover, Takeko Kawai. 1976. *China: an Anthropological Perspective*. Pacific Palisades, Calif.: Goodyear Publishing Co.

Strayer, Joseph R. 1966. The historical experience of nation building in

Europe. In *Nation Building*, ed. Karl W. Deutsch and W. J. Foltz, 17–26. New York: Atherton Press.

Strayer, Joseph R. 1970. *On the Medieval Origins of the Modern State*. Princeton: Princeton University Press.

Strayer, Joseph R. 1974. Notes on the origin of English and French export taxes. *Studia Gratiana* 15, 399–422.

Suyin, Han. 1965. *The Crippled Tree: China, Biography, History, Autobiography*. London: Jonathan Cape.

Taagepera, Rein. 1978. Size and duration of empires: systematics of size. *Social Science Research* 7, 108–27.

Tang, Anthony M. 1979. China's agricultural legacy. *Economic Development and Cultural Change* 28, 1–22.

Tannehill, I. R. 1956. *Hurricanes: Their Nature and History*. Princeton: Princeton University Press.

Tawney, R. H. 1932. *Land and Labour in China*. London: George Allen and Unwin.

Taylor, G. R. 1975. *How to Avoid the Future*. London: New English Library.

Tazieff, Haroun. 1962. *When the Earth Trembles*. New York: Harcourt, Brace and World.

Thapur, Romila. 1966. *A History of India*, vol. 1. Harmondsworth, Middlesex: Penguin Books.

Thesiger, Wilfrid. 1964. *Arabian Sands*. Harmondsworth, Middlesex: Penguin Books.

Tilly, Charles (ed.). 1975. *The Formation of the National State in Western Europe*. Princeton: Princeton University Press.

Timoshenko, S. P. 1953. *History of Strength of Materials*. New York: McGraw-Hill.

Tinker, Hugh. 1966. *South Asia: A Social History*. London: Pall Mall Press.

Tipton, Frank B. Jr. 1974. Farm labour and power politics: Germany, 1850–1914. *Journal of Economic History* 34, 951–79.

Toynbee, Arnold J. 1957. *A Study of History*, vols. 7–10, abridged. London: Oxford University Press.

Trevelyan, G. M. 1942. *History of England*. London: Longman, Green and Co.

Trevor-Roper, Hugh. 1965. *The Rise of Christian Europe*. London: Thames and Hudson.

Trevor-Roper, Hugh. 1967. *Religion, the Reformation and Social Change*. London: Macmillan.

Tuan, Yi-Fu. 1970. *China*. London: Longman.

Turnbull, Colin M. 1976. *Man in Africa*. Newton Abbot: David and Charles.

Udovitch, Abraham L. 1970. *Partnership and Profit in Medieval Islam*. Princeton: Princeton University Press.

Unwin, George. 1924. *Samuel Oldknow and the Arkwrights*. Manchester: Manchester University Press.

Unwin, George. 1963. *The Gilds and Companies of London*. London: Frank Cass.

Urness, Carol (ed.). 1967. *A Naturalist in Russia; letters from Peter Simon Pallas to Thomas Pennant*. Minneapolis: University of Minnesota Press.

Usher, A. P. 1930. The history of population and settlement in Eurasia. *Geographical Review* 20, 110–32.

Usher, A. P. 1973. *The History of the Grain Trade in France 1400–1710*. New York: Octagon Press.

Vagts, Alfred. 1959. *A History of Militarism*. New York: The Free Press.

van Beemelen, R. W. 1956. The influence of geologic events on human history. *Nederlands Geologisch Mynbouwkundig Genootschapp Verhandelingen* 16, 20–36.

van der Wee, Herman and van Cauwenberghe, Eddy (eds.). 1978. *Productivity of Land and Agricultural Innovation in the Low Countries (1250–1800)*. Louvain: Leuven University Press.

van Klaveren, Jacob. 1969. *General Economic History, 100–1760: From the Roman Empire to the Industrial Revolution*. Munich: Gerhard Kieckens.

Verlinden, Charles. 1953. Italian influence on Iberian colonization. *Hispanic American Historical Review* 33, 199–211.

Verlinden, Charles. 1972. From the Mediterranean to the Atlantic: aspects of an economic shift (12th–18th century). *Journal of European Economic History* 1, 625–46.

Vilar, Pierre. 1966. Problems of the formation of capitalism. In *The Rise of Capitalism*, ed. David Landes, 26–40. New York: Macmillan.

Wailes, Bernard. 1972. Plow and population in temperate Europe. In *Population Growth: Anthropological Implications*, ed. Brian Spooner, 154–79. Cambridge, Mass.: M.I.T. Press.

Walford, C. 1878 and 1879. The famines of the world: past and present. *Journal of the Statistical Society* 41, 433–535, and 42, 79–275.

Wallerstein, Immanuel. 1974. *The Modern World System: Capitalist Agriculture and the Origins of the European World-Economy in the Sixteenth Century*. New York: Academic Press.

Waterbolk, H. T. 1968. Food production in prehistoric Europe. *Science* 162, 1093–1102.

Watson, A. M. 1974. The Arab agricultural revolution and its diffusion, 700–1100. *Journal of Economic History* 34, 8–35.

Webb, Walter Prescott. 1952. *The Great Frontier*. Boston, Mass.: Houghton Mifflin.

Weber, Max. 1927. *General Economic History*. New York: Free Press.

Wesson, Robert. 1967. *The Imperial Order*. Berkeley, Calif.: University of California Press.

Wesson, Robert. 1978. *State Systems: International Pluralism, Politics, and Culture*. New York: The Free Press.

White, Lynn, Jr. 1962. *Medieval Technology and Social Change*. Oxford: Oxford University Press.

White, Lynn, Jr. 1972. The expansion of technology 500–1500. In *The Fontana Economic History of Europe: The Middle Ages*, ed. C. M. Cipolla. London: Collins/Fontana.

Whittlesey, Derwent S. 1944. *The Earth and State: a study of political geography*. New York: Holt.

Wight, Martin. 1977. *Systems of States*. Leicester: Leicester University Press.

Wightman, W. P. D. 1972. *Science in a Renaissance Society*. London: Hutchinson University Library.

Wilkinson, Richard G. 1973. *Poverty and Progress: an Ecological Model of Economic Development*. London: Methuen.

Wittfogel, Karl A. 1957. *Oriental Despotism: A Comparative Study of Total Power*. New Haven, Conn.: Yale University Press.

Wolf, John B. 1962. *The Emergence of the Great Powers 1685–1715*. New York: Harper and Row.

Wolpert, Stanley. 1965. *India*. Englewood Cliffs, N.J.: Prentice-Hall.

Woolf, S. J. 1970. The aristocracy in transition: a continental comparison. *Economic History Review* 2 ser. 23, 520–31.

Wrigley, E. A. 1962. The supply of raw materials in the industrial revolution. *Economic History Review* 2 ser. 15, 1–16.

Wrigley, E. A. 1966. Family limitation in pre-industrial England. *Economic History Review* 2 ser. 19, 82–109.

Wyman, W. D. and Kroeber, C. B. (eds.). 1965. *The Frontier in Perspective*. Madison, Wis.: Wisconsin University Press.

Wyrobisz, Andrzei. 1978. Resources and construction materials in pre-industrial Europe. In *Natural Resources in European History*, ed. Antoni Maczak and William N. Parker, 65–84. Washington, D.C.: Resources for the Future.

Young, Desmond. 1959. *Fountain of the Elephants*. London: Collins.

Zakythinos, D. A. 1976. *The Making of Modern Greece: From Byzantium to Independence*. Oxford: Basil Blackwell.

Ziman, John. 1968. *Public Knowledge: The Social Dimension of Science*. Cambridge: Cambridge University Press.

Zinkin, Maurice. 1951. *Asia and the West*. London: Chatto and Windus.

Supplementary bibliographical guide

To my surprise a number of books on economic change over the *very* long term came out soon after the manuscript of *The European Miracle* was completed or at about the time it was published. Others followed in the next year or two. I was working in isolation; so, obviously, were others. Lists of work in progress are too incomplete and narrow to enable one to keep abreast of the research under way in so many different academic professions or sub-professions, even when that work is on virtually global economic history.

The main comparable works of 1980 and 1981 were Ashok S. Guha, *An Evolutionary View of Economic Growth* (Oxford: Clarendon Press, 1981); W. H. McNeill, *The Human Condition: An Ecological and Historical View* (Princeton, N. J.: Princeton University Press, 1980); D. C. North, *Structure and Change in Economic History* (New York: W. W. Norton, 1981); L. S. Stavrianos, *Global Rift: The Third World Comes of Age* (New York: William Morrow & Co., 1981); and the second volume of Immanuel Wallerstein, *The Modern World System, Mercantilism and the Consolidation of the European World Economy, 1600–1750* (New York: Academic Press, 1980). There was also an interesting chapter on early economic change in Europe in Raymond Crotty, *Cattle, Economics, and Development* (Slough, Bucks: Commonwealth Agricultural Bureaux, 1980). Paul Colinvaux, *The Fate of Nations: A Biological Theory of History*, was likewise published by Simon & Schuster in New York in 1980, but I did not come across it until the edition of 1983 (Harmondsworth, Middlesex: Penguin Books).

In 1982 there appeared Michael Chisholm, *Modern World Development: A Geographical Perspective* (London: Hutchinson, 1982); John H. Kautsky, *The Politics of Aristocratic Empires* (Chapel Hill: University of North Carolina Press, 1982); Angus Maddison, *The Phases of Capitalist Development* (Oxford: Clarendon Press, 1982); Mancur Olson, *The Rise and Decline of Nations* (New Haven: Yale University Press, 1982); and Eric R. Wolf, *Europe and the People without History* (Berkeley: University of California Press, 1982). Norbert Elias, *State Formation and Civilization* (Oxford: Basil Blackwell, 1982) was published in English that year, having first appeared in German in Switzerland in the unpropitious year of 1939.

The output of new works in this field during the period 1980–82 was at two or three times the usual rate. Since then there has been a pause, but no doubt the spate will resume as the teaching of world history revives. Even so, we had Philip D. Curtin, *Cross-Cultural Trade in World History* (Cambridge: Cambridge University Press, 1984); an English edition of Yves Lacoste, *Ibn Khaldun: The Birth of History and the Past of the Third World* (London: Verso Editions, 1984, first published in French in 1966); Peter Worsley, *The Three Worlds: Culture and World Development* (London: Weidenfeld and Nicolson, 1984); and other works according to the strictness of definition of the field.

The baker's dozen of works listed here for 1980–82 are not of course exactly comparable. Some are more concerned with the modern industrial world than others, some are abstract, some historical. They are however general books tackling large, related themes, and most do include comparison with the non-Western world. It is worth considering the range of disciplines and approaches from which this rather distinct, yet wholly uncoordinated, revival of interest in *very* long-term, very broad gauge economic change has emerged. Guha is an economic theorist. Maddison and Olson are rather more empirical economists. Crotty is an agricultural and development economist. North and myself are economic historians (where is the rest of our sub-profession when we need them?). McNeill, Stavrianos, and Wallerstein each had previously written major books on world history; the first two are historians and Wallerstein is a sociologist originally concerned with African development. Wolf is an anthropologist formerly concerned with peasant society. Kautsky is a political scientist following in the footsteps of his grandfather, a major interpreter of Marx. Chisholm is a geographer. Colinvaux is a biologist.

All these are established scholars who had published extensively in specialist fields, and some already had attempts at very broad subjects to their credit. Chisholm, Colinvaux and myself are English in origin, although Colinvaux lives in the United States and I live in Australia. Crotty is Irish; McNeill is a Canadian long domiciled in the United States. North, Stavrianos, Wallerstein, and Wolf are, to the best of my knowledge, all Americans, although the names reveal a variety of family origins. Maddison is, I believe, an American now working in Holland. Guha is Indian and works in India, although he is a Harvard graduate. Eleven different publishers are involved, all major scholarly houses. I doubt that the publishers had spotted a trend in the market and suspect rather that the analysis of world history was supply driven. Publishers were not going to turn down major books offered by such well-established scholars.

What is of particular interest is that so many senior figures from so many different backgrounds, philosophies, scholarly fields and even countries, turned on their own account and under their own impetus in the same direction at once. They were not yet in their dotage and singing their swan songs (McNeill has published two major books since *The Human Condition*!), which is often the gibe when scholars move up from their lifetime research fields to some broader platform. They converged at the end of the 1970s on investigating and interpreting the history of economic development or some associated grand theme, often via comparative history. The scope of the treatments distinguishes them – the assumption that order must underlie all human economic experience. The books are also marked by their authors' realisation that there is a need to rise above the specialist studies which threaten to choke all our syllabuses, a need to offer students not broken meats but a diet from which they may choose throughout their lives.

However, there are real signs of a growth of demand, and of interest in world histories on the part of teachers. World histories have become one of the best-selling lines for English publishers, though many of the books are rather narrowly conceived studies of international politics since the French Revolution. A healthy interest is at any rate evidenced by the recent founding of the World History Association (President: Ross Dunn, San Diego State University, California) and the holding of a conference on the survey course in history at Michigan State University in April 1985. At that conference those of us who prefer to teach 'world history,' with all the attendant difficulties and risks, dominated, in my opinion, the older 'western civ' group, despite a forceful and amusing rearguard action by Jack Hexter.

Since putting down my pen in January 1980 I have come across four previously published general books I had missed. They are Jean Baechler, *The Origins of Capitalism* (Oxford: Basil Blackwell, 1975, first published in French in 1971); Shepard B. Clough, *The Rise and Fall of Civilization: An Inquiry into the Relation between Economic Development and Civilization* (New York: Columbia University Press, 1951, paperback edition 1961); Edward L. Farmer et al., *Comparative History of Civilization in Asia* (Reading, Mass.: Addison-Wesley, 1977); and the most remarkable comparative history I have ever read, Marshall Hodgson, *The Venture of Islam* (Chicago: University of Chicago Press, 1974, three volumes, with some earlier publishing history). A knowledge of all these would have made writing *The European Miracle* easier. It would however have deprived me of the fun of finding out much of the information, and coming to comparable conclusions, for myself.

Index

References are to Europe except where otherwise stated. Present-day authorities cited in the text are not usually indexed, neither are incidental references to aristocrats, sovereigns, individual towns, or countries.